W9-ALJ-058

PRO/CON VOLUME 16

EDUCATION

Published 2004 by Grolier,
an imprint of Scholastic Library Publishing
Old Sherman Turnpike
Danbury, Connecticut 06816

Library of Congress Cataloging-in-Publication Data
Pro/con
  p. cm
Includes bibliographical references and index.
  Contents: v. 13. U.S. History – v. 14. International Development – v. 15. Human
Rights – v.16. Education – v. 17. New Science – v. 18. Commerce and Trade.
  ISBN 0-7172-5927-7 (set : alk. paper) – ISBN 0-7172-5930-7 (vol. 13 : alk. paper) –
ISBN 0-7172-5929-3 (vol. 14 : alk. paper) – ISBN 0-7172-5931-5 (vol. 15 : alk. paper)
– ISBN 0-7172-5928-5 (vol. 16 : alk. paper) – ISBN 0-7172-5932-3 (vol. 17 : alk.
paper) – ISBN 0-7172-5933-1 (vol. 18 : alk. paper)
  1. Social problems. I. Scholastic Publishing Ltd Grolier (Firm)

HN17.5 P756 2002
361.1–dc21
                                                                    2001053234

Printed and bound in Singapore

SET ISBN 0-7172-5927-7
VOLUME ISBN 0-7172-5928-5

For The Brown Reference Group plc
Project Editor: Aruna Vasudevan
Editors: Chris Marshall, Lesley Henderson, Jonathan Dore, Rachel Bean
Consultant Editor: Lawrence M. Rudner, Director, ERIC Clearinghouse
on Assessment and Education,
Designer: Sarah Williams
Picture Researchers: Clare Newman, Susy Forbes
Set Index: Kay Ollerenshaw

Managing Editor: Tim Cooke
Art Director: Dave Goodman
Production Director: Alastair Gourlay

GENERAL PREFACE

"All that is necessary for evil to triumph is for good men to do nothing."
—Edmund Burke, 18th-century English political philosopher

Decisions

Life is full of choices and decisions. Some are more important than others. Some affect only your daily life—the route you take to school, for example, or what you prefer to eat for supper—while others are more abstract and concern questions of right and wrong rather than practicality. That does not mean that your choice of presidential candidate or your views on abortion are necessarily more important than your answers to purely personal questions. But it is likely that those wider questions are more complex and subtle and that you therefore will need to know more information about the subject before you can try to answer them. They are also likely to be questions where you might have to justify your views to other people. In order to do that you need to be able to make informed decisions, be able to analyze every fact at your disposal, and evaluate them in an unbiased manner.

What is *Pro/Con*?

Pro/Con is a collection of debates that presents conflicting views on some of the more complex and general issues facing Americans today. By bringing together extracts from a wide range of sources—mainstream newspapers and magazines, books, famous speeches, legal judgments, religious tracts, government surveys—the set reflects current informed attitudes toward dilemmas that range from the best

way to feed the world's growing population to gay rights, from the connection between political freedom and capitalism to the fate of Napster.

The people whose arguments make up the set are for the most part acknowledged experts in their fields, making the vast difference in their points of view even more remarkable. The arguments are presented in the form of debates for and against various propositions, such as "Should Americans Celebrate Columbus Day?" or "Are human rights women's rights?" This question format reflects the way in which ideas often occur in daily life: in the classroom, on TV shows, in business meetings, or even in state or federal politics.

The contents

The subjects of the six volumes of *Pro/Con 3—U.S. History, International Development, Human Rights, Education, New Science,* and *Commerce and Trade*—are issues on which it is preferable that people's opinions are based on information rather than personal bias.

Special boxes throughout *Pro/Con* comment on the debates as you are reading them, pointing out facts, explaining terms, or analyzing arguments to help you think about what is being said.

Introductions and summaries also provide background information that might help you reach your own conclusions. There are also tips about how to structure an argument that you can apply on an everyday basis to any debate or conversation, learning how to present your point of view as effectively and persuasively as possible.

VOLUME PREFACE
Education

Education is a topic that encourages passionate debate. Most people agree that education is a vital process for children and teenagers, but there are many issues about education on which people have opposing viewpoints. These include teaching methods, the subjects taught in schools, whether schools should be private or public, and types of education.

A hundred years ago education was very different. Schools taught Christianity, encouraged values based on white European beliefs, and enforced strict discipline in the class. Today such teaching methods are considered anachronistic. Most people believe that education should reflect the multicultural nature of contemporary society.

Education and multiculturalism
However, not all parents are happy to send their children to public schools. Since problems with antisocial behavior, especially drugs and violence, remain prevalent in many inner-city schools parents are increasingly choosing to educate their children at home. But is home education acceptable given the need for adults to interact fully in a multicultural society?

Education and immigration is also a controversial issue. Increases in the number of illegal immigrants coming to the United States have led some people to advocate the banning of public education for immigrants. In California efforts to exclude the children of illegal immigrants from public schools in 1994 were ruled unconstitutional by the Supreme Court.

Some people question what should be taught in schools. Is it still acceptable that religion should be taught in schools? And if so, which religion should be taught? Should schools be multifaith? In 2002 there was even a national debate over the constitutionality of the pledge of allegiance in schools. Critics argued that the phrase "one nation under God" could be seen as a state endorsement of religion, which is forbidden by the Constitution.

The politics of education
Politicians always have strong opinions about education, such as the size of classes and whether or not schools should be run by private firms. But is it a good thing to test children and rate schools based on the results? Do small school classes really make a difference to the effectiveness of teaching?

U.S. educational traditions are increasingly questioned by some commentators. Black universities have been accused of being outdated because segregation no longer exists in society. Supporters, on the other hand, argue that they provide a good education for students who would otherwise not be able to receive education in a nonblack college. Fraternities and sororities likewise have come under scrutiny. Critics argue that they encourage elitism and prejudice. Others believe that they offer benefits to all students. These issues and many others are discussed in *Education*, while an article on planning how to study gives useful tips about how best to prepare for exams.

HOW TO USE THIS BOOK

Each volume of *Pro/Con* is divided into sections, each of which has an introduction that examines its theme. Within each section are a series of debates that present arguments for and against a proposition, such as whether or not the death penalty should be abolished. An introduction to each debate puts it into its wider context, and a summary and key map (see below) highlight the main points of the debate clearly and concisely. Each debate has marginal boxes that focus on particular points, give tips on how to present an

argument, or help question the writer's case. The summary page to the debates contains supplementary material to help you do further research.

Boxes and other materials provide additional background information. There are also special spreads on how to improve your debating and writing skills. At the end of each book is a glossary and an index. The glossary provides explanations of key words in the volume. The index covers all 18 books, so it will help you trace topics in this set and the previous ones.

marginal boxes
Marginal boxes highlight key points of the argument, give extra information, or help you question the author's meaning.

summary boxes
Summary boxes are useful reminders of both sides of the argument.

further information
Further Reading lists for each debate direct you to related books, articles, and websites so you can do your own research.

other articles in the *Pro/Con* series
This box lists related debates throughout the *Pro/Con* series.

background information
Frequent text boxes provide background information on important concepts and key individuals or events.

key map
Key maps provide a graphic representation of the central points of the debate.

CONTENTS

ISSUES IN EDUCATION

INTRODUCTION

All Americans are entitled to a free education. They are also obliged to participate in some kind of formally assessed education up to high school level. According to the National Center for Statistics (NCS), in the fall of 2002 one in every four people in the United States—a quarter of the 288 million population—were participating in formal education. Approximately 69.2 million Americans were students in schools and colleges, while some 4.3 million men and women were employed as elementary and secondary school teachers and college faculty.

What is education for?

While most people agree that education matters, everyone has their own ideas about what should be taught and how schools should teach. People often have different views about the purpose and usefulness of education. Should it aim to produce good citizens who will contribute to their society? Would it be preferable if education taught people practical life skills, such as cooking or looking after children or elderly relatives? Should it concentrate on work-related subjects, like math or car mechanics, that can be usefully applied in the country's economy? Or what about the idea that education should be an end in itself, stimulating children into thinking for themselves and forming their own views, even if they are not those of the majority?

People may have their own opinions about the purpose and application of education, but they tend to agree that it is of great importance both for individuals and the nation. Many people believe that education is directly linked to better job opportunities and living standards. According to the National Institute for Literacy, almost half of all Americans with limited literacy skills live in poverty; of that number around three–quarters have no job.

System in crisis?

In 2002 UNICEF (the United Nations International Childrens' Education Fund) conducted a study of education systems in the developed world. The study set five tests for 14- and 15-year-olds to determine their ability in reading, math, and science. South Korea scored highest, with Japan in second place. The United States, however, came in nearer the bottom. U.S. students performed badly on all five tests.

Dewayne Matthews, vice president for state services of the Education Commission of the States, said that the U.S. rating was not surprising given that there was a "perception that schools are simply not good enough and they don't compare well with systems in other countries." Common reasons provided to explain the current shortcomings of the American education system include a lack of funding, poor or too few teachers, a dull curriculum, overcrowded classrooms, and too much bureaucracy. But how valid are these criticisms? Do they reflect media opinion rather than fact? And, more importantly, what are the answers?

The administration of President George W. Bush, which took office in 2001, sought to improve school funding. In 2002 it increased federal spending on elementary and high schools by $4.8 billion. It also introduced initiatives such as the

comes from either the federal or state government, so that makes any introduction of religion in schools potentially difficult. Spending government money on, say, a school that promoted Christianity might be interpreted as endorsing religion and therefore be seen as unconstitutional.

Another focus of debate is the recitation of the Pledge of Allegiance in schools. Some people believe that pledging to the flag encourages a kind

---

"It is in fact a part of the function of education to help us escape, not from our own time—for we are bound by that—but from the intellectual and emotional limitations of our time."

—T.S. ELIOT (1888–1965), POET

No Child Left Behind Act, which aims to make schools more accountable for student performance and to underpin a continued improvement in literacy and teacher quality. The first two topics in this book examine some of the central changes in education at the beginning of the 21st century. Topic 1 assesses the effectiveness of the No Child Left Behind Act, while Topic 2 asks whether it is feasible to cut class sizes at a time when school enrollment is growing.

Religion
The United States has a system in which the state and church are separate. There is no official state religion, and the Bill of Rights amended the Constitution to prevent the government from endorsing any one particular religion. All money in the public education system ultimately

of unquestioning patriotism that is inappropriate today. Others object to the inclusion in the pledge of the words "under God." Topic 3 considers the place of the pledge in schools.

The relationship between education and religion is examined in the final topic in this section. Some parents feel strongly that they should be free to educate their children in schools that promote a particular faith. However, the Establishment clause of the Constitution appears to make it impossible for the government to fund such schools. One answer is the voucher system, which gives parents the financial means to choose the school they want their child to attend. This has resulted in government indirectly funding religion-based schools and has led to much debate. Topic 4 asks whether the school voucher system works.

Topic 1
CAN THE NO CHILD LEFT BEHIND ACT WORK?

YES
"NEWS FROM THE COMMITTEE ON EDUCATION AND THE WORKFORCE"
RADIO ADDRESS, MARCH 2, 2002
GEORGE W. BUSH

NO
FROM "ALL CHILDREN TESTED, BUT MANY LEFT BEHIND"
CASCADE POLICY INSTITUTE, POLICY PERSPECTIVE NO. 1021, MARCH 2002
NICK WELLER

INTRODUCTION

On January 8, 2002, President George W. Bush signed into law the No Child Left Behind (NCLB) Act. For many its passage was the culmination of a long battle for a federal education program that would bring accountability and flexibility to an education system said to be in crisis. Critics, however, claimed that the act is flawed in its assumptions and that it is political rhetoric that will achieve little in the long run.

The new act promised great things and was backed in fiscal year 2002 (beginning October 1, 2001) by a record 27 percent increase of $4.8 billion in federal funding for elementary and secondary education. It aimed above all to improve the quality of education by making schools more accountable to students and parents through the introduction of state assessments that would closely monitor classroom achievement. In return the act promised to cut federal bureaucracy and allow school districts greater flexibility in the spending of federal funds. The act's Reading First plan was a substantial effort to tackle the national literacy problem by assisting states in providing effective and proven early reading programs. Among other measures, all states would also be required to improve English proficiency programs for bilingual students and to ensure a highly qualified teacher was in every classroom by 2005/6.

Even critics of the act agreed that reform of some kind was necessary. Teachers, politicians, and parents, in particular, have long been concerned about the quality of the education provided by the public school system. For some the nation's literacy problem showed how far the education system had failed both its citizens and the economy. In 1992 the National Adult Literacy Survey found that more than 40 million people aged 16 and over had "significant literacy needs." In practice that meant that 20 percent of adults read at or below fifth-grade level—far below the level that is usually judged necessary for employment. The National Institute for Literacy has stated that around 43 percent of those with low literacy skills live in poverty, and 70 percent have no full-time job. Statistics like these appear to support the case often made by businesspeople and politicians that improvements in education lead not only to more fulfilled individuals but also to better all-round economic performance.

> *"If you are planning for a year, sow rice; if you are planning for a decade, plant trees; if you are planning for a lifetime, educate people."*
> —CHINESE PROVERB

The origins of what has become known as "the accountability system" —central to the No Child Left Behind Act—can be traced back to a group of business and civic leaders in Texas in the 1980s. That group—which included the millionaire Ross Perot (1930-), who ran twice for the presidency in the 1990s—devised a system of testing that quickly raised education standards in a state where at the time public school children were performing in the bottom third of all children.

The new system involved testing children in grades three to eight and again in grade ten, and then publicly rating schools on those scores. If a school had a low performance rating

three years in a row, its teachers and its principal were held accountable and could lose their jobs.

Introduced in 1990, the Texas Assessment of Academic Skills (TAAS) test led to what supporters called "the Texas miracle," and it was fully endorsed by George W. Bush when he was Texas governor (1994-2001). He used it as the basis for the No Child Left Behind Act (NCLB) when he became president.

Advocates of the accountability system claim that more testing leads to better teaching, but critics argue that it is a further burden for teachers who are already overstretched. They argue that resources should be spent on teaching a more varied curriculum, not just on testing proficiency in a relatively standardized one.

Supporters of more accountability sometimes claim that it reduces the gap between white and minority students by ensuring that everyone is taught to the same standards. Critics, however— like Linda M. McNeil, the author of *Contradictions of School Reform* (2000)—argue that the new system only masks existing inequities. The emphasis on tests, they point out, may lead students to drop out of school altogether if they think they have little or no hope of passing. According to Walt Haney in "The Myth of the Texas Miracle in Education" (2000), there was a notable increase in the dropout rate in Texas after the TAAS reforms were introduced in the 1990s, especially among black and Hispanic students.

The following two articles look more closely at the NCLB Act. The first, a radio address by President George W. Bush, details the reforms themselves. The second, by policy analyst Nick Weller, argues that the new system excludes many children.

NEWS FROM THE COMMITTEE...
George W. Bush

George W. Bush (1946–) gave this radio address on March 2, 2002. Three days after becoming 43rd president of the United States on January 20, 2001, he announced that the No Child Left Behind (NCLB) Act would be "the cornerstone" of his administration. The NCLB Act passed into law less than a year later, on January 8, 2002.

YES

Good morning.

This coming week, I will be highlighting measures to help America's public schools carry out the education reforms we enacted in Washington earlier this year. Our education reforms require accountability and results, and give schools greater resources to achieve them.

Parents will have more information about the performance of their local schools and more say in how their children are educated. The No Child Left Behind Act is historic, ushering in a new era of accountability and education, but a lot of hard work is still ahead.

Good teachers in the classroom

The effectiveness of all education reform eventually comes down to a good teacher in a classroom. And America's teachers are eager to put higher standards into action and we must give them the tools to succeed. My administration has set a great goal for our public schools: a quality teacher in every classroom.

We can achieve this in two ways: by attracting capable men and women into the teaching profession, and providing teachers the training and support they deserve. Over the next decade, America will need more than 2 million new teachers. The budget I have signed into law for 2002 includes nearly $3 billion for teacher training, recruiting and hiring, an increase of more than 35 percent over the last year's budget.

We proposed to expand programs that recruit new math, science and special education teachers by forgiving part of their college loans in exchange for a commitment to teach in poor neighborhoods for at least five years. We should open up the teaching profession, allowing people who have achieved in other fields—including veterans and parents with grown children—to share their learning and experience. And we must upgrade the teaching colleges, where many teachers receive their training, the topic of a conference that will be hosted by our First Lady on Tuesday.

Today, only 36 percent of teachers themselves say they feel very well prepared for their jobs, so we'll focus on teacher training efforts where the need is greatest, in early childhood

Laura Welch Bush (1946–), George W. Bush's First Lady, hosted the White House conference "Preparing Tomorrow's Teachers" on March 5, 2002. Go to www.whitehouse.gov/firstlady/initiatives/education/teaching conference.html for more information.

Education was an important issue in George W. Bush's 2000 presidential campaign.

COMMENTARY: Solving the teaching crisis

The No Child Left Behind (NCLB) Act was passed in response to growing evidence of a national shortage in adequately skilled teachers. Many teachers do not have an educational background in the subjects for which they are responsible. The NCLB website, for example, cites both a 2002 survey, which shows that only 41 percent of 8th-grade math teachers had majored in the subject, and also a 1999 study that showed that a fifth of public school students from grade 7 through 12 were being taught English by teachers lacking even a minor in English literature, communications, or journalism. As part of the NCLB Act, George W. Bush promised to put a qualified teacher in every classroom. But while teacher quality is an acknowledged problem, the solution is more controversial.

Preparation

The traditional way to become a teacher is through state certification following a long preparation program at a college of education, but some education reformers have criticized such programs for failing to adequately prepare teachers. They argue that they focus too much on method at the expense of subject expertise. The NCLB Act helps states set up alternative fast-track certification routes, often involving internship in a school together with short, intensive training and subject-focused examinations. Supporters claim that these methods will attract both people already highly qualified in existing subjects, as well as experienced professionals from other fields who may have previously been discouraged from pursuing a career in teaching by long training programs. Critics, however, fear the new measures may result in new teachers learning their job in the classroom, which may be bad for students.

Rewards

Teachers' unions and other critics have long claimed that inadequate pay is one of the main reasons for the teacher crisis. They argue that teachers perform an essential but increasingly difficult job and are not rewarded properly in return. They cite growing classroom violence and the presence of an increasing number of immigrant students, many of whom are not native English speakers, as among the new challenges with which they have to contend. Faced with such issues, unions argue, better and more realistic wages are the only way to attract well-qualified staff. Supporters of the NCLB Act assert that it does that by authorizing performance-related pay ("merit pay"), so that outstanding teachers can be rewarded for doing a good job. Merit pay makes teaching more attractive to high achievers, they claim, and encourages good staff to stay in the classroom. Teachers' unions, however, oppose it. They believe that there is no reliable way to measure teaching performance because school standards vary so much.

education, special education, math, science and reading instruction. Through my administration's Reading First program, we are placing a new emphasis on the most basic of skills and many of our teachers will need training in the best and proven methods of reading instruction.

What are the "best" methods to teach reading skills? See Topic 10 Is phonics instruction the best way to teach students to read? for more information on one particular teaching method.

Helping teachers to do their jobs

Because learning only takes place in an atmosphere of order, we want our teachers to be in control of their classrooms. So we're protecting teachers from the threat of frivolous lawsuits that often result from enforcing reasonable discipline. Because committed teachers often buy school supplies for their students out of their own pockets, the budget I have proposed includes a tax deduction to cover some of those costs.

And because I strongly believe in local control of education, I'll implement new flexibility for school districts. They'll be able to use federal funds where the local need is greatest to reduce class sizes or improve teacher training or to increase teacher pay

Do you think school districts should be free to spend federal funds as they think fit?

A new era

In our new era of education reform we're asking a lot of our teachers, and we owe them something in return. We must treat them as the professionals they are. We must give them our respect and support. Teachers are among the most important people in our children's lives and a good teacher can literally make a lifelong difference.

Do teachers get the respect they deserve? Would you consider going into teaching yourself?

I have confidence in the education reforms we enacted because I have confidence in the teachers who will carry them out.

Thank you for listening.

ALL CHILDREN TESTED, BUT MANY LEFT BEHIND
Nick Weller

The No Child Left Behind Act is sometimes referred to as the ESEA because it reauthorized and amended the 1965 Elementary and Secondary Education Act (ESEA), the first national general-aid education program in the United States. In this article ESEA refers to the 2002 legislation, not the 1965 act.

Do you think national as well as state assessment is necessary? Go to http://nces.ed.gov/nationsreportcard/ for information about the NAEP.

The Certificate of Initial Mastery (CIM) is a voluntary state proficiency test for high-school students in Oregon. It was first introduced in 1998. Go to www.ode.state.or.us/cifs/cim/ for details. The author of this article is an analyst at the Cascade Policy Institute, based in Oregon.

NO

…The ESEA [Elementary and Secondary Education Act] is a mammoth document that totals over 1,000 pages and contains many obscure, specific rules the effects of which will only become clear over time. The centerpiece … of the bill, mandatory state testing, is complemented by a slew of other provisions that: give military recruiters access to students; authorize school districts to use federal money to test for illegal drug use and to inspect students' lockers for weapons, illegal drugs, or drug paraphernalia; expand federal support for charter schools; and increase federal funding for reading programs. The complexity and length of the bill makes it nearly impossible to understand its full ramifications.

Testing requirements

For the first time the federal government will require annual math and reading tests in grades three through eight; states can choose to develop and/or purchase appropriate tests…. Schools must define and track Adequate Yearly Progress towards having 100 percent of students achieve proficiency in math and reading within the next 12 years. To help the U.S. Department of Education verify statewide assessments a small sample of students in each state will participate in the fourth- and eighth-grade National Assessment of Educational Progress (NAEP) in reading and math every other year….

Testing effects on education

Critics of testing argue that American students are overtested and need fewer standardized tests, not more…. On the other hand, testing proponents argue that standardized exams create clear expectations for schools and students as well as collect precise information about performance. The biggest education effects come not from the tests themselves, but from the changes that the exams precipitate….

Unfortunately, classroom time devoted to the new exams is likely to be a waste. As is already the case with the CIM [Certificate of Initial Mastery] exams, students are unlikely to take the tests seriously. Commenting on the CIM, one high school student told *The Oregonian*, "There's a reward to yourself for doing the work, but it doesn't really mean anything." The federally-mandated exams will suffer from this fate, too, because performance on them is unconnected to ... rewards or penalties for students.

Do you think that all school tests "mean" something?

The effects of proficiency standards on students

The ESEA requires that states define a level of proficiency and bring 100 percent of students to it in both reading and math within 12 years. An objective definition of proficiency does not exist, however, and where the line is placed has major consequences. If standards are moderate to high, for example, schools may define more children as "learning disabled" to exempt them from the national exams, even though it might be more accurate to call the problem a disability of the rigid school system.

Go to www. ideapractices.org for further details about the 1997 Individuals with Disabilities Education Act, which provides for the education of children with disabilities— including learning disabilities— within the public school system.

The conference committee authoring the ESEA recognized that even in the current system "some children are being diagnosed as needing IDEA [Individuals with Disabilities Education Act] services simply because they did not receive proper early reading instruction...." The federal solution to the problem is the "Reading First" initiative designed to improve reading instruction in the early elementary grades. ...[That] may help some students, but the need to have 100 percent passage on the exams will likely cause even more students to be misidentified as learning disabled, forcing them to shoulder that potentially significant stigma.

A "stigma" is a mark of shame or discredit. Is that really how learning-disabled students are seen?

The 100 percent passage requirement means states will probably adopt relatively low standards for proficiency.... Curriculum will be adjusted to reflect the lowest common denominator, which will disproportionately affect advanced students who already exceed minimal proficiency standards and need a challenging environment....

Proficiency standards mask school performance

With a low proficiency standard the ESEA would provide lip service to accountability while masking poor school performance. Oregon's current school report cards show how meaningless the state's evaluations of school performance can be. According to the state Department of Education more than 99 percent of Oregon schools were rated satisfactory or above in the 2001 school report cards. However, in the average satisfactory school nearly fifty percent of students failed to meet state standards on one or more of the following tests: reading, writing, math multiple-choice and math problem-solving. A recent Manhattan

Founded in 2000, the Black Alliance for Educational Options educates African Americans and others about schooling choices available in the United States. Go to www.baeo.org for more details.

Institute report, prepared for the Washington, D.C.-based Black Alliance for Educational Options, showed that Oregon had a four-year high school completion rate of 67 percent, one of the lowest in the country. If these statistics warrant a satisfactory rating, the new proficiency standards will also have to be questioned....

Consequences tied to test results

The ESEA legislation provides immediate assistance for students trapped in chronically failing schools. The 1994 version of the ESEA identified nearly 3,000 underperforming schools across the country, but the data were never released and nothing was done once the schools were identified. The new ESEA is an improvement in that these failing schools will be publicly identified. In 2002-03, students at these schools will receive immediate access to intradistrict public school choice and supplemental private education services.

For all other schools, failure to meet the Adequate Yearly Progress (AYP) goals for two consecutive years requires the school district to provide intradistrict public school choice. If a school fails to meet AYP for a third year, the district must continue public school choice and additionally offer supplemental services to low-income children. If a school fails to make AYP for four consecutive years, the district must implement corrective actions, such as replacing staff members and implementing a new curriculum, as well as continue to provide public school choice and supplemental services. If a school is still failing after five consecutive years, it would be subject to alternative governance actions, such as state takeover, the hiring of a private management contractor, conversion to a charter school, or ... staff restructuring....

Do you think such drastic measures are the correct response to failing schools? Would it be better to try and solve the problems with the existing system first?

The corrective actions outlined in the ESEA for schools that fail to meet AYP for four or five years should ideally act as negative incentives to encourage school improvement. Unfortunately, the schools have not been given any commensurate freedom to improve their performance.

Professors Benjamin Scafidi and Catherine Freeman of Georgia State University and Stan DeJarnett of Morgan County (GA) Public Schools write:

Do you agree that schools should be given more control over their budget, personnel, and curricula? Who else might be better able to control these factors than the schools themselves?

Without a significant degree of control over the means for education improvement, such as budgets, personnel, and curriculum, local educators cannot ultimately be held accountable for achieving the assigned end of ... a high level of student learning....

Danger of national involvement in education

The newly reauthorized ESEA represents an increase in federal control over education. This fact should be of concern because millions of students will be affected by any poor policies that are adopted, perhaps for decades to come. Federal programs are incredibly difficult to change even after they are known to be harmful.

Although the ESEA explicitly rejects the notion of a national curriculum, it requires a sample of fourth and eighth graders to participate in the NAEP [National Assessment of Educational Progress] reading and math tests every other year. The NAEP is to provide an independent benchmark for the progress states are making. Supposedly, the results of the NAEP are not to exert "undue influence" on states to change their standards and/or assessments.

Do you agree that the No Child Left Behind Act increases federal control over education? Is that important?

What exactly undue influence is will be determined over the years, as will the reaction of federal officials when comparisons between NAEP and state tests reveal, as in Oregon, a 23 [sic] or 24 point difference in the percentage of students meeting proficiency standards. The difficulty of developing a proper standard for proficiency will likely cause disagreements between state and federal officials in the coming years.

The promises of the federal government notwithstanding, it is reasonable to suspect that many states will align their standards with the now-mandatory NAEP exam to avoid such a large discrepancy in performance, as well as to prepare for the possibility of sanctions and rewards connected to NAEP exams. If this happens the country's schools will be much closer to a national curriculum, which would be a major setback for education.... Because it is impossible to determine the one best curriculum, it is important that schools be free to adopt the best curriculum available....

Other countries have a national curriculum. Would introducing one in the United States really be a "major setback for education"?

Conclusion

The ESEA represents an important step by acknowledging that it is unacceptable for students to continually receive a low-quality education. According to the legislation schools must have all students scoring at or above proficiency within 12 years. Even if that outcome occurs and the level of proficiency is set at a reasonable level, what about the thousands of students who have been failed by the school in the interim period? It is ironic that legislation called No Child Left Behind accepts the fact that many children will continue to receive a poor education for the next 12 years. For [them], if improvement ever happens it will be too little, too late....

Summary

The No Child Left Behind Act was signed into law by George W. Bush in January 2002. Many have heralded it as the answer to the education problem in the United States; others claim it is deeply flawed.

In the first of the preceding articles—a radio address given by George W. Bush in 2002—the president discusses aspects of the new act. He claims it is "historic, ushering in a new era of accountability and education" but states that there is still much to do. Arguing that teachers are essential to reform, he promises to support them and help them do their jobs more effectively. He states that he will put a "quality" teacher in every classroom by providing the funds to attract more capable teachers and give them better training.

In the second article policy analyst Nick Weller criticizes the bill on a number of grounds. He claims that state proficiency standards will either be set too high or too low and thinks this will have adverse effects on students as well as masking poor school performance. He also warns of the dangers of increased federal involvement in education, claiming that it may lead to a standardized curriculum, which he does not favor. Although he praises the bill for recognizing that students should not be forced to attend continually failing schools, he doubts that the reforms themselves will work. Even if they do, he argues, they will only produce significant results after 12 years, and in the meantime many children will continue to receive a poor education.

FURTHER INFORMATION:

Books:

McNeil, Linda M., *Contradictions of School Reform: Educational Costs of Standardized Testing.* New York: Routledge, 2000.

Reeves, Douglas B., *Crusade In The Classroom: How George W. Bush's Education Policies Will Affect Your Children and Our Schools.* New York: Simon & Schuster/Kaplan, 2001.

Useful websites:

www.edexcellence.net/NCLBconference/NCLBconferenceindex.html
Thomas B. Fordham Foundation site. Papers by experts analyzing the No Child Left Behind Act.

www.edweek.org/context/topics/issuespage.cfm?id=59
Education Week on the Web site.

http://edworkforce.house.gov/issues/107th/education/nclb/nclb.
House of Representatives Committee on Education and the Workforce site. Section on No Child Left Behind Act.

www.nclb.gov
The Department of Education No Child Left Behind site.

www.whitehouse.gov/news/reports/no-child-left-behind.html
White House site. Section on No Child Left Behind Act.

The following debates in the Pro/Con series may also be of interest:

In this volume:

 Topic 2 Has the federal class reduction program improved student performance?

Topic 4 Do school vouchers work?

CAN THE NO CHILD LEFT BEHIND ACT WORK?

YES: Studies have shown that the two are related—below a certain reading level, for example, people cannot find jobs

YES: The case of Texas is often cited. After testing was introduced in the mid 1980s, the dropout rate rose by 10 percent.

ECONOMICS
Do educational standards improve economic performance?

DROPOUT RATE
Do standard tests lead to higher dropout rates among students?

NO: The problem with educational standards is that they do not account for those people with learning difficulties. Even people who cannot read and write can still work.

NO: People do not drop out of school just because of tests. That is too facile an explanation. Other factors are far more significant, such as home life, peer pressure, and so on.

CAN THE NO CHILD LEFT BEHIND ACT WORK?

KEY POINTS

YES: Inevitably, if you make people responsible for their performance, they will make sure they improve their work

YES: The situation has improved since everyone is taught in the same way to the same standard

ACCOUNTABILITY
Has accountability helped improve educational standards?

MINORITY STUDENTS
Has the No Child Left Behind Act helped minority students?

NO: It just puts extra pressure on already overstretched teachers and schools

NO: The high scores needed to pass tests has led to more children being marginalized as learning disabled

Topic 2

HAS THE FEDERAL CLASS REDUCTION PROGRAM IMPROVED STUDENT PERFORMANCE?

YES

"YES, SMALLER CLASS SIZES ARE A KEY TO EDUCATIONAL SUCCESS"
SPECTRUM, SUMMER 1998
KERRY MAZZONI

NO

FROM "THE DEBATE OVER CLASS SIZE, PART 2: THE CRITICS HAVE THEIR SAY"
EDUCATION WORLD, FEBRUARY 23, 1998
GARY HOPKINS

INTRODUCTION

Studies in the late 1970s seemed to show that schoolchildren of any age are happier in smaller classes. Research suggested that children in small classes perform better on exams and are more socially responsible, both in school and out of it, than children in bigger classes. Later studies showed that small classes also raised teacher morale and improved the quality of the whole school.

Specifically, researchers found that pupils in small classes attained a higher level of achievement at all grade levels, especially if their assignments were carefully controlled. Surveys concluded that the greatest benefits of reducing class size were in classes where the number of students was fewer than 20.

These ideas took root and gradually became the accepted wisdom. Educationists and politicians grew confident that once smaller classes were widely established in public schools, parents who sent their children to private schools would return them to the public system, and that would contribute to a further rise in standards. Some states decided to reduce class sizes even before any laws were passed.

In 1996 the federal government introduced legislation to reduce class sizes in kindergarten and grades 1–3 by helping pay for the recruitment of more teachers. Under the new rules there could be no more than 20 children per teacher.

For three years from 1998 Congress provided funds for a federal initiative to recruit, hire, and train qualified teachers specifically for the purpose of reducing class size in the four targeted grades. The aim was to ensure that every child received personal attention, got a solid foundation for further learning, and learned to read independently and well by the end of grade 3.

Eventually more than 1.7 million children in the early grades received instruction in smaller classes with more personal attention, and 90,000 teachers taught more manageably sized classes. Across the country 23,000 schools hired one or more additional teachers, and 15,000 school districts received funds to improve teacher recruitment, hiring, and professional development to help teachers maximize the benefits of smaller classes.

"Reducing class size is one of the most important investments we can make...."
—BILL CLINTON,
42ND PRESIDENT (1993–2001)

Studies seemed to show that the new plan was working well. Statistics suggested that academic achievement had increased, relations between teachers and parents had improved, and the number of disruptive children had been reduced.

But not everyone was happy. Critics questioned the validity of the cutoff point—why is 20 or fewer a good class number and 21 or more unacceptable? Why should we assume that a bad teacher with a class of 20 will produce better results than a good teacher with 30 pupils? Is there a difference between two classes of 20 with one teacher each and one class of 40 with two teachers?

In addition to those who questioned the basis of the scheme, others doubted the scheme's practicality. It is all very well, they said, to instruct schools to reduce their class sizes and pay for new teachers, but what good is that if there is no room in the school for more classes? Reducing class size requires building more classrooms, not simply hiring more staff. But construction work is more costly and time-consuming than recruiting more teachers. Skeptics saw the class reduction program as a typical politician's quick fix— prescribing a solution without really understanding the problem.

Moreover, critics ask, how can we be sure that the new recruits will be good enough? Some of the teachers hired had no previous experience. No matter how talented inexperienced teachers may be, it is easy to see that they might perform less effectively with a class of 18 than an old hand would with a class of 25. And what of the teachers who are returning to the profession or moving to new jobs? There is at least a possibility that they will be motivated by the desire for a quiet life away from jobs in industry or stressful, overcrowded inner-city schools. Are they—will they ever be—the right stuff?

The class-size reduction program was short-lived: Funding was restructured in fiscal year 2002. Schools are still allocated money that they can use for that purpose if they wish. In practice, however, current funding is insufficient to meet professional development needs and to allow for the recruitment, hiring, and training of enough new teachers to reduce class size. So there is no longer any assurance that the reduction of class size will remain a priority.

Former assembly member Kerry Mazzoni and founder and editor-in-chief of *Education World* Gary Hopkins debate the issue further.

YES, SMALLER CLASS SIZES ARE A KEY TO EDUCATIONAL SUCCESS
Kerry Mazzoni

YES

This article was originally published in Spectrum in 1998.

Class-size reduction is the most ambitious school reform program we have implemented in California in the past 20 years. Two years ago, the Governor and Legislature approved an incentive program to begin reducing classes to 20 pupils per teacher in kindergarten and first, second and third grades. In its first year, the program provided districts with $650 for each student in a class reduced to 20 students (the amount is now up to $800 per pupil). Despite the voluntary nature of the program, the response by school districts was overwhelming: 95 percent of all school districts chose to participate in some form in just the first year. As of last instructional year (1997–98), 84 percent of all students in grades kindergarten through third were in reduced class sizes of 20 pupils per teacher (8 percent of these students—mostly kindergartners—are in reduced class sizes for only half the day).

Does the number of schools that chose to enter the program actually say anything about its effectiveness?

I have been involved in public education for more than 10 years as a parent, a school board member, and now as a state legislator. As chair of the Committee on Education for the California State Assembly, I maintain that the state's annual expenditure of more than $1.5 billion for class-size reduction is a worthwhile investment in improving our public schools. Why do I believe it is an excellent investment? For three reasons:

Listing the central points of your argument at the start will make them clearer to your audience.

• Anecdotal and preliminary empirical evidence suggests it has improved achievement;
• Class-size reduction has positively affected the relationship between the public schools and their "clients"—parents and the community at large; and
• Class-size reduction has been accompanied by other reform efforts.

Improving educational achievement
First and foremost, preliminary data and some anecdotal evidence suggest that the reduction in class sizes in the early grades has led to considerable improvement in achievement for children in these grades. The third largest district in the

state, Long Beach Unified, reported that the percentage of first-graders scoring at grade level in reading increased from 40.3 percent to 58.6 percent in only one year, when they reduced the size of all first grade classes to 20. Another large district, San Juan Unified, reported a significant reduction (19 percent) in the number of students suspended in grades 1 through 3, as well as significantly improved math test scores for the 1996–97 school year when compared to the previous year without class-size reduction. San Francisco Unified reported a net gain of 7.0 Normal Curve Equivalents in first grade reading scores when comparing achievement before and after class-size reduction.

A Normal Curve Equivalent (NCE) score expresses an original test result as a value on a scale from 1 to 99. NCEs are used to make comparisons between different kinds of tests.

And anecdotal evidence abounds. School districts report that class-size reduction has attracted children back from private schools. Teachers report achievement gains and fewer discipline problems. And administrators report happier teachers [who] receive satisfaction from being able to provide individualized attention to their young students.

And of course, there are studies from other states that show that smaller class sizes result in improved student performance, the most commonly cited study being the evaluation of the Tennessee Project STAR that compared the achievement of randomly assigned groups of children in classes of 13–17 and 22–25. The Project STAR evaluation showed that children in the smaller classes consistently outperformed children in the larger classes. Although some critics of class-size reduction point to studies that conclude that smaller class sizes have a negligible effect on achievement, these studies are in the minority and many use student/teacher ratio as a proxy for class size, which is problematic. The majority of studies conclude that smaller class sizes are linked to greater student achievement.

Project STAR (student-teacher achievement ratio) studied pupils' achievement in kindergarten and first-, second-, and third-grade classrooms in Tennessee. The study, which began in 1985, followed pupils through four years of schooling in each given class size.

Improving school and community relations

Secondly, class-size reduction is a worthwhile investment because of the positive effect it has had on relations between schools and local communities. When the Legislature approved funding for class-size reduction in the summer of 1996, districts had only 2 to 6 months to hire thousands of additional teachers and find thousands of additional classrooms, in order to participate in the first year. But despite these formidable obstacles, districts responded overwhelmingly to implement what they perceived as a priority among parents and the public. Class-size reduction provided an opportunity for public school districts to demonstrate that they can respond quickly and effectively

Does the need for more teachers carry a danger that they will not be so well qualified?

to public demands. In return, the public has become very engaged and interested in the public schools. For example, public awareness has increased about the facilities needs of our schools and the need for qualified teachers. In short, class-size reduction has proved to be an important catalyst in increasing the involvement of the community in the schools.

Some may say that government programs should not spend money … just to please the public. Clearly, public popularity should not be the only reason to implement class-size reduction. However, there are empirical reasons to support class-size reduction, and parents know this. Smaller class sizes in the early grades are popular with parents because they know that they increase individualized attention for their children. When both research and the public support a particular reform effort, there is even more reason to support the effort. Public support is extremely important to have in implementing any reform.

"Empirical" means based on observation or experience.

Maximizing other educational reforms

And lastly, class-size reduction is one of the best investments we can make in improving our schools, especially when it is paired with other school reform efforts. To those that say that class-size reduction is not a panacea, I wholeheartedly agree! Class-size reduction was never intended to fix all problems in the state's schools, and that's why in the past five years the state had adopted other major reforms. Most importantly, we adopted statewide content standards in Math and Language Arts, which have been described as some of the most rigorous in the country. We adopted reforms in the way we teach reading, to emphasize decoding and phonemic awareness. We provided intensive math training for teachers and the adoption of a statewide test that is nationally normed. And, we are in the process of developing a statewide accountability system to identify low-performing schools and require improvements over time.

For more on phonemic awareness see Topic 10 Is phonics instruction the best way of teaching students to read?

But I cannot overemphasize the important role that class-size reduction plays in allowing room for these reforms to work. More importantly, it helps these reforms to work in the early grades, when children learn the gateway skills of reading and basic math concepts. Success in the early grades determines success in later grades, and California's program currently invests in lowering class size only in these early grades, to maximize the opportunity for teachers to implement the reforms I cited above. Without class-size reduction and the opportunity to work more intensively with children, teachers may never fully be able to reap the benefits of these reforms.

And the importance of small class sizes in maximizing opportunities for reform will become more important in the coming years, as the state embarks upon a statewide accountability system. Our hope is that such a system will encourage teachers and administrators to utilize all the resources and tools they have to improve student achievement. Class-size reduction provides a ready tool for schools to try to improve their performance.

The importance of longitudinal studies

But the question remains: Are smaller class sizes the key to educational success? A formal, longitudinal evaluation of California's program is obviously of crucial importance in definitively answering this question. And, as responsible policy-makers, my fellow lawmakers and I welcome evaluation—not just of the class-size reduction program, but of other programs as well. Last year, I authored successful legislation (AB 354, Mazzoni) to require the California Department of Education to develop a methodology for a longitudinal evaluation of the effects of the state's class-size reduction program on academic achievement. This and other evaluations are imperative to the success and credibility of class-size reduction.

As we finalize the second year of the program and enter into the third, it is important for lawmakers and educators to reflect on the returns on our investment in class-size reduction in California. Preliminary data and anecdotal evidence suggest it has positive returns on student achievement. And the positive public reaction, combined with the state's adoption of other education reforms, lead me to conclude that for now it is best to continue on the course we have set in reducing class sizes in the early grades in California.

A longitudinal evaluation is one that assesses pupils' achievement over time. Project STAR in Tennessee is an example of a longitudinal study (see page 25).

AB (assembly bill) 354 also required that a method for assessing other issues related to the class-size reduction program be developed. These issues included teacher and parent satisfaction and the effect on other educational programs.

THE DEBATE OVER CLASS SIZE, PART 2: THE CRITICS HAVE THEIR SAY
Gary Hopkins

NO

Smaller classes have some critics too!

This article first appeared in February 1998.

… President Clinton's plan has fueled anew the longstanding debate over the issue of class size. His plan has lots of skeptics wondering aloud—and loudly!

- Many critics point to conflicting research about the benefits of smaller classes.
- Many wonder where school administrators will find the classroom space for new classes and the *quality* teachers needed to fill them.
- Other critics take issue with the cost of Clinton's proposal. The money, they say, might be better spent on other programs.

The balance of this story will examine these concerns and others that surround the Clinton class-size reduction initiative …

Go to www. education-world. comla_adminl admin049.shtml to read Part 1 of this article.

Reducing class size in California

Last week, in Part 1 of this story, we took a look at California's CSR (Class Size Reduction) program. In little more than a year, 18,000 new classes were created in the state's schools. Today, about a million of the state's pupils are in classes of 20 students or fewer. Reports of participation rates and early test results indicate that the program has had some success. But that doesn't mean that everybody in California is singing the praises of CSR.

The biggest concern for many school administrators has been finding the teachers to fill the new openings created by the program.

Is it better to have an inexperienced teacher teaching a class of 18 students or an experienced teacher teaching a class of 25?, critics wonder.

How much experience does a teacher really need? Is knowledge of their academic subject enough?

Some school administrators are being forced to dip low into the applicant pool to fill many new openings. Almost two-thirds of the teachers hired to fill new slots in California have little or no teaching experience, according to some reports. Many of those inexperienced teachers, critics add, are poorly prepared.

Inner-city schools—where the need is arguably greatest—have been hit especially hard. Many new teachers don't want to teach in inner-city schools. And many experienced teachers are leaving the cities to take higher-paying and less stressful jobs in suburban schools. The "raiding" of experienced teachers by wealthier school districts just exacerbates the problem city schools face in providing a quality education to hard-to-reach students.

The focus on smaller classes is happening at an inopportune time, some California administrators add. It's happening at a time when enrollments are growing. Baby-boomers are having kids before it's too late and Generation Xers are starting families. An expected boom in retirements in the decade ahead adds to the dilemma.

We need classrooms!

"If I've got the math right, more teachers teaching smaller classes requires more classrooms," President Clinton said in his State of the Union Address. "So I also propose a school construction tax cut to help communities modernize or build 5,000 schools."

Clinton's initiative calls for 100,000 new K–3 teachers. But, critics say, 100,000 new classrooms won't get built overnight! Many school administrators will face a "class struggle" as they attempt to make space to accommodate new teachers and new classes.

In California, finding space for 18,000 new classrooms last year was one of the biggest challenges school administrators faced. Many schools had to give up libraries, art and music classrooms, science labs, and computer labs to create new class space. Many others turned playground space into parking lots for portable classrooms. Some other schools, especially crowded inner-city schools, have no space for portables—so they haven't been able to participate in the CSR program....

Philadelphia's Superintendent of Schools David Hornbeck knows that simply reducing class size will "not solve all the city's education problems." But the "biggest challenge" will be recruiting qualified teachers and finding space to house the new teachers and classes (*Philadelphia Inquirer*, 1/30/98)....

President Clinton's initiative—which includes money to support construction of new schools and classrooms—might help schools like those in Miami, Philadelphia, Bridgeport, and other large cities. That remains to be seen.

President Clinton has placed a $12 billion pricetag on his education initiative. The pricetag on California's two-year CSR program is $2.5 billion.

"Baby boomers" are people who were born between 1946 and 1964. Generation Xers are the generation born after the baby boomers. The term "Generation X" was first used in 1964 in a sociological survey and in the same year was also used in the novel of the same name by Jane Deverson and Charles Hamblett. The novel portrayed children who would come of age toward the end of the 20th century as apathetic and materialistic.

Are there signs in your local schools of a shortage of classrooms?

The Public School Parent's Network website at www.psparents.net/ Class%20Size.htm has excerpts from and links to reports about the class-size reduction program.

Reducing class size is one of the most expensive approaches to school reform, critics argue. Cutting class size drains money that might be spent on better programs, they add.

Perhaps *U.S. News & World Report* summed it up best in their special report last October, "Does Class Size Matter?":

Smaller classes could be one of the most important school reforms of recent years—or a colossal waste of money. States that shrink class size by only a few students across the board will probably be throwing their money down the drain.

See page 25 for more information about Project STAR.

An awful lot of attention is being paid to a few studies—especially Project STAR. But do a few studies make a definitive case for small classes? skeptics ask, adding, researchers have published findings from more than 1,100 studies on class size over the years. Those studies offer mixed and contradictory findings.

"I don't think a single study proves that much," Herbert J. Walberg, a professor at the University of Illinois at Chicago, told *Education Week* of the STAR study. "You can find some studies that indicate that bigger classes have better effects on learning."

Go to www. edweek.org/ew/ vol-14/40 small.h14 to read this article.

One of the leading critics of class-size reduction plans is Eric A. Hanushek, a University of Rochester economist and public-policy professor. *Education Week* reports ("Less Is More," 7/12/95) that Hanushek "has analyzed 300 studies and concluded that across-the-board reductions in class size are not worth the expense."

"Dropping a class from 25 to 22 students increases classroom expenditures by more than 10 percent," Hanushek wrote in his 1994 book, *Making Schools Work: Improving Performance and Controlling Cost....*

Alternatives to reducing class size

Cooperative learning is an approach to teaching that stresses teamwork in small groups in which each student is dependent on all others on their team. See www.clcrc.com/ for further information.

In what other more beneficial ways might $12 billion be spent? Critics offer all kinds of suggestions. Train teachers in better intervention strategies and teaching techniques, such as cooperative learning, some critics suggest. Add aides and special teachers whose job it will be to focus on helping students in need, others say. Focus on low-achieving schools first, individual tutoring, early childhood programs.... Suggestions abound....

In Montgomery County (Virginia), school superintendent Paul L. Vance recently announced a $9.2 million plan to reduce class size. The proposal would add 238 teachers, according to a *Washington Post* report ("Should Classes Be Smaller?", 12/15/97). Officials said it would cost $7 million to lower the average class size in Montgomery County by one student.

> *Instead of recommending an across-the-board reduction, Vance proposed hiring more teachers for elementary reading, middle school math, and high school algebra, saying that those were the students who would benefit most from smaller classes,* the Post reported. *The plan would reduce the average student-teacher ratio for first- and second-grade reading instruction to 15 to 1, from the current 24 to 1.*

Robert Slavin, a Johns Hopkins University professor, agrees that money could be better focused. Slavin, in *U.S. News Online*'s "Does Class Size Matter?" says:

> *California could have improved instruction in its elementary schools dramatically for a fraction of the money it spent simply by hiring and carefully training retired teachers and other part-timers as reading instructors to reduce the size of classes during the time reading is taught.*
>
> *Reducing class size seems to be most effective in combination with other reforms.... Evidence comes from a study of 16 low-income schools in Austin, Texas. In the late 1980s, each of the schools was awarded an extra $300,000 a year for five years as part of a desegregation case. Fourteen of the schools spent the money to reduce class size and yet in five years didn't manage to improve student attendance or test scores. But the other two schools reduced class size, set higher standards, provided intensive teacher training, and established health clinics on their grounds to address physical problems that were keeping students from learning. Test scores and attendance both improved significantly at those schools. ...*

Ronald Ferguson, a lecturer at Harvard University's John F. Kennedy School of Government, told the *Washington Post* last December (see "Should Classes Be Smaller?") that his research shows that "teacher quality, not class size is the most important factor in education."

"The issue is whether teachers teach any differently to a small class than to a large class," he said. "If you cut class size and the teachers don't teach any differently, it won't matter." ...

Funds for the class-size reduction program were last handed out to states on October 1, 2001, and the program was then incorporated into a new teacher quality grant. *See* Topic 1 Can the No Child Left Behind Act work? *for more information about funding for reducing class size.*

How might the teaching methods used to instruct a small class differ from those used to teach a larger class?

Summary

In the first article Kerry Mazzoni gives a positive account of the effect of reductions in class sizes in the state of California. According to her, the high cost of the program—which she puts at $1.5 billion a year—was worth it because it improved pupils' educational performance (especially in reading proficiency), inspired better behavior by pupils, and had a beneficial effect on the triangular relationship between schools, parents, and the community as a whole. Mazzoni stresses that for the class reduction program to be fully effective, it has to be accompanied by other reform initiatives, such as the introduction of statewide standards in math and language, and improved methods of recruiting teachers.

In the second article Gary Hopkins points out that not all research indicated that the reduction of class size was necessarily a good thing. He also argues that smaller classes mean not only more teachers but also more classrooms and wonders how they were going to be funded and where they were going to be built. Although President Bill Clinton gave tax breaks to help communities modernize existing schools or construct new ones, even where there was a local will there was not necessarily a way—many schools could accommodate the new, smaller classes only by cutting libraries, art and music rooms, and other existing facilities. Hopkins also questions whether the level of federal funding was adequate—how could $12 billion have been enough for the whole country when the class-size reduction program cost $2.5 billion over two years in California alone?

FURTHER INFORMATION:

Books:

Achilles, Charles M., *Let's Put Kids First, Finally: Getting Class Size Right*. Thousand Oaks, CA: Corwin Press, 1999.

Blatchford, Peter, *The Class Size Debate: Is Small Better?* Milton Keynes, Buckinghamshire: Open University Press, 2003.

Finn, Jeremy D., *Class Size and Students at Risk*. Upland, PA: DIANE Publishing Co., 1999.

Finn, Jeremy D., and Margaret C. Wang (eds.), *Taking Small Classes One Step Further*. Greenwich, CT: Information Age Publishing, 2002.

Jepsen, Christopher, and Steven G. Rivkin, *Class-Size Reduction, Teacher Quality, and Academic Achievement in California Public Elementary Schools*. San Francisco, CA: Public Policy Institute of California, 2002.

Mishel, Lawrence, et al. (eds.), *The Class Size Debate*. Washington, D.C.: Economic Policy Institute, 2002.

 Useful websites:

www.ed.gov/index.jsp
Department of Education

www.education-world.com/a_admin/admin140.shtml
Article on class-size reduction.

http://eric.uoregon.edu/publications/policy_reports/class_size/alternatives.html
"Alternatives to Class-Size Reduction," by Lawrence O. Picus, College of Education, University of Oregon.

The following debates in the Pro/Con series may also be of interest:

In this volume:
 Topic 1 Can the No Child Left Behind Act work?

HAS THE FEDERAL CLASS REDUCTION PROGRAM IMPROVED STUDENT PERFORMANCE?

YES: Children learn to read more quickly in classes of 20 or fewer pupils

YES: Research showed that reducing class size would improve teacher and student performance

SMALL IS BEAUTIFUL
Is size of class inversely proportional to achievement of pupils?

LEVEL OF FUNDING
The program was a federal initiative, but has Washington done enough?

NO: There is no necessary correlation—a class of 30 will perform better with a good teacher than a class of 15 with a bad one

NO: The amount of money put into the program was insufficient for it to be practicable—the emphasis was too much on new teachers, not enough on adequate facilities

HAS THE FEDERAL CLASS REDUCTION PROGRAM IMPROVED STUDENT PERFORMANCE?
KEY POINTS

YES: Research shows that the smaller the ratio between pupils and teachers, the better the academic performance

YES: Teaching and learning both improve in smaller classes

IS THE DIAGNOSIS CORRECT?
Do we need smaller classes or more and better teachers?

NO: The data is insufficient to prove a correlation

NO: It is better to recruit more experienced teachers than to reduce class sizes in the hope that pupils will then improve regardless of who is teaching them

33

Topic 3

IS SWEARING ALLEGIANCE TO THE FLAG IN SCHOOLS UNCONSTITUTIONAL?

YES

FROM "WHAT IS WRONG WITH THE PLEDGE OF ALLEGIANCE"
ATHEISM AWARENESS
BLAIR SCOTT

NO

FROM "UNDER GOD"
SERMON, NEW YORK AVENUE PRESBYTERIAN CHURCH, WASHINGTON, D.C.,
FEBRUARY 7, 1954
DR. GEORGE M. DOCHERTY

INTRODUCTION

On June 26, 2002, a ruling by the Ninth Circuit Court of Appeals in California in the case *Newdow v. Congress of the United States*, provoked a national debate over the constitutionality of the Pledge of Allegiance. The court, in a two-to-one decision, found in favor of Michael Newdow, who stated that "the Pledge of Allegiance is unconstitutional because it includes the phrase 'under God.'" It was thus, he argued, in violation of the Establishment Clause of the First Amendment, which states that "Congress shall make no law respecting an establishment of religion." That clause, in essence, makes it illegal for the government to pass legislation to establish an official religion or to prefer one religion over another.

Newdow, who is an atheist and does not believe in any god, has a daughter who attends a public elementary school in California. He brought the case because, although no pupil can be made to recite the Pledge, he objected to his daughter being forced to "watch and listen as her state-employed teacher in her state-run school leads her classmates in a ritual proclaiming that there is a god and that our's is 'one nation under God.'"

Judges Alfred T. Goodwin and Stephen Reinhardt found that "In the context of the Pledge, the statement that the United States is a nation 'under God' is an endorsement of religion." The court concluded that the Pledge in its current form is unconstitutional and therefore must not be recited in schools. The third judge, Ferdinand Fernandez, disagreed, saying that "Such phrases as 'under God' and 'In God we trust' have no tendency to establish a religion in this country."

Many lawmakers and politicians condemned the court decision and predicted that the ruling would be overturned either by the full Ninth Circuit Court of Appeals or by the Supreme Court, but the case has led many people to question whether swearing allegiance to the flag is unconstitutional.

Francis Bellamy (1855–1941), a former Baptist minister, wrote the original Pledge of Allegiance in 1892 for the public schools' celebrations of the 400th anniversary of the discovery of America by Christopher Columbus. It was first published in the September 8, 1892, issue of *The Youth's Companion* in Boston, stating, "I pledge allegiance to my Flag and the Republic for which it stands, one nation, indivisible, with liberty and justice for all."

---

*"I pledge allegiance
to the flag of the United
States of America,
and to the Republic
for which it stands,
one nation under God,
indivisible, with
liberty and justice for all."*
—PLEDGE OF ALLEGIANCE (1954)

The National Flag Conference in 1923 changed the words "my Flag" to "the Flag of the United States," and in 1924 again to "the Flag of the United States of America," reasoning that immigrants might otherwise pledge their allegiance to the flag of the country of their birth rather than to the flag of the United States. In 1942 Congress codified the Pledge to the Flag in the United States

Flag Code. In 1945 the Pledge received its official title as the Pledge of Allegiance. The words "under God" were added in June 1954, leading President Dwight Eisenhower to state "in this way we are reaffirming the transcendence of religious faith in America's heritage."

Some advocates, including religious groups, argue that the religious significance of the phrase "under God" is minimal and that the *Newdow* decision is an overreaction that could lead to the removal of every mention of God and religion from the public arena. They maintain that there are many precedents for the recognition of the existence of God by the government, including the Declaration of Independence itself.

Others interpret the decision as an attack on religion and the fundamental values on which America was founded. They argue that it is especially vital since September 11, 2001, that the United States support the ideals that reflect the culture of the nation and, by attacking the Pledge, the court is attacking those fundamental values.

Some critics of the current pledge propose that it be returned to its pre-1954 wording. They argue that they are not antireligion, but maintain that they want to uphold the Constitution, and that the inclusion of the words "under God" violates the First Amendment separation of church and state.

Blair Scott, director of Atheism Awareness, in the first of the following pieces, supports the ruling of the Ninth Circuit Court. However, Dr. George M. Docherty, in an extract from his 1954 sermon, argues that the words "under God" should be added to the Pledge because they define the essential character of the United States.

WHAT IS WRONG WITH THE PLEDGE OF ALLEGIANCE
Blair Scott

YES

The fact that it contains the words "under God" is what is wrong with the Pledge of Allegiance. It is a common misconception that the Pledge of Allegiance was written as it is said today. Let us clear up that misconception right now. The Pledge of Allegiance as it was originally written goes like this: "I pledge allegiance to my Flag and the Republic for which it stands, one nation indivisible, with liberty and justice for all." This was as it appeared in a Boston based magazine called *The Youth's Companion* back in 1892. The words were put there for students to repeat on Columbus Day. The magazine's circulation manager, Francis Bellamy, wrote it. Columbus Day fell on October 12, 1892, and children recited the Pledge of Allegiance—beginning the tradition of reciting the Pledge of Allegiance at the beginning of each school day.

Pledge of allegiance modified

On June 14, 1923, at a National Flag Conference in Washington, the Pledge of Allegiance was modified. The words "my flag" were replaced with "the flag of the United States of America."

In 1942 Congress officially recognized the Pledge of Allegiance. In 1943 the Supreme Court ruled that school children could not be forced to recite the Pledge of Allegiance. In June of 1954 the words "under God" were added. President Dwight Eisenhower said:

> *In this way we are reaffirming the transcendence of religious faith in America's heritage and future; in this way we shall constantly strengthen those spiritual weapons which forever will be our country's most powerful resource in peace and war.*

The change was made after the Knights of Columbus (self-proclaimed "Strong Right Arm of the Church") campaigned for the change (during the era of McCarthyism and the "Red Scare"). Bellamy's granddaughter said that Bellamy would have resented the second change because it went against his

---

Scott gets straight to the point of his argument in the first sentence. That is a very effective way of getting the reader's attention.

Francis Bellamy (1855–1941) wrote the Pledge of Allegiance for the public schools' celebration of the 400th anniversary of the discovery of America by the Italian explorer Christopher Columbus (1451–1506).

The Knights of Columbus is a Roman Catholic society for men. It was founded in 1882 by Father Michael J. McGivney at St. Mary's Church, New Haven, Connecticut. Its mission is to protect the interests of the church and to promote civic loyalty among its members.

original intent for the Pledge of Allegiance. Bellamy was the circulation manager for the magazine because he walked away from his church as a Baptist minister the year before. Reverend Bellamy left the church in 1891 because of public views about his socialist sermons and because he thought the church was bigoted and racist. After he retired to Florida, Bellamy discussed what he was thinking when he wrote [it]:

Does Francis Bellamy's original intention matter to the debate about the Pledge?

> *It began as an intensive communing with salient points of our national history, from the Declaration of Independence onwards; with the makings of the Constitution ... with the meaning of the Civil War; with the aspiration of the people.... The true reason for allegiance to the Flag is the 'republic for which it stands.' ... And what does that vast thing, the Republic mean? It is the concise political word for the Nation— the One Nation, which the Civil War was fought to prove. To make that One Nation idea clear, we must specify that it is indivisible, as Webster and Lincoln used to repeat in their great speeches. And its future? Just here arose the temptation of the historic slogan of the French Revolution which meant so much to Jefferson and his friends, 'Liberty, equality, fraternity.' No, that would be too fanciful, too many thousands of years off in realization. But we as a nation do stand square on the doctrine of liberty and justice for all...*

"Liberty, equality, fraternity" was the motto of the French Revolution, which began in 1798. When the French constitution was drafted in 1848, those words defined the main principles of the republic.

The addition of "under God" is a clear violation of the separation of Church and State. The law was changed ... when a small group of Strong Arm Catholics made a stink when everyone was afraid of those "godless communists". The Supreme Court has already ruled that children cannot be forced to say the Pledge of Allegiance, and yet schools continue to defy that decision. Students have been suspended from school for refusing to say the Pledge—even though the Supreme Court said they don't have to say it.

Is there still a fear of communism in the United States? Is it justified? See Volume 13, U.S. History, Topic 11 Did the United States overestimate the threat of communism in the 1950s?

When the 9th Circuit Court in California ruled that the phrase "under God" was unconstitutional it created a national uproar. The timing, because of the post-9/11 environment, could have been better, but the fact remains that the court was correct. Immediately after the decision the leaders of Christianity were on the airwaves rallying against the court. Congress rallied against the court and called the judges such mature words as "idiots," "morons," and other adjectives. The Congressional ploy was so obviously motivated by politics, yet the public didn't seem to realize it.

The court ruling came after the terrorist attacks of September 11, 2001. What difference, if any, do you think the timing made to the decision?

Scott claims that those with opposing views speak "babbling nonsense." Is using this kind of language about those who disagree with his views counterproductive?

The immediate claims on the airwaves were simple arguments and pleading to the emotionalism of Americans. Only those that supported the court's decision actually had any facts or law to back up their view. The religionists only had emotional pleas and babbling nonsense, such as claims that "under God" was a generic statement and didn't support a particular religion. The historical ignorance of the phrase became obvious in letters and on the airwaves. It wasn't until after a few weeks that the majority of Christians at least acknowledged that the phrase was inserted in 1954.

Even the judge that ruled against the phrase, a Republican, stated in his opinion that he disagreed with it and felt it should be there, but he had no choice but to follow the law. None of the opponents of the decisions ever mentioned that. Of course, none of the proponents of the decision seemed to mention it, either. It seemed that both sides were missing the key points. Even the media swayed away from the decision and started pinging on the personal life of Mike Newdow, the plaintiff in the case. ...

Is the phrase "under God" generic?

Is the phrase "under God" generic or does it promote a specific religion? If you consider the source of the phrase and the historical origins thereof, it is clear that it promotes not only a specific religion, but a specific sect; Catholicism. It was a Catholic strong-arm group, the Knights of Columbus, which persuaded and pushed for the phrase to be added during the height of the scare of those "Godless Communists". If the phrase is generic then it should fit every religion as the Christians would have you believe. So let's take a closer look at the way different religions spell the name of their god(s) and write it out.

Close examination of specific words and their meanings is an important debating technique. Slight changes of meaning can often alter the whole meaning of an argument.

"G-d" is the way that god is written out in Judaism. It is considered blasphemous to spell out the name of god, so the hyphen is inserted. We can eliminate Judaism as the endorsed or sponsored religion because the phrase is not "under G-d".

Islam uses the phrase "The God" (Allah). We can eliminate Islam as the endorsed or sponsored religion because the phrase is not "under The God" or "under Allah".

Deism believes in an impersonal god that is spelled with a lowercase "g". We can eliminate deism and related religions as the endorsed or sponsored religion because the phrase is not "under god". Paganism, Shamanism, Wicca or similar religions use "goddess" or the proper names of individual goddesses. Earth-based religions would not call "Mother Earth" such a sexist term as "God". We can eliminate

Paganism and related religions as the endorsed or sponsored religion because the phrase is not "under Goddess" or "atop Mother Earth".

Hinduism talks about the "gods" or uses the specific and proper name of the incarnation of Vishnu, depending on what sect you are referring to. We can eliminate Hinduism as the endorsed or sponsored religion because the phrase is not "under gods".

Endorsement of Christianity

What does that leave? What religion spells god with a capital G? Christianity is the religion that spells their concept of god with a capital G and is not blasphemous to spell it out. Christians are the only ones up in arms over the decision. A Christian sect strong-armed the government to make the change. The Christian mindset of fear of godlessness is what setup the environment that brought on the change. These things combined clearly show that the phrase "under God" in the Pledge of Allegiance is a direct endorsement and promotion of Christianity by the government... It is therefore an unconstitutional phrase and should be removed.

There are a lot of Christians that say by removing " under God" from the Pledge that the government is endorsing "the religion of atheism". To endorse their concept of what religious atheism is (the disbelief in God), the phrase wouldn't be removed—it would be changed to "under no God". The removal of the phrase doesn't endorse any religion or non-religion. It makes no statement either pro or con of any god or goddess concept. The Pledge, without that phrase, remains neutral to all religions.

Do you think the Pledge is still relevant to contemporary U.S. society? Should it be replaced with something more modern?

Pledge to an icon

I'm often surprised that Christians endorse the Pledge of Allegiance in the first place. After all, pledge to an icon (the flag) is in violation of their Ten Commandments. Shouldn't they only be pledging to their god? Of course that goes for any religionist—not just Christians.

The Ten Commandments are fundamental to Judaism and Christianity. The author is referring to the First Commandment, which prohibits idolatry and the worship of anything other than God.

Freedom of religion

This country is founded on the freedom of religion, and as we have already learned, religion does not mean god. Buddhism is a religion without a god and others as well. To pledge to this country by way of its flag with a law written to endorse a single religion (which it does by capitalizing the word god) is a clear violation of the Separation of Church and State....

multitude of Muslim, Jewish, African American, secular, and other homeschooling organizations are popping up across the country. And homeschooling has become an increasingly respected option. Between 1985 and 1997, the percentage of Americans who said they approved of it increased from 16 to 36 percent. Homeschooling, in short, has gone mainstream.

A positive alternative?

What accounts for the trend? In some cases parents see homeschooling as a remedy for the overcrowded classrooms, cookie-cutter curricula, and indifferent teachers that plague so many public school systems. In other cases parents don't trust the public schools to educate their little geniuses, or perhaps they have a child who has been diagnosed with a learning disability and want to customize his education to meet his needs. Private schooling used to be the solution to many of these problems. But, at just a couple of hundred dollars a year for texts and learning materials, homeschooling is a better bargain.

Why do you think these parents are inclined to remove their children from school rather than seeking to improve what they see as the drawbacks of the public school system?

And, to be sure, homeschooling is not necessarily a prescription for domestic disaster. In fact, there are some stunning success stories. Take Andy of Washington, D.C., who is marching through the fourth-grade curriculum of the Calvert School in Baltimore—one of several reputable correspondence schools that offers graders, transcripts, and diplomas to homeschoolers. Andy is a sweet and highly social kid. He participates in a chess club, arts-and-crafts classes, and group field trips. He has studied the stock market and Latin. He is fascinated by idioms. All this, at seven years old.

Do you think there is a way children like Andy could flourish and find fulfillment in a public school?

Better results?—the missing information

But, while homeschooling enthusiasts insist that children taught at home score higher on tests and get into better colleges, a closer look at the research suggests there is little evidence either way. What few studies have been done may be flawed. The most commonly cited study, sponsored by the National Home Education Research Institute, is a case in point. According to that report, the average public school student scores in the 50th percentile on national tests, while the average homeschooler scores in the 80th to 87th percentile—regardless of race. That sounds like an open-and-shut case for homeschooling. But Glen Cutlip, an official of the National Education Association, points out that the study averages percentiles from several different tests, comparing the scores of homeschoolers nationwide with those of public school students ... only [from] the state of Virginia. In

UNDER GOD
Dr. George M. Docherty

NO

X …[Lincoln] claims that it is under God that this Nation shall know a new birth of freedom. And by implication, it is under God that "government of the people, by the people, and for the people shall not perish from the earth." For Lincoln, since God was in His Heaven, all must ultimately be right for his country.

Salute to the flag

Now, all this may seem obvious until one sits down and takes these implications of freedom really seriously. For me, it came in a flash one day sometime ago when our children came home from school. Almost casually, I asked what happened at school when they arrived there in the morning. They described to me, in great detail and with strange solemnity, the ritual of the salute to the flag. The children turn to the flag, and with their hand across their heart, they repeat the words: "I pledge allegiance to the flag of the United States and the Republic for which it stands; one nation, indivisible, with liberty and justice for all."

Docherty was born and brought up in Glasgow, Scotland, and therefore did not have the words of the Pledge of Allegiance stamped on his memory.

I don't suppose you fathers would have paid [as] much attention to that as I did. I had the advantage over you. I could listen to those noble words as if for the first time. You have learned them so long ago, like the arithmetic table or the shorter catechism, something you can repeat without realizing what it all really means. But I could sit down and brood upon it, going over each work slowly in my mind.

And I came to a strange conclusion. There was something missing in this pledge, and that which was missing was the characteristic and definitive facto in the American way of life. Indeed, apart from the mention of the phrase, the United States of America, this could be a pledge of any republic. In fact, I could hear little Muscovites repeat a similar pledge to their hammer-and-sickle flag in Moscow with equal solemnity, for Russia is also a republic that claims to have overthrown the tyranny of kingship.…

Why do you think Docherty mentions Moscow, and why is he worried that Muscovites could recite a similar pledge? Do you think Docherty is motivated by anticommunist sentiments?

What, therefore, is missing in the pledge of allegiance that Americans have been saying off and on since 1892, and officially since 1942? The one fundamental concept that completely and ultimately separates Communist Russia from the democratic institutions of this county. This was seen clearly by Lincoln. Under God this people shall know a new birth of freedom, and "under god" are the definitive words.

Now, Lincoln was not being original in that phrase. He was simply reminding the people of the basis upon which the Nation won its freedom in its declaration of Independence. He went back to Jefferson as he did in so much of his thinking. Indeed, he acknowledges his debt to Jefferson in a famous speech delivered at Independence Hall in Philadelphia on February 22, 1861, two years before the Gettysburg Address. "All the political sentiments I entertain have been drawn from the sentiments which originated and were given to the world from this hall. I have never had a feeling politically that did not spring from sentiments embodied in the Declaration of Independence."

Listen again to the fundamentals of this Declaration:

We hold these truths to be self-evident, that all men are created equal, that they are endowed by their Creator with certain unalienable rights; that among these are life liberty, and the pursuit of happiness.

At Gettysburg Lincoln poses the question: "Now we are engaged in a great civil war, testing whether that nation, or any nation so conceived and so dedicated, can long endure."…

Definitive character of the American way of life

The pledge of allegiance seems to me to commit this theological implication that is fundamental to the American way of life. It should be "One nation, indivisible, under God." Once "under God," then we can define what we mean by "liberty and justice for all." To omit the words "under God" in the pledge of allegiance is to omit the definitive character of the American way of life.

Some might assert this to be a violation of the first amendment to the Constitution. It is quite the opposite. The first amendment states concerning the question of religion: "Congress shall make no law respecting the establishment of religion."

Now, "establishment of religion" is a technical term. It means Congress will permit no state church in this land such as exists in England. In England the bishops are appointed by her Majesty. The church, by law, is supported by teinds or rent. The church, therefore, can call upon the support of the law of the land to carry out its own ecclesiastical laws. What

---

Docherty is quoting from Abraham Lincoln's (1809–1865) memorable Gettysburg Address (1863) in which he said, "…this nation, under God, shall have a new birth of freedom and that government of the people, by the people, for the people, shall not perish from the earth." Why do you think Docherty only used parts of the quotation?

Do the words of the Declaration of Independence suggest a fundamental belief in God?

Is Docherty stating that the United States is a predominantly Christian country? Look at www.census.gov, and see if you can find out if that was true in 1954. Is it the case today?

Do you think that the author's assertion that the "establishment of religion" is a "technical term" is a valid one?

41

Why does Docherty make a distinction between religion and the church? Is the question which religion or which god not the same as which church?

the declaration says, in effect, is that no state church shall exist in this land. This is separation of church and state; it is not, and never was meant to be, a separation of religion and life. Such objection is a confusion of the first amendment with the First Commandment.

If we were to add the phrase "under the church," that would be different. In fact, it would be dangerous. The question arises, which church? Now, I could give good Methodists an excellent dissertation upon the virtues of the Presbyterian Church, and show how much superior John Knox was to John Wesley. But the whole sad story of church history shows how, of all tyrants, often the church could be the worst for the best of reasons. The Jewish Church persecuted unto death the Christian Church in the first decade of Christianity; and for 1,200 years the Christian Church persecuted the Jewish Church. The Roman Church persecuted the Protestants; and the Protestants, in turn, persecuted the Roman Church; the Presbyterians and the Episcopalians brought low the very name of Christian charity, both in Scotland and America. It is not for nothing that Thomas Jefferson, on his tombstone at Monticello, claimed that one of the three achievements of his life was his fight for religious freedom in Virginia—that even above the exalted office as President of these United States. No church is infallible; and no churchman is infallible.

Of course, as Christians, we might include the words "under Jesus Christ" or "under the King of Kings." But one of the glories of this land is that it has opened its gates to all men of every religious faith….

There is no religious examination on entering the United States of America—no persecution because a man's faith differs even from the Christian religion. So, it must be "under God" to include the great Jewish community, and the people of the Moslem faith, and the myriad of denominations of Christians in the land.

Is it possible to be both an atheist and a citizen of the United States? Does it boil down to a matter of individual choice?

What then of the honest atheist?

Philosophically speaking, an atheistic American is a contradiction in terms. Now don't misunderstand me. This age has thrown up a new type of man—we call him a secular; he does not believe in God; not because he is a wicked man, but because he is dialectically honest, and would rather walk with the unbelievers than sit hypocritically with people of the faith. These men, and many have I known, are fine in character; and in their obligations as citizens and good neighbors, quite excellent.

But they really are spiritual parasites. And I mean no term of abuse in this. I'm simply classifying them. A parasite is an organism that lives upon the life force of another organism without contributing to the life of the other. These excellent ethical seculars are living upon the accumulated spiritual capital of Judaeo-Christian civilization, and at the same time, deny the God who revealed the divine principles upon which the ethics of this country grow. The dilemma of the secular is quite simple. He cannot deny the Christian revelation and logically live by the Christian ethic. And if he denies the Christian ethic, he falls short of the American ideal of life.

A God fearing nation

In Jefferson's phrase, if we deny the existence of the god who gave us life how can we live by the liberty he gave us at the same time? This is a God-fearing nation. On our coins, bearing the imprint of Lincoln and Jefferson are the words "In God we trust." Congress is opened with prayer. It is upon the Holy Bible the President takes his oath of office. Naturalized citizens, when they take their oath of allegiance, conclude solemnly, with the words "so help me God."

This is the issue we face today: A freedom that respects the rights of the minorities, but is defined by a fundamental belief in God. A way of life that sees man, not as the ultimate outcome of a mysterious concatenation of evolutionary process, but a sentient being created by God and seeking to know His will, and "Whose soul is restless till he rest in God."

In this land, there is neither Jew nor Greek, neither bond nor free, neither male nor female, for we are one nation indivisible under God, and humbly as God has given us the light we seek liberty and justice for all. This quest is not only within these United States, but to the four corners of the glove wherever man will lift up his head toward the vision of his true and divine manhood.

During her history of more than a century and a half this church has adhered steadfastly to the purpose for which it was organized, the christianizing of her home community and the world. The extent of her influence for good is inestimable and her accomplishments have been many and great. ... As the single purpose for her justification of existence, she has always held on high, Christ and His Gospel as the way of salvation for the world. ... Her course has always been Godward and her influence has extended to "the utmost parts of the earth" in many churches and many denominations.

Is Docherty's reference to atheists being "spiritual parasites" insulting? Does it detract from his argument?

Given that the United States is a multicultural and multidenominational country, is it correct to state that the American ideal is based on the Christian ethic?

Does the fact that the president is sworn into office on the Bible necessarily make the United States a God-fearing nation? Should the Bible be replaced by a nonreligious text?

Summary

What is wrong with the Pledge of Allegiance? Blair Scott, the director of Atheism Awareness, spells out point by point exactly why he thinks the Pledge of Allegiance is unconstitutional. He reminds us that the wording of the Pledge was altered three times and that its original form did not contain the phrase "under God." The Pledge was written in 1892 by a former Baptist minister, James Bellamy, to celebrate Columbus Day. Bellamy gives his reasons for writing the Pledge as "the true reason for allegiance to the flag is the 'republic for which it stands'… it is the concise political word for the nation—the one nation, which the Civil War was fought to prove." The words "under God," which were added to the Pledge by Congress in 1954, violated the First Amendment to the Constitution. Scott also makes the point that "under God" is a direct endorsement of Christianity rather than Buddhism, Hinduism, or other religions and as such is a clear violation of the separation of church and state.

In the second article Dr. George M. Docherty, preaching in 1954, argues for the inclusion of the words "under God" in the Pledge of Allegiance. He puts forward the case that in its original form the Pledge could be meaningfully recited in any country, including communist Russia. Docherty believes that what ultimately sets the United States apart from communist regimes is the nation's fundamental belief in God. He cites Jefferson and Lincoln to back up his view that the United States is a God-fearing nation. He points out that belief in God is central to American life—the president takes his oath of office on the Bible, and coins carry the words "In God We Trust."

FURTHER INFORMATION:

Books:

Baer, John W., *The Pledge of Allegiance: A Centennial History, 1892–1992*. Annapolis, MD: Free State Press, 1992.

Hamburger, Philip, *Separation of Church and State*. Cambridge, MA: Harvard University Press, 2002.

Marshall, Paul A., *God and the Constitution: Christianity and American Politics*. Lanham, MD: Rowman and Littlefield, 2002.

Miller, Margarette S. (ed.), *Twenty-Three Words: The Life Story of the Author of the Pledge of Allegiance as Told in His Own Words*. Portsmouth. VA: Printcraft Press, 1976.

Useful websites:

www.religioustolerance.org/nat_pled3.htm
Site that contains comprehensive information on comparative religions and promotes religious tolerance.

The pages on the *Newdow v. U.S. Congress* case include pointers for further research.

dir.yahoo.com/Society_and_Culture/Religion_and_Spirituality/Church_State_Issues/
A whole directory of issues relating to church and state.

www.atheism.about.com/library/decisions/religion/bl_l_NewdowUSCongress.htm?terms=newdow
Detailed information on the Newdow case.

The following debates in the Pro/Con series may also be of interest:

In this volume:

Topic 12 Should religion be taught in schools?

IS SWEARING ALLEGIANCE TO THE FLAG IN SCHOOLS UNCONSTITUTIONAL?

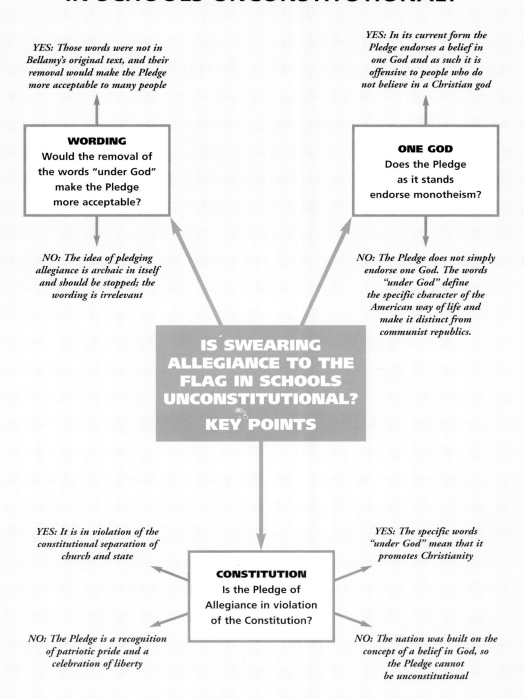

YES: Those words were not in Bellamy's original text, and their removal would make the Pledge more acceptable to many people

YES: In its current form the Pledge endorses a belief in one God and as such it is offensive to people who do not believe in a Christian god

WORDING
Would the removal of the words "under God" make the Pledge more acceptable?

ONE GOD
Does the Pledge as it stands endorse monotheism?

NO: The idea of pledging allegiance is archaic in itself and should be stopped; the wording is irrelevant

NO: The Pledge does not simply endorse one God. The words "under God" define the specific character of the American way of life and make it distinct from communist republics.

IS SWEARING ALLEGIANCE TO THE FLAG IN SCHOOLS UNCONSTITUTIONAL? KEY POINTS

YES: It is in violation of the constitutional separation of church and state

YES: The specific words "under God" mean that it promotes Christianity

CONSTITUTION
Is the Pledge of Allegiance in violation of the Constitution?

NO: The Pledge is a recognition of patriotic pride and a celebration of liberty

NO: The nation was built on the concept of a belief in God, so the Pledge cannot be unconstitutional

PLANNING HOW TO STUDY

*"It's only when you have to use what you've studied
that you regret not studying more."*
—CHINESE PROVERB

*Exams are important, but preparing for one can be very stressful. In an
attempt to retain information, students often cram days—or the night—
before the event. Statistics show that our brain will better remember
information if we review what we have learned each day. Without reviewing,
our brains will only retain about 20 percent of the data seen.
It can be difficult to remember facts and figures, especially when stressed or
nervous. We can help the "remembering" part of our brains by making
connections, linking new information to existing knowledge and concepts.*

Exams

Exams are a part of school life, and the success of future aims and ambitions can
depend on their outcome. That pressure can make it difficult to give the best
performance on the test day. Blind panic can make some people stay up all
night, desperately cramming, and that in itself may result in them performing
badly. The key to good exam study is calm preparation and planning.

Preparation

Study notes are important. Always make your own notes either by typing them
or writing them out neatly. That process will actually help you absorb the
information. Try to summarize your notes as key words and phrases, and then
expand them into more detailed notes from memory. Get into the habit of
reading through your notes each day; that will make it easier to remember
during the exam. Make a plan of what you need to learn for each exam. When
you are confident in your subject knowledge, practice with past test papers.
Use study guides and Internet sites to support your work. Discuss review topics
with friends, or devise tests that other people can give you.

Planning

- Study plans are a good way to ease the stress of review. Write out a study plan
(or review timetable), and stick to it.
- Start your study about 2–3 months before your exams. Set achievable goals,
and dedicate a realistic amount of time to your studies.
- Study with other people (see opposite) if that helps you retain information.
- Study in blocks of 30–40 minutes, and have regular breaks in between.
- Vary your timetable to include your weakest and your strongest subjects. Alter
your learning activities to avoid boredom and to keep your brain stimulated.
- Do not work late into the night; it is better to go to an exam fresh.
- Use exercise and breathing techniques to relieve stress.
- Plan some evenings off with friends to help you relax.

LEARNING STRATEGIES

There are three main ways in which we learn. *Auditory* (taking in information by listening to speech or sound), *visual* (retaining information by looking at words or images), and *kinesthetic* (acquiring knowledge through physically engaging with objects). No one uses one of these styles exclusively, and there is a significant overlap in learning styles. What senses do you prefer to use as you learn? Understanding your own preferences can help you study and learn.

Auditory
Audio learners can take in concepts delivered through speech. They learn best by listening to information. Auditory study aids include taping lectures or putting review notes on tape and listening to them on a recorder; working in groups to discuss what you have read, ideas, and opinions; asking questions and listening to the radio or television.

Visual
Visual learners think in terms of pictures. They often learn best by seeing information. Visual study aids include mind-maps (a diagram that maps the relationship between key elements of the information), study cards, interactive multimedia, illustrated books, charts and graphs, or videos.

Kinesthetic
Kinesthetic learners learn best through touch, movement, and space. They absorb information most successfully by doing. Kinesthetic learning is often hands-on, and learners like sports or working with their hands.

Study groups
Working in a study group can be a productive review technique, but there are several points to remember in order to make it a successful experience:
- Avoid working just with your friends; choose people who stimulate you.
- Work in groups of no more than five people.
- Keep notes on what you have studied and what you plan to do next.
- Test each other.
- Make the most of individual strengths within the group—one person may be an excellent researcher, another a good typist, and so on.

USEFUL WEBSITES

Visit www.homeworkspot.com for more information on learning strategies, tips on exam preparation, and how to study.

Topic 4
DO SCHOOL VOUCHERS WORK?

NO
FROM "DO SCHOOL VOUCHERS VIOLATE THE ESTABLISHMENT CLAUSE?
ARE THEY GOOD PUBLIC POLICY?"
RUTGERS JOURNAL OF LAW AND RELIGION WEBSITE
ELIZABETH J. COLEMAN

YES
FROM "DO SCHOOL VOUCHERS VIOLATE THE ESTABLISHMENT CLAUSE?
ARE THEY GOOD PUBLIC POLICY?"
RUTGERS JOURNAL OF LAW AND RELIGION WEBSITE
STEPHEN D. SUGARMAN

INTRODUCTION

Public schools in the United States have come under criticism in recent years from parents and educators, among others, who believe that their standards have fallen, and that they are failing their students. Many people have come to believe that public education can be improved only if public schools are subject to competition, giving parents a choice of schools for their children.

Wealthy people already have such a choice, critics argue. If they do not like a local public school, they can move or pay to educate their children privately. In order to extend that freedom to everyone, educators suggested that people earning less than a certain income should receive vouchers in order to send their children to schools they could not otherwise afford.

The theory was first put into practice in 1990 when Milwaukee, Wisconsin, allowed a limited number of families whose incomes were less than 1.75

times the poverty level to send their children to private schools at public expense thanks to a voucher worth up to $4,400 a year. Parents were not allowed to choose religious schools because state funding of any religion might be construed as a violation of the First Amendment, which guarantees the separation of church and state. About 1,000 families joined the plan.

In 1995 the Wisconsin legislature expanded the program to allow up to 15,000 students to receive vouchers. It also permitted families to use the vouchers to enrol their children in religious schools. By 1996 nearly three-fourths of the participants were African American, and nearly one-fifth were Hispanic. Opponents went to court to challenge the use of vouchers in religious schools; but in June 1998 the Wisconsin Supreme Court ruled against them, and in the fall of the same year the U.S. Supreme Court refused to review the case. As a result, Wisconsin families were free to use the vouchers in religious schools, and by 1999 approximately 6,000 students were attending nonpublic schools with the aid of publicly funded vouchers.

> *"In large states public education will always be mediocre, for the same reason that in large kitchens the cooking is usually bad."*
> —FRIEDRICH NIETZSCHE
> (1844–1900), PHILOSOPHER

The voucher program for low-income students in Cleveland, Ohio, created in 1995, awarded vouchers of up to $2,250 and allowed them to be used in religious schools. As in Milwaukee, eligibility was based on income. By the spring of 1997 nearly 2,000 students were using vouchers in 46 religious schools and 9 other private schools. During the 1998–99 school year about 3,500 students were enrolled in the program. The Cleveland program was also challenged in court; and although the Ohio state appeals court upheld the challenge, the Ohio Supreme Court let the program continue while it reviewed the case. Efforts to determine whether the achievement levels of voucher students were higher or lower than those of public school students were inconclusive.

Those who object to programs that allow vouchers to be used in religious schools on the grounds that the practice violates the First Amendment prohibition of state-supported religion received a setback in 2002, when the U.S. Supreme Court, by a 5–4 vote, upheld the constitutionality of the Cleveland program. Chief Justice William Rehnquist recognized that 96 percent of participants used the vouchers to attend religious schools, but ruled that the percentage was not constitutionally significant because the program was "entirely neutral in regard to religion." He found that parents did have "true private choice" in how and where to have their children educated.

The first statewide voucher plan was Florida's Opportunity Scholarship Program, enacted in 1999. It offered a yearly voucher worth up to $3,500 to any student enrolled in schools the state judged as worst-performing. The voucher could be used for any school willing to accept the students. In August 2002, however, a Tallahassee circuit court judge ruled that the state's program was unconstitutional on the grounds that it violated a 117-year-old provision in Florida's constitution that prohibits the use of public funds for religious institutions.

The voucher scheme has thus become one of the most controversial issues in U.S. education. Vouchers are generally opposed by teachers' organizations, and a 2002 PDK/Gallup opinion poll found that their view is shared by 52 percent of Americans. One of the greatest fears that opponents have is that vouchers will cause racial and class segregation in schools. Elizabeth J. Coleman, the author of the first of the following articles, argues that the voucher program is unconstitutional. But Stephen D. Sugarman, the second author, disagrees, claiming that voucher programs can only improve public schools and make education more fair.

DO SCHOOL VOUCHERS VIOLATE THE ESTABLISHMENT CLAUSE? ARE THEY GOOD PUBLIC POLICY?
Elizabeth J. Coleman

NO

Summary:

Private school vouchers violate the First Amendment's Establishment Clause, harm public schools, and effect state regulation of religious institutions, according to Anti-Defamation League ["ADL"] Civil Rights Director, Elizabeth J. Coleman....

MS. COLEMAN:

...I am afraid that the ADL's position has already been given away, so there are no surprises here. We are opposed to vouchers both on constitutional and policy grounds....

Vouchers are a very emotional issue.... [W]e look at vouchers through three lenses: through the lens of the Constitution, through the lens of public policy, and inevitably, through a very personal lens.

When one looks at something so emotionally, I think it is easy to look for simple solutions to extraordinarily complex constitutional and policy questions. One of the things we wanted to try to do today was to add some depth to a very important societal discussion.

The importance of separation

As has been so eloquently stated by people who have come before me on this panel, our founding fathers had the wisdom to know that the union of government and religion tends to degrade religion and to destroy government. A person should absolutely not be taxed to pay for the religious indoctrination of others. Over 80% of vouchers for private schools would be used in schools whose central mission is religious training....

Vouchers would do what the Supreme Court has so clearly said is unconstitutional: they would force citizens, Christians, Jews, Muslims, and Atheists to pay for religious indoctrination of students at schools with [a] specific parochial agenda.... There is, however, something particularly important and

---

Elizabeth J. Coleman and Stephen D. Sugarman were two of five panelists who took part in a debate called "Do School Vouchers Violate the Establishment Clause? Are They Good Policy?" These extracts are taken from Coleman's and Sugarman's speeches.

Do taxpayers have a right to decide what their money is spent on. Are state and federal authorities the best people to make such decisions?

troubling about vouchers in relation to other assaults on the wall [separating church and state]. They are a bad idea not just because they hammer at the wall…; they are a bad idea because they harm another pillar of American democracy, the public school. The glory of American public education is that it is for all children, regardless of religion, academic talents, or ability to pay a fee.

As Jews, we know the crucial role public schools have played over the years in helping immigrants become part of America by teaching the common political process and the common values of freedom and tolerance. Vouchers take money from public schools at a time when public schools desperately need money to be fixed.

It is really very simple. Government must not fund religion, and public schools must be enhanced, improved, and treasured, not short-changed in any way at this crucial time.

Are public schools desperately short of funds? If so, why do you think that is? See www.nasvf. org/web/allpress. nsf/pages/5938 for an article on the subject published by the New York Times.

Forces pressuring for change

Unfortunately, forces coming from three groups of people have converged at this time to create societal pressure for vouchers. First, there are those who want to have their religious views permeate every aspect of public life. Second are those who want to privatize the public business of our country, regardless of whether they have a historic interest in inner city and minority children. Third are those who care deeply and rightly about a good education for their children, but fear that that education is not available to them through the public schools now and believe vouchers will help.

Anti-voucher is not anti-religion

To the first group I say, as a religious-based organization, we also value deeply the role religion can play in people's lives and in society, and we believe that religious schools, from Catholic schools to Jewish day schools, are an important option for families. They are a necessary part of our educational mosaic. The government, however, must not pay for this education.

Let us stick with the American tradition of separation. It has served us, the religious and nonreligious, magnificently for 200 years, and serves us even better as we become more religiously diverse. Besides, as was discussed earlier, state regulation of religious schools may well follow state funding, something deeply religious people should find particularly odious, thus compromising another great constitutional principle, religious freedom. The flip side of that, of course, is inadequate accountability. Neither situation is palatable, the

Harvard University's Pluralism Project is a long-term study of "the growing religious diversity of the United States." Go to www.fas. harvard.edu/ ~pluralsm/ for more information.

51

regulation of federally funded parochial schools or the lack thereof. Finally, once down that road, there is divisiveness, as was said earlier, for scarce federal funds. Religious minorities will never win a political battle over scarce federal funds.

Defending the public realm

To the second group, I say we are better off leaving the public schools in the hands of government. The government has been doing this for 200 years. Furthermore, any perception that the general American public does not share this view would be misplaced. Public schools are part of our American tradition. Like separation of church and state, they are cornerstones of our democracy. When we take money and talented students from them, we leave people behind, because many private schools do not accept people with learning disabilities, special language needs, low academic achievement, those who might not meet a religious criterion, et cetera. People would be at risk of being left out of the American dream altogether. This can harm those left behind, their communities, and ultimately, our greater American community. Also, they risk separating communities, vulcanizing them, taking away historically the most important thing that brings us together, at a time when increasing diversity makes this even more important. Ultimately, this is bad for all of us.

There are, of course, enormous issues about whether competition works in this setting. I am still puzzled by how taking money away from the schools improves the schools. Finally, it is unpalatable to try to save just a few children, as not every child can go to private schools.

Doing the best for our children

To the third group, I say—and this is the hardest, the very hardest to say—apart from the fact that it is unclear vouchers improve academic achievement, you are right, everyone deserves a great education. It is part of our birthright as Americans, and everyone has to look after his or her children and do the best for them. How can parents not seek vouchers for their children, if they can do so and believe that it is the children's best hope? But the jury is far from out on whether vouchers work. Besides, from a societal standpoint, it is an unacceptable choice, because so many children will not have the choice. They will not be able to afford the schools even with vouchers; will not be chosen by private schools for a specific reason, or for no reason at all, or perhaps for a socially unacceptable reason like race or religion; or maybe

Should private schools be obliged to take any pupil in return for receiving money through vouchers? What do they have to gain by doing this?

The fact that private schools are not required to publish their results makes comparison of academic standards difficult. Should private schools that take vouchers be bound by the same rules of accountability that apply to public schools?

their parents will not be able to afford the transportation, the uniform, or the school trips.

It is unpalatable for a parent to have to choose between giving up his child's religious upbringing and getting the child the education he or she needs. To call vouchers school choice is a misnomer, for they merely leave many with a worse choice or no choice. The poorest are left behind in schools that are even more bound to fail.

So, to the third group I say ... let us work together to fix the public schools. I think Elliot Mincberg has been very involved with People for the American Way in some extraordinary ideas. There is an enormous amount of creativity out there on what to do with the public schools within the public system. I think we need to grab onto that and go with those types of efforts and really treat that issue like the emergency it is....

Let us fix our public schools and leave our Constitution alone. Thank you.

Elliot Mincberg is vice president and legal director of People for the American Way, which promotes the public support of public schools. See www.pfaw.org/ pfaw/general/ for further information.

DO SCHOOL VOUCHERS VIOLATE THE ESTABLISHMENT CLAUSE? ARE THEY GOOD PUBLIC POLICY?
Stephen D. Sugarman

YES

JUDGE ADAMS:
Our next speaker is Professor Steve Sugarman, Boalt Hall, University of California.

PROFESSOR SUGARMAN:
Thank you.

The President of the United States sent his daughter to a private school. I read recently that a majority of the members of the Senate and the Congress have sent their children to private schools. A startling proportion of public schoolteachers sends their children to private school.

What is the message here? The message is that the poor cannot be trusted to make choices for their children. And it is really bad when you hear the message from the people who view themselves as self-styled defenders of the civil rights and civil liberties of the poor.

Another source of dismay of mine is that liberal opponents of school vouchers attack Milton Friedman's plan, an unregulated voucher scheme, in which half the money that we now spend on public school kids would go to every kid in the country. That is not what the public wants. That is not what school choice is becoming. It is not what the publicly funded private school choice programs in states like Florida and cities like Milwaukee and Cleveland are about. It is not what privately funded school voucher programs in Indianapolis, San Antonio, and seventy-five other cities around the country are about.

Those plans are all about giving choice to working class and poor families. It is choice for those families that we liberals ought to be concerned about, and it is choice that the children in those families desperately need.

Extending choice to the poor
People who have means can already move to the fancy suburbs and send their kids to what are purported to be

Economist Milton Friedman first proposed using vouchers in schools in the mid-1950s. Go to www.cato.org/ pubs/briefs/ bp-023.html for a more recent statement of his views on the subject.

A 2002 report by the General Accounting Office gives background on the history and performance of privately funded school voucher plans operating in many U.S. cities. See www.gao.gov/new. items/d02752.pdf for more information.

public schools, or they can send their kids to private schools. Of course, those schools do not generally admit poor kids from the cities. Poor families do not usually have a choice.

What happens when you do give poor families a choice for their kids? They jump at the opportunity. John Walton and Ted Forstmann recently offered 40,000 school vouchers to poor families, and one million families around the country signed up in a very short time.

How do the poor feel about the choices they make once they are given the opportunity to choose?

They think their choices are great. They think the schools they have selected for their kids are better. Their kids like it better. The kids go more often. The teachers are more demanding. The curriculum is more central to the kids' lives. Plus, if the kids stick with it, the kids do much better. The literature also demonstrates that poor children who attend private schools graduate from high school and go on to college at a far higher rate than their counterparts who stay in the public schools.

Elizabeth Coleman charged that voucher plans skim off the cream. It is a charge often made by liberals. These programs I am talking about do not skim off the cream.

First of all, to start with, we are talking about poor people. Second, among poor families whose kids are doing very well in public schools, do they leave when they are given these choices?

No, they stay where their kids are succeeding. Who leaves in these typical programs that are now in place around the country? It is the single mother whose kid is being treated very badly and failing miserably in the school. She is the one who moves her child to a place where the child has a chance to do better.

A price worth paying

Now, will some private schools go bankrupt or rip off their families through fraud under a school voucher plan?

Yes, a few will. That is also true for some car dealers and some department stores, but no one is suggesting that we have Soviet-style government ownership of the distribution of clothes and automobiles in this country.

In any event, the real bankruptcy and fraud are in many of our urban public schools, where the push-out/drop-out rate, in public schools like those in New York City for example, is more than 50%,18 and many of those who so-called graduate end up functionally illiterate. That is where the real bankruptcy and fraud are.

John Walton and Ted Forstmann are businessmen who founded the Children's Scholarship Fund in 1998. See www.scholarship fund.org/index.asp/ for more information.

Could public schools be improved in the ways that Sugarman lists? If so, would there still be a need for private schools?

If schools can be viewed in the same way as private businesses, should they receive money via the voucher program? Car dealers and department stores do not receive public funds.

Will some parents make poor choices for their children? Yes, some will. But, of course, under a choice plan, if your first choice does not work out very well, you can change your choice and go somewhere else. That is not what our public schools are about. They are very, very reluctant to let you transfer out of the local school if your child is not doing well. Often your only real choice is to try to move. But if you are poor and living even in quasi-decent, low-income housing, the last thing you want to do is to move. And if you are living in government-subsidized housing, you probably cannot move at all.

Will we get more racial isolation by having school choice? Well, the reality is that we have a tremendous and growing amount of racial isolation in our public schools today. Although private schools and charter schools have considerable racial isolation, it is less than the public schools have. We will get some more appealing sorts of racial isolation, I suspect, with choice. Some African-American families will choose Afro-centric schools. Some Hispanic families will choose bilingual schools. I think that is great. They should be able to get what they want for their kids. In fact, they will probably be moving their kids from one racially isolated school to another racially isolated school.

Is racial isolation more acceptable when it is chosen than when it is forced on children?

Challenging public schools to do better

Will the public schools get better? Elizabeth Coleman makes the usual complaint that we are siphoning money from the public schools with these plans, neglecting to note, of course, that children are leaving, so there are fewer children over whom to spread the money. In fact, in the last two decades we have [had] more than doubled spending in public schools—that is, real, inflation-adjusted spending. Alas, our public schools are not doing significantly better. Most people think they are doing worse.

Is it only a question of funding per pupil, or are there also some fixed costs that do not drop even when fewer children are enrolled?

If we have widespread school choice, public schools will get better. They will get better because they will want to hold on to their enrollment. In order to hold on to their pupils, they will be more responsive to the needs of kids— needs that are neglected now. We see this already with charter schools. When charter schools begin to spring up in substantial numbers in the community, the public schools respond and the public schools do more.

Charter schools are publicly funded and are accountable for their results, but are largely independent in their operation. See www.suntimes.com/special_sections/skul/charter.html for more background.

Within the constitution

Now, let me just say a few words about the constitutionality of school choice. The purpose of these plans is to give some measure of choice to the poor that other families, like those of most of us in this room, have long had for our children. Is this worthy and legal purpose somehow made illegal because some of those children will be sent to religious schools? I do not think so.

Is the Food Stamp program illegal because some poor people use their food stamps to buy matzo for use in their Passover Seder? I do not think so. No one would say that.

Some people say, "Well, that is different, because only a little bit of the food stamp program's money is used for religious ritual purposes." And they say, "Look at all the school choice that will be used for religious schools." Elizabeth Coleman said 80%. But that is the wrong way to understand school choice plans. Most people who are given choice in a sensible school choice plan will choose to stay in their local public schools. That is where most of the choice will be made. Some will choose charter schools. Some will choose magnet schools. Some will choose an inter-district transfer, in the states that allow it, to out-of-district schools in the suburbs. Some will choose private, nonreligious schools. And, yes, some will choose private religious schools. In the bigger picture, relatively few of the people who have the choice will make that choice.

Magnet schools are public schools that specialize in particular subject areas, like math or the arts. See www.magnet.edu/ for more information.

Would Sugarman benefit from citing statistics here? Coleman gave a percentage figure. Is her argument more convincing?

Let me emphasize that the people who choose to keep their kids in public schools will also be making a choice, and their choice will change the milieu of the public schools. This is because their children will now be there by choice, and not by force. In turn, those public schools will get a benefit that private schools now have. They will get the loyalty of their families, because the families will be there because they want to be there. And if you choose to be there, the schools can make more demands on you as a family and more demands on your child. That, I think, is part of the secret as to why private schools do so well.

Now, you could say, "Well, we could create vouchers that could only be used in nonreligious private schools. What would be wrong with that?" I would certainly be in favor of such a plan, as compared to what we have now. But why, I say, should we limit it to that? If there are some families who want religious schools for their children, why should they be singled out and treated worse because that is the kind of choice they want to make? That is what the free exercise of religion is about. That is the sort of position that I would have thought that the Anti-Defamation League, our cosponsor today, would have been supporting—that is, endorsing the free exercise rights of all of American families. Thank you.

Summary

The first article is the text of a speech given by Elizabeth J. Coleman, civil rights director of the Anti-Defamation League, during a debate on the school voucher program held at Rutgers University, New Jersey. Her main objection to the plan is that it is unconstitutional. The Framers wanted the church and state to be separate. Coleman says that public education should be for all children regardless of their religion, and that no one should be taxed to pay for the religious indoctrination of others. School vouchers—80 percent of which, she says, would be used in religious schools—are therefore a violation of the First Amendment. Moreover, state subsidy for private education undermines public schools by depriving them of funds that they would otherwise receive.

The second article is a transcript of Professor Stephen D. Sugarman's reply to Coleman in the same debate. He believes that all children should have the opportunity to attend the best schools available regardless of their parents' financial means. The only way to achieve this is by subsidizing those who cannot afford to send their children to their schools of choice. He disputes Coleman's view that voucher programs will skim off the best pupils from public schools: On the contrary, he asserts that the greater the available choice of schools, the better public schools will become because they will work harder to hang onto their enrollment. Sugarman also disputes Coleman's objection to the voucher scheme on constitutional grounds—if some parents want their children to be educated in religious schools, they will only be a minority, and that, after all, is what religious freedom is all about.

FURTHER INFORMATION:

Books:

Bonsteel, Alan, and Carlos Bonilla, *A Choice for Our Children: Curing the Crisis in America's Schools*. San Francisco, CA: ICS Press, 1997.

Good, Thomas L., and Jennifer S. Braden, *The Great School Debate: Choice, Vouchers, and Charters*, Mahwah, NJ; L. Erlbaum, 2000.

Useful websites:

www-camlaw.rutgers.edu/publications/law-religion/debate_3.htm

A transcript of the debate from which these papers derive.

www.geocities.com/Athens/Cyprus/6547/articles.html

School Funding Equity page of articles against vouchers.

http://edreform.com/school_choice/facts/

The Center for Education Reform resource page of articles giving the case for vouchers.

The following debates in the Pro/Con series may also be of interest:

In this volume:
Part 1: Issues in U.S. education

Topic 1 Can the No Child Left Behind Act work?

In *The Constitution*:

Topic 9 Does the Constitution protect religious freedom?

DO SCHOOL VOUCHERS WORK?

YES: Without vouchers the rich have a greater choice of schools than the poor

RANGE OF CHOICE
Do vouchers give everyone access to the school of their choice?

NO: Even with the voucher program private schools can reject applicants, and that limits their choice

YES: The state should not finance education that instructs students in any particular religion

CONSTITUTIONAL CONSIDERATIONS
Do vouchers conflict with the First Amendment?

NO: Freedom of religion is also enshrined in the First Amendment; the voucher system protects and empowers that freedom

DO SCHOOL VOUCHERS WORK?
KEY POINTS

YES: The fear of losing good pupils will galvanize public schools into raising standards

THE EFFECT ON EDUCATION
Do vouchers benefit public schools and pupils?

NO: Good pupils will move to better schools, making the bad schools worse

YES: They empower poor parents to send their children to better schools

NO: Minorities often select schools that teach their own language and culture, which breaks the U.S. tradition of unifying disparate cultural elements

THE PUBLIC SCHOOL SYSTEM

INTRODUCTION

The American educational system is split between public schools, funded by state and federal money, and private schools, which get their income from sources such as parental fees or grants from private foundations. The vast majority of Americans are educated in the public school system. For that reason public schools are fundamental to education. For that reason too, however, they receive a lot of criticism.

A question of size

One of the main challenges facing the public school system is its sheer size. In 2003 *The Washington Post* reported that there were around 53 million children in American public schools. Department of Education figures reveal that enrollment is growing, and is growing more quickly in public schools than in private schools. Between 1985 and 2001 enrollment in public elementary and secondary schools rose by 20 percent; in contrast, private school enrollment rose by only 7 percent. To cope with such numbers, public schools are now extremely large. Throughout the 20th century there was a trend to consolidate small schools into larger bodies; from 1930 to 2003, the total number of public schools fell from almost 250,000 to only 85,000.

Critics of the public school system argue that large schools contribute to the commonly perceived failings of American schools. Those failings include discipline problems, particularly with regard to the presence of drugs and firearms in schools, and problems deciding how best to deal with America's multiethnic society.

Some of these problems reflect broader dilemmas in American society. Even though black Americans make up 12 percent of the population, for example, their representation in higher education is only 6 percent. For critics, this is evidence that minorities receive fewer educational opportunities than their white counterparts, beginning in public schools.

Schools are also on the frontline of the interaction between settled Americans and non-English-speaking ethnic groups, particularly Hispanics and East Asians. Although schools do mirror the wider problems of society, some people believe that they also—because they are a controlled environment—offer the best chance to tackle them.

Privatization

The rise in enrollment and the reduction in the number of schools were accompanied by fluctuating levels of state funding for elementary and secondary schools, although the general trend was upward. Critics complain that the system remains underfunded, and that funds are wasted on bureaucracy and bad management. They associate the public school system with inefficiency, a lack of competition, and poor teachers. For some the answer lies in treating schools like other services: Take them out of government hands, and put them in the private sector, which, because it is profit driven, is more business oriented, competitive, and efficient. Privatization in public schools is the subject of Topic 5.

Education to solve social ills?

The social problems in public schools include violence, as highlighted by such events as the Columbine High School shootings in Colorado in April 1999, and the high rate of teenage pregnancy. Around one million young women between 15 and 18 become pregnant each year; around 70 percent of them drop out of high school.

attended one of the 2,700 charter schools. But critics question how accountable the schools really are and whether they should be state-funded.

For other parents home schooling is the answer. It has become much more popular in the last 20 years or so. Some estimates claim that between 500,000 and 1.23 million children are being taught at home by their parents Advocates of home schooling argue that not only does it strengthen family bonds, but it also allows the parent to monitor exactly what his or her child is learning. Topic 7 considers home schooling further.

The problem of the "other"

Certain commentators argue that parents should not have to look outside the public school system. They assert

"Today's public education system is a failed monopoly; bureaucratic [and] rigid."
—DAVID T. KEARNS, BUSINESSMAN AND EDUCATIONALIST

Faced with what they perceive as this social failure in the school system, some parents seek alternatives. Charter schools, examined in Topic 6, are a popular option. They are publicly funded, but are allowed to operate under their own charter, normally devised by parents, teachers, and community leaders. Charter schools are accountable for the academic performance of students and the running of the schools, but operate, for the most part, outside of the rules that most public schools have to abide by. In 2003 the Center for Educational Reform estimated that almost 700,000 students

that many problems could be solved by increased funding or lower enrollment. They claim that money can be saved by preventing the children of illegal immigrants—many from Mexico or Central America—from attending school. This would help deal with the problems of large classes, overstretched resources, bored students, truancy, and unacceptable social behavior. Opponents argue that this argument goes against the ethos of a universal public school system. The last topic in this section looks at whether the children of illegal immigrants should be allowed to attend public schools.

Topic 5
SHOULD PRIVATE BUSINESSES RUN PUBLIC SCHOOLS?

YES

FROM "CLASSROOMS, INC.: WILL PRIVATIZATION SAVE PUBLIC SCHOOLS?"
ED. MAGAZINE (HARVARD GRADUATE SCHOOL OF
EDUCATION IN THE NEWS), DECEMBER 1, 2002
REBECCA POLLARD

NO

"PRIVATE OPERATOR OF U.S. PUBLIC SCHOOLS FACING FINANCIAL CRISIS"
WORLD SOCIALIST WEBSITE, MAY 29, 2002
PETER DANIELS

INTRODUCTION

In a recent survey of 20 developed countries United States 12th-graders came 15th out of 20 on international math tests and 12th in science. Many Americans believe that such results constitute an educational crisis. They believe that reform of the public education system is necessary in order to change matters. But what shape should that reform take?

Increasing numbers of people believe that privatizing the public education system could be the answer. "Privatization" generally means moving the services performed by public employees to private businesses. That usually happens in the form of "contracting out," in which public organizations enter into private contracts for the delivery of services. School districts have been contracting out certain education support services, such as maintenance, transportation, and catering, for decades. The same

approach is now being extended to teaching and administration. Contracting out services usually leads to lower costs, and supporters of privatization say that those savings can be diverted back into the classroom, where they are badly needed.

Attempts to improve the situation in public schools have been made before. A voucher system whereby parents are given public money to help send their children to private schools has been posed but has not met with much enthusiasm among the public. Some people feel that such a system will only further marginalize less-advantaged students. Charter schools, where a school is given public money but allowed to apply for its own charter and operate independently of the rules that govern most public schools, have proved more popular. Plans to privatize the education system, though, have caused the most controversy to date.

Some critics see public schools as wasteful and bureaucratic, with poor teaching standards. And more and more people argue that for-profit schools, or educational management organizations (EMOs), can offer the flexibility, efficiency, and expertise that schools need to succeed. For-profit schools, supporters argue, are more accountable than public schools. At a for-profit school, if results drop, the company running the school stands to lose its contract and also its investors' support. Advocates of privatization argue, therefore, that running schools for profits provides educators with greater incentives to achieve.

"If all the rich and all of the church people should send their children to the public schools they would feel bound to concentrate their money on improving these schools until they met the highest ideals."
—SUSAN B. ANTHONY (1820–1906),
SOCIAL REFORMER

EMOs can design their own school curriculum. New York-based EMO Edison Schools claims that it has raised academic achievement through initiatives it has introduced such as the Success for All reading program, the provision of computers for students at home, and the generous allowance of time teachers are allocated on a daily basis for their professional development.

But there are as many voices against privatizing schools as there are in support. The National Education Association is opposed to privatization because it believes it is a threat to the quality of education, the accountability of public schools to their communities, and the welfare of schoolchildren. Civil liberties groups have also expressed concerns about the nature of some of the right-wing political backing the move to privatization has attracted. There is often an ideological as well as an economic motivation for investors to support for-profit schools.

There are further concerns about the implications of a corporate takeover of the education system. Will privatization lead to profit being the primary concern in education—questions of who controls the budget, who has the power to award contracts, and so on—rather than the interests of students? Proposals by companies to take over public schools have included plans to cut the teaching staff to save cost. Some people question how education can be improved by having fewer teachers and pushing class sizes above the limit of 33. Evidence of these concerns can be seen in the numbers of worried parents and students who are protesting against privatization.

For-profit schools currently teach around 100,000 of America's 53 million children from kindergarten through 12th grade. And they are growing rapidly. But is this the best course for U.S. education?

The following articles debate the issue of privatizing public education and focus on Edison Schools. Rebecca Pollard in the first argues that private businesses work, but Peter Daniels disagrees in the second extract.

CLASSROOMS, INC.: WILL PRIVATIZATION SAVE PUBLIC SCHOOLS?
Rebecca Pollard

YES

On an unusually hot morning in the South Bronx something strange was happening at the Harriet Tubman Charter School. … A small parade of teachers and aides formed behind a triumphant-looking five-year-old girl [who has] just finished reading her 25th book…

As Avgayil burst into the principal's office, Michele Pierce, Ed.M.'95, the school's founding director, greeted her with clamorous applause.…

With few exceptions, all of the kindergartners read and write at a first-grade level. That is especially remarkable given that students in the South Bronx have a history of scoring lower on reading and writing tests than any other students in the country.

There is one other unusual aspect to the learning that is taking place at Harriet Tubman: somebody is making a profit on it—or at least trying to. The school is operated by Edison Schools, Inc., the single largest for-profit educational management organization—or EMO—in the United States. The company manages some 150 public schools in 23 states from its headquarters on Manhattan's Fifth Avenue. Its student population, at close to 85,000, dwarfs all but a few dozen school districts in the country. Despite plummeting stock values, high debt, and a recent investigation by the Securities Exchange Commission, Edison plans to keep growing.

See www. edisonschools.com/ for the company's website.

But the idea that a company might attempt to make a profit from learning—albeit a small one—has sparked tremendous controversy. In Philadelphia … that controversy has come to a head. Since the state seized control of the city's troubled schools last December, Pennsylvania's plan to yield a number of them to for-profit EMOs has made front-page news.…

Governor Mark Schweikert announced that the government of Pennsylvania was taking control of the Philadelphia School District on December 22, 2001. See www.edweek. org/ew/newstory. cfm?slug=16philly. h21 for more background on this story.

School ties

Edison Schools has … found itself caught in a fiery debate in which both sides claim to want the same thing: to improve K-12 education, particularly for poor, urban children. On one side, Edison and other privatization enthusiasts believe that running schools for profit will give educators greater incentives to raise achievement. On the other side, critics of for-profit schools argue that doing well and doing good are mutually exclusive endeavors.

Still, according to Stephen Tracy, Ed.D.'84, Edison's chief architect behind the deal, Edison's potential success in Philadelphia could give the for-profit EMO movement its biggest opportunity to date to prove its worth and open up a new channel for urban school reform....

Edison's philosophy and its school design were enough to convince Tracy to join the private sector after nearly a quarter-century in public schools. "Public schools change slowly, even under great pressure. Given all the talk about A Nation at Risk and school reform in the 1980s and 1990s, it's incredible to me how much public schools have resisted true reform," he says....At an Edison school, if test scores droop, parents complain or teachers quit, the company stands to lose its contract with that school system's board. Edison is also beholden to its investors, who have supplied some $500 million for the research behind the company's design....

> In April 1983 the National Commission on Excellence in Education report entitled A Nation at Risk warned against "a rising tide of mediocrity" in education. See www.ed.gov/pubs/NatAtRisk/ for the text of the original report.

Conservative education pundit Chester E. Finn, Jr., M.A.T.'67, Ed.D.'70, the president of the Thomas B. Fordham Foundation, also joined the Edison Project during its inception. Finn recalls how the group envisioned the ideal school "completely uncontaminated" by the clutches of government. "It was great fun," he says. "We essentially got paid to brainstorm the perfect school design." That design has remained largely intact to this day, says Finn. It includes, among other elements, the Success for All reading curriculum, Spanish instruction in every grade, monthly computer-based assessments, and a whopping 90 minutes of professional development time for each teacher, every day. The company also mandates an eight-hour school day, as well as a longer school year. Since it opened its first school in 1995, Edison has purchased more than 30,000 computers for its students' families. These efforts have added up to success in most Edison schools: the company boasts that it has raised achievement in 84 percent of them.

> Pollard carefully lists the qualifications of the people she mentions. Why?

> What do you think would be the advantages and disadvantages for students of a longer school day and school year?

The potential for profit

The financial payoff, however, may take some time.... As anyone at the company would freely admit, Edison does not foresee making money until it assumes management of many more schools; it would do well, say company sources, to capture around 1 or 2 percent of the 92,000 public schools in the country. Since Edison receives the same public funding, per pupil, that district schools receive, it can make a profit only by running its schools more efficiently—that is, for less money. The more schools it manages, the more cheaply it can purchase computers, curriculum packages, and supplies. Edison also curbs costs by having just one central administrative office, where a staff of about 350 oversee operations at all of its schools. In contrast, [school] districts of comparable size have as many as 1,500 administrators on the payroll.

Yet if and when Edison does turn a profit, it will be a relatively small one. The profit margin for EMOs hovers at around 7 percent....But EMOs are the love child of a new kind of venture capitalist, says Peter Stokes, the executive vice president of Eduventures, Inc., a research and financial advising firm that specializes in educational markets. "These are investors who believe they are challenging the status quo. It's really a politicized investment," he says.

Whether or not the private sector should plunge its sticky fingers into the public pot is not a new debate—and doing so is not a new phenomenon. The past two decades have seen privatization in the postal service, energy services, and many parts of public education outside of whole-school management....For-profit companies have had a large and relatively inconspicuous role in education for a long time, says Edison's chief development officer Manuel Rivera, Ed.M.'75, Ed.D.'94, who, like Tracy, works to develop new Edison partnerships with schools. "I remember when I was a superintendent," says Rivera, who led the Rochester (New York) Public Schools from 1992 to 1994. "I would sign million-dollar contracts with textbook companies or companies that provided school lunches. They were making profits, and with no accountability. No one was out there holding a sign that said, 'Hey, you're profiting off our kids.'"

Do you think it matters what motivates investors in a company like Edison? How might that have an effect on the way the company operates?

Rivera argues that private companies have been making money in public education for a long time. Do you think there are any important differences between such companies and EMOs like Edison?

Building an empire—and holding it accountable

Last year, the education industry brought in over $100 billion in revenues—a number that must have appealed to Edison's founder and CEO, Christopher Whittle, media entrepreneur and former chairman of *Esquire* magazine. In the late 1980s, Whittle ... launched *Channel One*, a TV program produced by and for teens that delivered 10 minutes of news with 2 minutes of commercials to classrooms across the country.

Since Whittle founded the Edison Project in 1992, a number of EMOs have started, and many have folded. About 35 remain, but mergers and acquisitions keep this number in constant flux. Edison is, by far, the largest EMO, and one of few that has also started managing public, noncharter schools, such as the ones in Philadelphia. But almost none of the EMOs has turned a profit....

The results

Edison management does not hide the fact that some of its schools have incurred a bevy of grievances, low scores, and bad press. More than 20 schools have ended contracts with the company for a host of reasons. ... "No one here will tell you that we've hit the ball out of the park every time. Far from it, in some cases. But the fact is that we are improving achievement in the majority of our schools," says R. Gaynor McCown, Ed.M.'87, Edison's senior vice president for business development and a former senior education policy analyst for the Clinton administration.

Edison recently hired RAND, a nonprofit, nonpartisan research organization, to conduct an independent evaluation of achievement in the company's schools and of claims in its annual reports. RAND will not complete the study until 2003, although it has released preliminary findings that verify scores listed in Edison's annual reports. "Edison is an institution that is committed to learning. We want to learn from our mistakes, and we have to stay afloat," says McCown. "That's how any business works."...

> RAND was founded in 1948 with the aim of promoting "scientific, educational, and charitable purposes for the public welfare and security of the United States." See its website at www.rand.org/ for further details.

In the end, what runs the school?

...A recent National Education Association-funded study conducted by Peter W. Cookson Jr., C.A.S.'91, of Columbia University's Teachers College, found that the "striking investments" that Edison makes in teachers often result in high morale. Teachers attend yearly professional development seminars, for instance, and take part in career-ladder programs. Teacher pay at Edison varies from district to district, but Edison sources say it is competitive with district salaries, often higher to compensate for the longer school day and year. The Cookson study suggests that the extra teaching time may contribute to teacher burnout, though. Some Edison schools do have high teacher attrition rates, but the average attrition rate for Edison schools has dropped to around 17 percent, only slightly higher than the national average....

> The National Education Association was founded in 1857 "to ... advance the interests of the profession of teaching and to promote the cause of popular education." See its website at www.nea.org for further details.

...Perhaps Michele Pierce puts it best when she explains what really underlies the learning at Harriet Tubman: "This school works because the people here care a lot about it. We're a community here, a family, and we believe that learning is about relationships," she says. "EMOs don't really run schools in the end—people do."

> Do you think there is any connection between this sense of community and the fact that the school is run by an EMO? If so, what do you think that connection is?

PRIVATE OPERATOR OF U.S. PUBLIC SCHOOLS FACING FINANCIAL CRISIS
Peter Daniels

NO

Edison Schools, the for-profit company that was handed control of 20 schools in the city of Philadelphia only a month ago [April 2002, after the state had taken control of Philadelphia School District in December 2001], is reported to be facing a severe cash crisis that imperils its plans for expansion and may even jeopardize its current operations.

The company has grown substantially in recent years, with the help of sympathetic local and state politicians. Its revenue for the fiscal year that ended in June 2001 was $375.8 million, compared to $38.6 million five years earlier. It currently manages schools enrolling some 75,000 students in 22 different U.S. states, including nearly all the largest states—California, Illinois, Michigan, New Jersey, Pennsylvania, Texas and New York.

Would the use of EMOs open up schools to financial insecurities that might disrupt the education of their students?

This rapid growth has not translated into profits for Edison, however. It has reported continuous losses, with its cumulative losses now amounting to more than $240 million. The shortfalls have been made up by infusions of cash raised primarily from sales of company stock. Its initial public offering in November 1999 raised more than $120 million, and second and third offerings, in August 2000 and March 2001 respectively, raised another several hundred million dollars.

What safeguards should schools have to ensure that education can continue regardless of the state of the stock market?

Falling on hard times

Now, however, Edison must raise at least another $50 million at a time when its stock price has completely collapsed. Like some of the dot.com casualties and other high-flying firms from the late 1990s, its shares have fallen more than 95 percent from their high of several years ago. Edison stock traded at $35 a share in early 2001, fell to $20 by the beginning of 2002, and is now less than $1.50. Thus the sale of new stock is obviously not now an option, but other alternatives appear to be equally unpalatable. Edison had to pledge $61 million in assets last fall as collateral for a loan of only $20 million. It has also been paying as much as 20 percent interest on some loans.

The company may turn again to wealthy investors whose primary motive is an ideological one. Edison has become the standard bearer of the campaign, backed by growing sections of the wealthy and big business, to privatize the education system. Its supporters have argued that the introduction of the profit motive is necessary to provide a decent education. At the very least, they have claimed, the element of competition will shake up the "public school monopoly" and force the public schools to improve.

Edison Schools was founded by L. Christopher Whittle about 10 years ago [in 1992]. It first proposed a national network of private schools. It made a tactical shift, however, in response to critics who pointed out that simply shifting public funds to private schools via a voucher system or privately-run "charter schools" would leave the vast majority of students behind in public schools that were being essentially abandoned. The proposal to take over the management of public schools enabled Edison to present itself as the savior of all public school students, and the school system as a whole. Inveighing against bureaucracy, waste and poor teaching, the company claimed it would make a profit while operating schools for less money than currently budgeted.

Whittle recruited high-profile backers, most notably Benno Schmidt, the president of Yale University, who became president of Edison. Meanwhile, amid the increasingly desperate situation in many public schools, especially in urban and working class areas, parents were told that profit-making schools would introduce efficiency and dynamism into the system.

Do you think that it is inevitable that public schools become complacent unless they are challenged by private schools or EMOs? If so, where does the complacency come from?

Charter schools are publicly funded but are administered independently of the local school district. See www.suntimes.com/ special_sections/ skul/charter.html for further background.

Part of a larger agenda

In an era of "welfare reform," of the virtual demonization of government social programs and public services, the prevailing free-market dogma was that there was nothing in the world that couldn't be improved with a dose of the profit motive. Big-city mayors like Republican Rudolph Giuliani in New York and Democrat Ed Rendell in Philadelphia did their best to encourage privatization of mass transit, sanitation and other services, and if they had limited initial success it was not for lack of trying.

In this atmosphere Edison grew despite its lack of profits. Investors saw it as a potential profit center. What could be better than feeding off the dismantling of public services, a process that had already generated super profits in Latin America and other "emerging markets"? Government money

COMMENTARY: The origins of EMOs

As Manuel Rivera notes in Rebecca Pollard's article reprinted here, some private businesses have been involved in education in the United States (and around the world) for a long time. In fact, for as long as teachers have used textbooks, publishers have been making money from education. Since the early 1980s some countries have also begun to use private companies to provide services such as cleaning and catering. At the same time, there was a growing feeling in the United States that public schools were failing, especially in urban areas with mainly poor populations. In response private schools began to play a greater role in public education with the introduction of voucher plans and the establishment of charter schools and magnet schools, which received public funds but operated outside the normal mechanisms of local government control. In the late 1980s these trends came together in the first proposals to use private, for-profit companies—Educational Management Organizations (EMOs)—receiving public funds to perform the core functions of a public school: providing the teaching staff and developing the curriculum.

Entrepreneurs such as John Golle, who founded Education Alternatives Inc. (now Tessaract) in 1986, and Chris Whittle, who founded the Edison Project (now Edison Schools Inc.) in 1992, presented their proposals as the next logical step in the introduction of private-sector expertise: a common-sense choice to address what was basically a problem of poor management. As a beneficial side effect, EMOs would also challenge public schools to do better themselves. Those who opposed EMOs, however, felt they posed a fundamentally hostile challenge to the very idea of the public school. Many who supported or financed EMOs made no secret of their belief that private organizations are always superior to public in principle, or even that governments have no legitimate role in the provision of education. That is what gives the debate about EMOs such a strong emotional charge.

would be used to directly reward the wealthy investors in Edison.

Edison enjoyed certain unique advantages. It was able to arrange for some of its schools to be assisted by private charities, giving it an advantage over public schools. It also charged fees that were based on an average of the money spent on all the students in a given district, thus getting higher fees based on high-school spending, while running elementary and middle schools that require less funding.

Nonetheless, Edison never made a profit, and a number of careful studies showed that Edison students were not doing any better academically than their counterparts at public schools. One study of ten Edison schools published in 2000

What do you think would be the fairest way to work out the fees that EMOs receive from school districts?

found that students at only three of the ten schools were doing better than the comparison schools, while three others scored below public schools and the remaining four showed mixed results.

The text of this study, by Gary Miron and Brooks Applegate, can be seen online at www.wmich.edu/ evalctr/edison/ edison.html

The collapse of Edison's stock price has led to a number of developments that are typical of other firms in desperate financial straits. Investors are up in arms, and the company has also suddenly attracted the interest and attention of regulatory authorities.

The Securities and Exchange Commission, for instance, announced last week that Edison had provided false information about its past revenues and had maintained inadequate financial controls. According to the SEC, Edison agreed to a settlement that, without admitting wrongdoing, committed the company to various changes in its financial methods and procedures.

See www.sec.gov/ news/press/2002- 67.htm for the SEC's press release about these findings.

In addition, at least three class-action lawsuits were filed against Edison last week in Federal District Court in Manhattan. The suits, similar to others involving companies whose stock price has collapsed, seek compensation for massive losses, and are sure to keep Edison tied up in court for some time.

Parents are unconvinced

Around the country, the skepticism of parents over Edison's promises is rapidly turning to worry and anger. The company was never able to turn all of its political backing into broad community support for its privatization plans. In New York City a year ago, a proposal to turn over five schools to Edison went down to a humiliating and overwhelming defeat in a local vote by parents. The deal to turn over 20 Philadelphia schools was imposed in the face of strong local opposition. Now the state commission overseeing the Philadelphia schools claims it will secure procedures safeguarding the schools if Edison is unable to fulfill its contract. One commission member suggested that the district would ensure that Edison did not remove computers and other equipment if it pulled out of its Philadelphia operation.

Do you think parents should always have a chance to vote on the use of an EMO, as in New York?

While Edison's financial crisis has exposed as a fraud the firm's claim that privatization is the solution to the schools crisis, the dismantling of public education continues apace. Recently in New York City, the Board of Education spelled out a "worst-case scenario" to local school districts, forecasting that proposed budget cuts will mean a loss of "almost a billion dollars in services to students compared to the funding levels of a year ago."

Summary

Rebecca Pollard, writing for the the Harvard Graduate School of Education magazine, argues that the privatization of public schools is necessary for children to get a decent education. She says that public schools have resisted reform and that for-profit schools can improve the situation faster and at a lower cost. Pollard points to initiatives run by Edison Schools (an educational management organization, or EMO), such as the purchase of computers for home use, which Edison claims has raised achievement in 84 percent of students. There is also a potential for schools run by EMOs to run at a profit, although Pollard concedes that Edison has yet to do so. She contends that profits will come in the future, but that in any case, investors in for-profit schools are not doing it so much for the profits as because it is a political investment. They believe that private enterprise could be the answer to the schools crisis.

In the other article, taken from the World Socialist Website, Peter Daniels identifies the privatization of education as part of a wider trend toward free-market reform. He points out that for-profit schools do not seem to be making much profit—Edison Schools is, he contends, a financially unviable business that has reported continuous losses. Daniels argues that for-profit schools have attracted low scores and bad press, and have failed to win over most parents. Edison Schools also favor a longer school day and year, which may lead to teacher burnout. He says that because the public school system is in such a desperate condition, companies such as Edison Schools have wooed parents with promises of efficiency and dynamism. He concludes that claims of privatization being the solution to the schools crisis are fraudulent.

FURTHER INFORMATION:

 Books:

Bracey, Gerald W., *The War against America's Public Schools: Privatizing Schools, Commercializing Education*, Boston, MA: Allyn and Bacon, 2002.
Ravitch, Diane, and Joseph Viteritti, *New Schools for a New Century: The Redesign of Urban Education*, Hartford, CT: Yale University Press, 1999.
Private Management of Public Schools: Early Experiences in Four School Districts, Washington, D.C.: United States General Accounting Office, 1996.

 Useful websites:

www.horizon.unc.edu/edsp287/1998/Turner/webpages/emo-issue.htm
Paper by Andrew Sherman and Celeste Turner putting EMOs in the broader context of school privatization.

www.ncspe.org/keepout/papers/00014/7_OP14.pdf
A paper by Henry Levin considering the challenges that EMOs such as Edison face in attempting to make K-12 education profitable.

The following debates in the Pro/Con series may also be of interest:

In this volume:
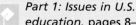 *Part 1: Issues in U.S. education*, pages 8–9

 Part 2: The public education system

SHOULD PRIVATE BUSINESSES RUN PUBLIC SCHOOLS?

YES: By contracting out services and streamlining school administration, for-profit schools save money that can be redirected to the classroom

YES: People have been making a profit out of children's education for decades. For-profit schools will do so with more accountability.

COST
Can for-profit companies run public schools more cheaply?

STUDENTS' INTERESTS
Can for-profit schools put the interests of children before profit?

NO: For-profit schools such as Edison's have been running at a continuous loss and are being investigated by regulatory authorities because of the collapse of their stock price

NO: The profit motive has to be the primary concern of for-profit schools because they have to satisfy investors

SHOULD PRIVATE BUSINESSES RUN PUBLIC SCHOOLS?
KEY POINTS

YES: A for-profit school can raise achievement levels even in the poorest urban setting by raising teacher and student morale through its own specially designed school curriculum

YES: For-profit schools have more incentives to achieve because if results drop, they will lose contracts and investors

QUALITY OF EDUCATION
Can for-profit schools raise education standards?

NO: Studies have shown that students at for-profit Edison Schools are doing no better academically than their counterparts at public schools

NO: For-profit schools advocate cutting the number of teachers, which leads to bigger classes and thus cannot improve educational standards

Topic 6

DO CHARTER SCHOOLS PROVIDE A BETTER EDUCATION THAN TRADITIONAL PUBLIC SCHOOLS?

YES
FROM "CHARTER SCHOOLS PLEDGE SUCCESS"
USA TODAY, NOVEMBER 14, 2001
TAMARA HENRY

NO
FROM "CHARTER SCHOOLS TAKE US BACKWARD, NOT FORWARD"
CCPA EDUCATION MONITOR, SUMMER 1997
HEATHER-JANE ROBERTSON

INTRODUCTION

The public school system in the United States guarantees every child a free education. The government pays for public schools out of public taxation, and local school districts own and operate the schools under the governance of the state boards of education. Many people, however, have become dissatisfied with the way the public school system is working. They want less bureaucracy, greater accountability, and more parental choice; but they still want schools to be funded through public taxation rather than private tuition fees. Some people argue that charter schools meet all these criteria. They also assert that charter schools provide a "better" education than traditional public schools. But is that really the case?

Charter schools are part of the public school system and receive the same sum of money per pupil in funding as the traditional public schools. However, charter schools are independent institutions, and the education authorities grant them a certain amount of freedom from the rules and regulations imposed on other public schools. In return charter schools are held accountable for the academic achievement of their students.

Groups of parents, teachers, and community leaders are normally responsible for setting up charter schools. The schools get their name from the *charter*, or agreement, that they receive from their sponsor, usually the state or local school board. The charter, which is typically for a term of between three and five years, details how the school is to be run, what the curriculum will cover, what the students should achieve, and how that achievement will be measured. Schools face suspension or closure if the charter-granting body judges that they have not attained accepted standards of performance.

Minnesota passed the first charter school law in 1991. According to the Center for Educational Reform, in January 2003 there were around 2,700 charter schools in operation in America serving more than 684,000 students. The District of Columbia, Puerto Rico, and 39 states have passed charter school laws, and 36 states, the District of Columbia, and Puerto Rico have had charter schools in operation since September 2002. The laws governing the establishment and running of charter schools vary from state to state.

> "Next to our free political institutions, our free public-school system ranks as the greatest achievement of democratic life in America."
> —AGNES E. MEYER (1887–1970), JOURNALIST

Charter school supporters maintain that the public school system is overcentralized and overregulated—it is failing children and is in need of reform. They point to several key areas in which charter schools best other public schools. First, because charter schools are accountable for the academic performance of their students and for the responsible operation of the schools themselves, their supporters believe that these schools are more goal oriented, achieve better academic results, and are more efficiently run

than traditional public schools. Second, because charter schools are more autonomous than most schools, they have the freedom to innovate. They can focus on the quality of teaching and learning, instead of spending time dealing with bureaucracy. Third, and most important, the introduction of charter schools expands choice for parents and teachers.

Charter schools, however, have many opponents who feel that these institutions are a betrayal of the philosophy behind universal public school education. These people oppose the idea of education as a marketplace with consumer choice placed at the center. They question whether charter schools are any more accountable than other public schools and accuse charter schools of employing uncertified teachers at low wages. They do not see the public school system as a failure, but believe that the funds being diverted to charter schools should be used to make the traditional system work better for all students.

The following articles take different positions on whether charter schools provide a better education than traditional public schools. Tamara Henry reports on the success enjoyed by Cherry Creek Academy, a charter school in Arapahoe County, Colorado. Writing in 2001, Henry noted that Cherry Creek had a waiting list of 1,300 students. Heather-Jane Robertson, on the other hand, taking a Canadian perspective, fears that the ultimate objective of some of the supporters of charter schools "is to dismantle public education, weaken teachers and their unions, use public funds for private benefit, and channel our school system into the service of the social, economic and religious 'chosen.'"

CHARTER SCHOOLS PLEDGE SUCCESS
Tamara Henry

✓ The Cherry Creek Academy, a public charter school created seven years ago by disgruntled parents who wanted a more fundamental curriculum, has racked up some of the highest standardized test scores in Arapahoe County. Largely because of its success, the academy now is viewed by some educators in this community of pricey homes and luxurious condominiums as a threat. Since the summer, the school board presidents of Cherry Creek and five surrounding districts have been meeting to discuss ways to strengthen the public school system to prevent a flood of students to the other 88 charter schools in the state.

Currently, the charters serve 2.5% of Colorado's public school enrollment and represent 4.3% of all the state's public schools. Most of the charters are showing academic performance that meets or exceeds the average performance of their respective districts, says the League of Charter Schools, a non-profit advocacy group. And an evaluation study last year showed that the level of parental involvement, waiting lists and satisfaction were all high at the charter schools. Across the nation, educators are watching Colorado's charter school movement, because it comes closest to proponents' goals of what works in education. Colorado charters "are not all doing wonderfully," says the league's Jim Griffin. "But a very healthy percentage of them are."

Fewer rules and regulations

The idea behind charter schools is simple: They are public schools operated by parents, teachers, community groups— anyone who agrees to improve student achievement in exchange for fewer rules and regulations and promises to handle their budgets wisely....

Ideally, these schools serve as laboratories where new education models are tested in all sorts of environments, from the inner cities to the suburbs. School sizes vary from just a few dozen students to thousands.

There is the Colorado Virtual Academy, where elementary-school students telecommute with the state's first online instructional program. The California Charter Academy, with more than 7,000 students in mostly high school completion

This article was published in 2001. The Colorado League of Charter Schools (www.colorado league.org) listed 95 schools operating across the state in 2003.

The Colorado Virtual Academy (COVA; www.covcs. org) has no school buildings as such. Students "attend" via the Internet, and most schoolwork takes place in the home. Do you think virtual schools will be the schools of the future?

programs, is geared to specific populations in the different communities. A recently approved charter school in St. Louis will prepare students for construction work.

Unlike voucher programs, in which public money is used to pay private school tuition, charters do not remove students from the public school system. But charters compete with neighboring schools for students and the per-pupil funds they bring.

Charter school proponents long have argued that traditional public schools will improve if they have to compete for students. "Charter schools do not just help the students they serve directly, they also prod the entire system to improve," says Education Secretary Rod Paige.

Voucher or school-choice programs operate in the cities of Cleveland and Milwaukee and in the state of Florida. For more details visit www.school choiceinfo.org, and see Topic 4 Do school vouchers work?

Healthy tensions

The tensions generated by competition between traditional and charter schools are healthy, adds Joe Nathan of the Center for School Change at the University of Minnesota. "Cooperation and competition can occur at the same time."

But critics say charter schools are divisive and divert attention from the needs of public schools. And they don't always work. Charter school history nationwide is marked by sketchy progress, mixed academic results and questionable management practices.

As of December, the Center for Education Reform [CER] says that the number of failed charter schools stands at 86— 4% of all the charter schools ever opened in the USA.

As far as educational performance is concerned, those eyeing the charter movement as a whole are skeptical. Charter test scores in such places as Michigan, Texas, and Ohio have lagged behind the scores of other children in the same district.

In Colorado, though, charter schools as a group tend to perform well on the state standardized tests called Colorado Student Assessment Program (CSAP)....

In the Denver Public School District, however, test results were mixed for both traditional and charter schools. Most of them scored below the state average. Historically, charter schools in Denver have faced fierce opposition. ...

Elaine Berman, president of the Denver Public Schools Board of Education, favors the concept of charter schools and says there's a lot to be learned from them. "As a district, I don't think we've figured out how to do that yet. I'm not sure that we've taken their good work and incorporated it," she says. Part of the problem, Berman says, is that charter schools can be nuisances for policymakers who have to deal

Are cooperation and competition compatible? What might go wrong?

CER's latest figures indicate that 194 charter schools (6.7 percent of those opened) had closed by October 2002.

Go to www.cde.state. co.us/cdechart/ charsurv.htm for both up-to-date and historical comparisons of public and charter school performance in CSAP.

with application hearings, appeals of rulings and the expenses of contracting attorneys to handle appeals. "Charter schools generally take a disproportionate amount of our time. Just the whole process of approving a charter school is somewhat challenging."

Efforts to ease tensions

Still, understanding the lure of charter schools is a key goal for Berman. "One of my frustrations is there's a reason why charter schools are becoming charter schools," she says. "As a school board member governing and making policy decisions, I want to know what those reasons are. Why go the charter route? What is it that they (parents) feel that they can do in that venue that we can't do as a school district? Is there anything we should be doing to change the way we do business?"

Seven years ago, parents in the Cherry Creek district sought to create a charter when many of their children weren't learning to read. Already, there was heated debate over whether reading should be taught using the whole language or phonics approach. Parents wanted a curriculum that focused on the basics. Their dissatisfaction with the suburban schools challenged the schools' generally accepted reputation for excellence. Charter school critics asked the disgruntled parents: "What possibly could you be unhappy with, and why in the world do you think that you could do something better or be better than what we already are?" recalls Donna Fitzgerald, director of the Cherry Creek Academy.

Animosity gives way to respect

Fitzgerald, who worked in the school's library and as a fourth-grade teacher before becoming director, remembers the days the charter school proposal was before the local district. "These were angry parents and ... a superintendent and a board of a school district that's top in the state. There was some animosity."

But over time, relations have improved between the charter and traditional public schools in Cherry Creek's district. "We have worked on this relationship," says assistant superintendent Nola Wellman. "I would say our respect for them and how they've learned has grown. Their respect for us in how difficult it is to run a school has grown. That relationship has developed more respect."

Education experts acknowledge that charter schools hold many attractions for parents. Generally, there is a common goal, a focus, a well-defined mission.

The whole-language and phonics approaches are the two major methods of teaching children to read. For an explanation of these terms and a discussion of the reading debate go to www.sedl.org/reading/topics/balancedliteracy.pdf—also see Topic 10 Is phonics instruction the best way of teaching students to read?

Try to explain the qualifications of people you quote to judge an issue because it gives your argument more credence.

And accountability. They are "more vulnerable to the consequences for performance" in a way that traditional public schools are not, says Ted Kolderie of the Charter Friends National Network. A school's charter may not get renewed if terms are violated, if students don't improve academically or if finances are mishandled, Kolderie says. A death knell sounds when unhappy parents pull their children out, in effect taking away the school's source of funding.

With charter schools, Wellman says, there is "a reinforcement of values. Children do so much better when their parents have a vested interest in their education. (Cherry Creek Academy) has an excellent school there, and the parents are very active."

Parents of academy students sign pledges to work in the school 40 hours a year, limit their child's time watching television and meet with teachers at least twice a semester.

"There's not a lot of red tape and bureaucracy. We see a need and fix it," says Fitzgerald, who notes the school has 1,300 names on a waiting list.

This attraction is not lost on Denver Board of Education president Berman. Already, she says, the district's newly appointed school superintendent is working to reduce the number of regulations plaguing public schools—rules that charters already are free from by their charter agreements. This effort may ease the tensions between traditional and charter schools.

Politics of funding

The flow of public school dollars to charter schools has increased as major political parties warm to the idea of these non-traditional programs. President Bush's education bill being negotiated in Congress calls for spending $200 million on 680 new charter schools and on 1,100 of the existing ones. Besides providing money for "start-up costs," the legislation also calls for $175 million for charter school facilities—one of the biggest problems faced by charter schools because they often are left to find their own locations. The bill also would give students in low-performing public schools the option and some money to transfer to charters, and regular public schools that fail for three years could be closed and reopened as charters.

A Gallup Poll conducted for the Phi Delta Kappa education fraternity this year found that fewer than 1% of schoolchildren in the USA attend charter schools today. Even so, the fiercest opponents concede that charter schools are not fads, but permanent fixtures on the education scene.

The Charter Friends National Network (CFNN) is a charter-supporting organization set up in 1996. Visit www. charterfriends.org. for more information.

Is parental involvement in schools a good thing? Could it also lead to conflict if the curriculum conflicts with a parent's personal beliefs or ideals?

Why do public schools have so many rules?

The author uses statistics to back up her argument. Does that make it more convincing?

CHARTER SCHOOLS TAKE US BACKWARD, NOT FORWARD
Heather-Jane Robertson

NO

The author begins her argument by immediately stating the questions in which she sees the debate.

Charter schools should be tested, not in the context of "choice," but on how they answer two straightforward questions: "What are schools for?" and "Whom should public education serve?"...

Most of us see public education as much more than an efficient means of providing our young with remarkable levels of literacy and proficiency—although it is, in part. We see it as a shared undertaking, the means of carrying out the social contract between one generation and the next.

This is not a "product–customer" relationship. It is not a private transaction. We have a collective interest—morally, not just financially—in the success of schools. We reinforce public education's importance in a democracy by publicly governing schools, not just publicly funding them.

The United States has a tradition of individualism. Is that compatible with collective responsibility?

Some read this as a statement that diminishes parents' responsibility for their children; but in fact it is the only way to discharge our collective responsibility for everyone's children.

Do we assume and discharge this responsibility perfectly? Of course not. But that doesn't mean we should walk away from the obligation.

A filter in the education system

Those who would govern charter schools have, by definition, no need to worry about what happens to other people's children in other charter schools....

[Charter] schools provide a mechanism to disaggregate not just kids, but public purpose. Their effect (and to a large extent their goal) is to insert into public education a filter or screen through which only some kids, and their parents, can pass.

Visit www.pbs.org/kcet/publicschool to read the history of public education in the United States.

This filter is fundamentally and explicitly contrary to the modern objectives of public education. I say "modern" objectives because the roots of public education in North America are embedded in some rather unsavoury purposes—the sorting, training and "taming" of children so that they would forever after "know their station."

Charter schools, then, take us not forward in an innovative leap, but backwards—back to a time when opportunity was closely rationed, when health and well-being—and education—could be afforded only by the rich and the lucky, and when the poor were scapegoated for their own failures....

The "promises" of charter schools sound pretty good, on the surface; and some of the promise-makers may even believe their own rhetoric. The language of "quality" and "choice" is hard to resist. But charter schools must be judged, not by their expressed goals, but by their actual effects. And when these charter school effects are measured against any egalitarian answer to our question about whom schools should serve, or by any democratic answer to what schools are for, the charter schools fail. Good intentions are not a defence....

The argument for charter schools rests on the flawed premise of school failure, and we have to deal effectively and assertively with bizarre and unfounded criticism. The enemies of public education understand only too well that if you're going to take something away from the public, you first have to convince them it was worthless in the first place....

Much of what has been written in praise of charter schools reads like a time-share brochure—and, like that kind of brochure, the small print about costs, liabilities and hurricane damage tend to be avoided. Let's deal with a few of these promises.

The back-to-the-basics model

The most popular model proposed by charter school supporters is that of "back-to-the-basics"—a fundamental (if not fundamentalist) curriculum, learned in a teacher-centred, authoritarian classroom. The same place I learned Latin, along with the virtues of the British Empire, racism, homophobia, sexism, how to cheat, how to give the answers the teacher wanted, and how to pretend to care about what I was learning.

When the charter school proponents talk about "busting the public school bureaucracy"—i.e., school boards, teachers and their unions—they are really using a code for resisting (and reversing) most of the educational and social progress of the past three decades. Which is not to say there is a teacher anywhere who has never been angered or frustrated by some "dumb" decision made by some dumb decision-maker in the administrative branches of the education system. I would

"Rhetoric" in this sense means talk that sounds impressive but is insincere and exaggerated.

Using a well-known analogy may capture your audience's imagination and help your argument.

The "back-to-basics" movement in U.S. education arose in the 1950s amid concerns about America's ability to wage the Cold War and compete with the Soviet Union in the space race. The movement resurfaced in the 1970s and 1980s, with the country this time in recession and facing economic competition from Japan.

suggest, however, that the private sector experience is virtually identical. Indeed, there is a growing literature about the "bloated bureaucracy" in the private sector—the same sector which the charter school advocates are so fond of holding up as the model we should emulate....

[T]hose who favour charter schools say they are inevitable.... They point to other countries, such as the United States and New Zealand, which have experimented with charter schools. What they don't tell us is how these experiments have turned out....

The author is a noted Canadian education activist and is writing on charter schools from a Canadian point of view.

Choice increases separation

Among the recent literature on the subject is "Who Chooses, Who Loses: Culture, Institutions and the Unequal Effects of School Choice," a collection of 10 studies by senior researchers in the U.S. commissioned to find empirical rather than rhetorical evaluations of school choice.

Go to www.school choices.org/ roo/elm_i.htm to read the concluding chapter, Who Chooses? Who Loses?

The editors, in summarizing their conclusions, reported that "increasing educational choice is increasing the separation of students by race, social class, and cultural background." This happens "even when they [charter schools] are explicitly designed to remedy inequality." A paper by three of the researchers reinforced this conclusion, observing that "increasing parental choice will accelerate both the social stratification of schools and the gap in student performance."

Research findings such as these confirm the logic—and the fears—of those who oppose charter schools. We have argued that school-by-school competition would create high demand for the students who already have the greatest chance of success in our schools, while creating disincentives to avoid serving harder-to-teach kids and those with disabilities. Indeed, exactly these effects were found in a study of charter schools in Arizona. The researcher found that fewer than 4% of the 7,000 students in that state's charter schools had learning disabilities....

Do you think disabled students should be taught in separate educational facilities? If so, why?

It's the same story in California, where some school principals said they might be able to accommodate learning disabilities, but a student with greater needs would be a problem. One principal even told the researcher that "one severely disabled special-ed kid would put me out of business." This, despite charter school promises that there will be no discrimination, and that "choice" will be equally available to all.

We teacher union representatives have been dismissed by some charter advocates as "union bosses" who are simply trying to cling to our "monopoly." It is easy to make this charge of self-interest, and to promise the teachers recruited for charter schools that they will be "liberated" from their unions. What they are not told is that the ideal teacher envisioned by the charter school enthusiasts is one who will also agree to work at lower wages and with no job security, and who would not even need to hold a teaching certificate....

I would be less annoyed by this union and teacher bashing if it weren't cloaked in lies about "teacher empowerment." To dismiss the need for sophisticated professional and pedagogical knowledge among teachers, and to call it "giving teachers respect" is an insult.

The myth of the parent–teacher "partnership"

To talk about parents and teachers "jointly" creating a charter school—while ignoring the fact that one group is entirely dependent on pleasing the other group to stay employed—to call this a "partnership" is simply a lie. To indulge in union-bashing in the name of "liberating" teachers is an affront to Canada's teaching profession.

The charter school supporters will no doubt point out that, where charter schools exist, they have had no difficulty recruiting teachers. I'm not at all surprised. There are thousands of teachers in this country who are tired of being criticized, asked to do the very difficult if not the impossible, and then denied the tools to do it with. That some, when promised they can avoid all this frustration in a charter school, believe such promises is hardly extraordinary. Of course, charter schools don't solve these problems; they just enable some lucky people to avoid them—all through the magic of "choice."

"Choice" is the mantra of corporatism. It makes a good deal of sense when buying refrigerators.... But when this market model for choosing goods is applied to public institutions and services—how we govern ourselves—it quickly breaks down.... The fact is that, in the public interest, every society restricts the choices of its citizens—when those choices affect the well-being of others....

It is not coincidence ... that the emergence of charter schools has the support of the business-funded Fraser and C.D. Howe Institutes and the Donner Foundation. Their ultimate objective, through the charter schools, is to dismantle public education, weaken teachers and their unions, use public funds for private benefit, and channel our school system into the service of the social, economic and religious "chosen."

For a debate on teachers' unions see Topic 9 Do teachers' unions hinder educational performance?

"Pedagogical" means "relating to teaching." "Pedagogue," meaning a teacher, derives from the Greek word for a slave who accompanied a child to school.

The Fraser Institute (www.fraser institute.ca) and the C.D. Howe Institute (www.cdhowe.org) are Canadian policy-research organizations. The Donner Canadian Foundation (www. donnerfoundation. org) is a grant-making body whose fields of interest include public policy.

Summary

Tamara Henry and Heather-Jane Robertson set out powerful arguments for and against the question: "Do charter schools provide a better education than traditional public schools?" Henry explores the impact of the success of charter schools in Colorado. She reports that the success of one particular school, Cherry Creek Academy, has prompted school boards in the area to look for ways of strengthening the public school system to prevent students from moving to charter schools. She states that Elaine Berman, president of the Denver Public Schools Board of Education, "favors the concept of charter schools and says there's a lot to be learned from them." Berman cited the example of the Cherry Creek district's new school superintendent, who was working to reduce the number of public school regulations—"rules that charters already are free from by their charter agreements."

Heather-Jane Robertson disagrees fundamentally with the concept of charter schools. She believes that children's education is the responsibility of society as a whole. Society, through government, should not only fund schools but also govern them. She believes this "is the only way to discharge our collective responsibility for everyone's children." Robertson goes on to accuse charter schools of trying to resist (and reverse) "most of the educational and social progress of the past three decades" with the aim of "busting the public school bureaucracy." She also says that, contrary to the claims of the charter school movement, recent research supports the view that "school-by-school competition would create high demand for the students who already have the greatest chance of success in our schools, while creating disincentives to avoid serving harder-to-teach kids and those with disabilities." She believes that, as the title of her article sums up: "Charter schools take us backward, not forward."

FURTHER INFORMATION:

Books:

Fuller, Bruce, Richard F. Elmore, and Gary Orfield (eds.), *Who Chooses? Who Loses?: Culture, Institutions, and the Unequal Effects of School Choice*. New York: Teachers College Press, 1996.

Moe, Terry M., *Schools, Vouchers, and the American Public*. Washington, D.C.: The Brookings Institution, 2001.

Useful websites:

www.rppintl.com/divisions/education/charter.html
RPP International site concerning National Study of Charter Schools.
www.uscharterschools.org
U.S. charter schools site.

The following debates in the Pro/Con series may also be of interest:

In this volume:
Part 1: Issues in U.S. education, pages 8–9

Topic 4 Do school vouchers work?

Part 2: The public education system

DO CHARTER SCHOOLS PROVIDE A BETTER EDUCATION THAN TRADITIONAL PUBLIC SCHOOLS?

YES: Parents should be able to send their children to a charter school if the local public school is failing

CHOICE
Should charter schools be one of the educational options available to parents?

NO: Charter schools divert attention and funding from traditional public schools

YES: Charter schools are free of many of the rules and regulations that fetter traditional public schools

BUREAUCRACY
Have charter schools succeeded in "busting the public school bureaucracy"?

NO: "Bureaucracy busting" is just code for hiring uncertified teachers and then exploiting them. Besides, the private sector is not free from bureaucracy.

DO CHARTER SCHOOLS PROVIDE A BETTER EDUCATION THAN TRADITIONAL PUBLIC SCHOOLS?

KEY POINTS

YES: Charter schools can take an innovative approach to teaching. They also have more incentives to reach an accepted level of performance.

PERFORMANCE
Do charter schools outperform traditional public schools academically?

NO: Charter schools often follow "back-to-basics," an authoritarian teaching model. Also, test scores in several states show charter school students lag behind those attending traditional public schools.

YES: Making traditional public schools compete with charter schools for children (and their funding) will cause all schools to improve

COMPETITION
Is competition between charter schools and traditional public schools healthy?

NO: Such competition serves only to create a high demand for students who already have a great chance of success in school

Topic 7

IS HOME EDUCATION AN ACCEPTABLE ALTERNATIVE TO PUBLIC EDUCATION?

YES

FROM: "TEACH YOUR OWN CHILDREN ... AT HOME"
WWW.BLOOMINGTON.IN.US/~LEARN/HOLT.HTM
ORIGINALLY PUBLISHED AS "PLOWBOY INTERVIEW"
THE MOTHER EARTH NEWS, JULY/AUGUST 1980
JOHN HOLT

NO

"SCHOOL'S OUT: DOES HOMESCHOOLING MAKE THE GRADE?"
THE NEW REPUBLIC, APRIL 6, 1998
KATHERINE PFLEGER

INTRODUCTION

The Department of Education defines homeschooling or home education as "the education of school-aged children at home rather than at school." Most people associate home education with an alternative lifestyle, but in reality the homeschooling movement has grown rapidly since the 1980s among a wide variety of people.

Current statistics on the numbers of homeschooled children in the United States vary widely, some sources citing as many as 1.23 million students. The Cato Institute claimed in 2003 that the most realistic estimate was 500,000–750,000 students, compared to 60 million students in approximately 85,000 public schools and 26,000 private schools.

Although religious freedom, academic excellence, and the strengthening of family bonds are among the most often stated reasons of supporters of the

movement, for others the real reason for the rise in home education is the failure of the public school system to provide an adequate education. But many educationists have queried whether home education is really an effective alternative to the public school system. Does it, as some critics claim, just add to existing problems by creating a generation of unsocialized young adults with behavioral problems who are ill prepared for the real world?

Although there have always been examples of parents teaching their children at home—for example, among families living in isolated places—the modern homeschooling movement originated in the 1960s and 1970s in the ideas of educationists coming from two very different perspectives. Raymond and Dorothy Moore published two influential books—*Home Grown Kids* (1981) and *Home-Spun Schools*

(1982)—based on research into the optimum age at which children should start school. They concluded that setting continuous academic tasks too early resulted in learning and physical problems in young children, and recommended that formal education should not begin until the age of at least 8, and preferably 10 or 12.

Although the Moores' books were written from a Christian perspective, their supporters argue that they provide reliable advice to any parent on the best way to be a home educator.

> *"I have never let my schooling interfere with my education."*
> —MARK TWAIN (1835–1910),
> NOVELIST

Similarly, John Holt was an advocate of school reform who had worked as a teacher for many years. Holt wrote *How Children Fail* (1964) after concluding that schools mold children into obedient but unthinking future citizens. He espoused what he called "learning by living," claiming that the most important factor in homeschooling was that the home provided a "natural" and "organic" base for "children's growth into the world."

The parental educators that Holt and the Moores have inspired teach their children in a variety of ways, from curricula published in special books to enrollment in long-distance programs. Others develop their own program based on existing state curricula and library and national reading lists.

However, many people argue that this very educational freedom is what makes home education problematic. It is difficult to judge its success when there is no federal code of practice for home education, and different states have different standards, ranging from established curricula and educational standards monitored by testing to simply filing basic paperwork. They also argue that children's education should not be limited to the intellectual resources of their parents, whatever the benefit of remote learning aids.

Among the other criticisms of homeschooling is that it holds back the social development of children, since they are often educated alone and lack peers. However, a 1992 study carried out by University of Florida psychotherapist Larry Shyers on the socialization practices of 35 home schoolers and 35 public school students seemed to show that there was little if any difference between the children. If anything, the homeschooled children were more patient and more likely to exchange contact numbers with other students. Critics point out, however, that the opportunities to make such contact with other children are inevitably fewer, and that to focus on learning is to ignore that education is also fundamentally about how to interact with one's peers.

Since the 1980s the largest growth in homeschooling has been among Christian Fundamentalists, leading some critics to query whether it is desirable for a society to allow citizens to withdraw their children for what seem to be antisocial motives—to ensure that they do not mix with people who have a different view of the world.

The following two articles examine the debate in greater depth.

TEACH YOUR OWN CHILDREN … AT HOME
John Holt

YES

Do you agree that learning only results from curiosity? How might students become curious about a new subject unless a teacher introduces it to them first?

☑ …**PLOWBOY:** Can you expand on your concept of what home schooling should be?

HOLT: I think that learning is not the result of teaching, but of the curiosity and activity of the learner. A teacher's intervention in this process should be mostly to provide the learner with access to the various kinds of places, people, experiences, tools, and books that will correspond with that student's interest … answer questions when they're asked … and demonstrate physical skills. I also feel that learning is not an activity that's separate from the rest of life. People learn best when they're involved with doing real and valuable work, which requires skill and judgment.

Growing Without Schooling magazine was published from 1977 to 2001.

These concepts are my basic philosophy of learning—and are mirrored in my magazine, *Growing Without Schooling*— but I'm in favor of having people teach their children at home and don't insist that they have my reasons for doing it or even follow my methods. As a result, the readers of *Growing Without Schooling*, or *GWS*, include a variety of people … ranging from leftist counterculturists to right-wing fundamentalists.

PLOWBOY: Is the home-schooling movement entirely a negative reaction against established educational systems?

HOLT: No, indeed … because it has such incredible positive benefits for children. True, people often start teaching their children at home because they see bad things happening to the youngsters at school. Many such parents, though, find that their children soon become happier, nicer, and more inquisitive human beings than they were when enrolled in educational institutions.

Do you think it is understandable that parents might feel this way? Or do you think it is worrying that some parents do not want their children to be away from the home at all?

Home schooling can be beneficial to the entire family, too. A lot of people write me to say that—when their children were sent off to school each day—the parents almost felt their families were being broken up. For such people, home schooling is a family-saving movement.

PLOWBOY: But aren't a lot of parents nervous about trying to educate their youngsters themselves? I can imagine someone thinking, "I don't know how to teach!"

HOLT: I run across that fear all the time, and in people with Ph.D.s just as often as in Joe Blow from Kokomo. I tell such folks that teaching is not a mystery … anybody who knows something can help anybody else who wants to learn it. In fact, what passes for official "teacher training" often makes people much less effective educators than they would have been if they hadn't had it.

> How could training make someone a less effective educator?

PLOWBOY: But what if you don't know a subject? Suppose the child gets interested in something that's over your head … like, possibly, physics?

HOLT: The youngster doesn't have to learn physics from you … there are plenty of available books on the subject. Besides that, lots of other people in the world know something about physics. If a 12-year-old, say, types a letter to somebody—and, by the way, knowing how to touch-type is a valuable skill for children to possess, and I've never in my life known a youngster who's had access to an electric typewriter who didn't learn to use it—and if the letter is neatly typed, asks a question, and doesn't admit that the writer is 12 years old, the chances are that the child will get an answer....

> Is that the best way to learn a difficult subject? What other methods can you think of?

PLOWBOY: But how can people find the time to teach their children for six hours a day, as the schools do?

HOLT: Name a school that teaches children for six hours a day! Observers who've used stop watches to time classes have shown that about 35 minutes out of every classroom hour are devoted simply to maneuvering around and getting ready to work. And the rest of the time consists mainly of either teacher demonstration or repetitive drill in a workbook.

> It is not clear what study Holt is referring to. Would his statement have more credibility if he gave the citation for the study?

I know from my own schooling—and I was a good student in good schools—that I rarely got 15 minutes of real teaching a day. Furthermore, the schools themselves admit this by their own actions. When a sick or injured pupil has to stay home for a while, the youngster's school will often send a tutor around to keep the child caught up in her or his schoolwork. And how much time does a tutor spend with one youngster? From as little as an hour and a half to a top figure of five hours a week!

> Why might a tutor in a one-to-one situation with a child at home not need as much time as when teaching a class?

PLOWBOY: Have you considered that, nowadays, few families can even afford to keep a parent at home all day?

HOLT: The question of how working parents can raise a home-schooled child is important, but you should realize that the problem is basically a custodial one … because the parents can easily provide enough adult help in the evenings to keep a child's learning progressing. When I meet people who are disturbed by the "day care" dilemma, I say, "If you have a very young child, you'll have to find someone—like one of your own parents, or a live-in baby sitter—to be at home while you're both at work. But you ought to be able to get your child to the point where, at age eight, the youngster can occupy her- or himself perfectly happily and usefully during those hours of the day when you're away."

Do you think children who are left to occupy themselves are likely to spend the time as effectively as those who are in school?

PLOWBOY: You would recommend leaving a child alone for eight or nine hours every day?

HOLT: It doesn't have to be that long a time. Remember, once school hours are over, the youngster will no longer be an "outlaw" and can go to a friend's house, the local library, etc. In addition, you could probably find an older person or hire a student to spend a couple of hours doing something interesting with your child to give the youngster a break in the day. But even leaving a child to her or his own activities for the full working day is better than sending the youngster off to a destructive school.

In most states the law on leaving children unsupervised is unclear. However, guidelines suggest that 11–12 is the minimum age at which a child can be left at home alone for any amount of time, and no reputable authority suggests that any child should be left alone for the whole day.

PLOWBOY: What about providing a child with the chance to learn social skills? Don't parents ever worry that a home-schooled boy or girl may not have the chance to make friends?

HOLT: Most of the children I know who are learning at home do have social lives. They see peers after school and on weekends, and have the chance to experience friendships, arguments, and all the ups and downs of true social life. When youngsters live a long, long way from anyone their own age, groups of parents can make arrangements to bring their children together to solve this problem. In fact, we print a directory of home schoolers in *GWS*, partly to help such folks get in touch with each other.

Do you think it is possible for a home-educated child to have a close friendship with other children without sharing the school experience with them?

More important, though, I think the social life of most schools is so competitive and snobbish and status-oriented, and so full of meanness and teasing and ganging up, that—

even if I didn't have any other reason for wanting to keep a child out of school—that very "society" would be reason enough to educate the youngster at home! I don't think schools teach young people anything about friendship, intimacy, and trust.

For years and years … I've seen evidence of the harmful desocializing effects schools have on children. Even my sister, who certainly is not an educational critic, told me that her five-year-old never knew how to do anything really mean, sneaky, or dishonest until after the tot had gone to school.

Is it your experience that schools teach "nothing about friendship, intimacy, and trust"? Do you think your experience is typical of "most schools"?

PLOWBOY: Suppose the children want to go back to school when they get older. Do they have peer problems then?

HOLT: Actually, they'll be in better shape for coping with school, because they're going there by choice and for their own reasons. It's like the difference between a prisoner in jail and a sociologist who goes in to study prison conditions. Both people are in the same building, but they're in very different frames of mind.

Do you agree that going to school feels like going to prison? Is this a good analogy?

PLOWBOY: What other worries do parents express about the consequences of home schooling?

HOLT: Some are concerned about whether their children will be able to get into college or land a good job without an "official" diploma. However, anyone can take the high school equivalency exam to earn a secondary diploma … and anyone can get into college—a good college—if she or he scores well on the Scholastic Aptitude Test.…

…Many of you folks who read this magazine believe—and with good reason—that government interferes too much in our lives. Well, I think that there is no place where this interference is less justified, more harmful, and more easily resisted than in the education of children. So it would seem to me that those who want to minimize the power the government has over their lives would find the area of their youngsters' learning to be the first place where they'd want to work toward that goal.

And I'd like to emphasize one last point very strongly. People, if you're smart enough to build your own home, design your own solar system, make your own fuel, redesign your car, raise your own food, and do all the things that many MOTHER-readers are doing … then you sure as hell are smart enough to teach your own children!

Do you agree that "government interferes too much in our lives"? Do you think this argument is consistent with Holt's earlier claim that the home schooling movement is not simply "a negative reaction against established educational systems"?

SCHOOL'S OUT: DOES HOMESCHOOLING MAKE THE GRADE?
Katherine Pfleger

NO

Carole Kennedy is a principal at one of the local schools in Columbia, Missouri. But one of the students she says worries her the most isn't even enrolled there. "This boy was in our school in the fourth and fifth grade and had behavior problems. His parents never had an interest in his education. They'd miss parent–teacher conferences. They'd drop him off at concerts and then not pick him up. When he got to middle school, he had attendance problems. His parents got tired of the calls from the attendance office and announced that they were going to pull him out of school and teach him at home." Homeschooling laws vary widely from state to state—some require that parents follow an approved curriculum or bring in their children for annual testing. But, in Missouri, all the boy's parents have to do is file some paperwork. "Now," says Kennedy, "his former friends say he's doing nothing all day."

Do you think all states should require homeschoolers to show that their children are being properly educated? Or do you think that is less important than simply respecting parents' wishes?

Stories like this may not be as rare as we'd like to imagine. Once a relatively limited phenomenon, homeschooling is on the rise. Between 1990 and 1995 the number of children taught at home more than doubled—today it stands at over one million. And, as the popularity of homeschooling continues to increase, so does the likelihood that well-meaning parents who lack the know-how, time, or resources to be effective teachers—or, worse, parents who actually have malign motives for keeping their kids out of school—will deprive their children of needed social skills and a decent education.

A charter for zealots?

Homeschooling used to be the province of the religious right. During the 1980s, Christian conservatives seized on it as a way to insulate their children from what they perceived to be the anti-family culture of public schools. These parents, generally full-time mothers, relied on religious groups to provide them with a curriculum and contacts with other homeschooling families. But, over the past few years, homeschooling has spread well beyond the Christian right; a

Do public schools have an "antifamily culture"? What does the author mean?

COMMENTARY: John Holt and homeschooling

John Holt (1923–1985) is seen as the father of the homeschool movement in the United States. He served in the U.S. Navy during World War II, then drifted into teaching in the early 1950s. He never earned a teaching qualification, which he believed was an advantage because it did not give him any preconceptions about what children could or could not do.

His experiences as a teacher, recounted in his 1964 bestselling book *How Children Fail*, led him to believe that the classroom situation, in which children were continually being tested and were obliged to perform to certain standards, ensured that most children failed to learn anything useful because stress and fear replaced the natural desire to learn. His solution, beginning in *How Children Learn* (1967), was an approach that used the child's own natural curiosity as a vehicle through which to learn.

Holt became strongly influenced by the ideas of Ivan Illich (1926–2002), following the publication of his book *Deschooling Society* in 1971, particularly by Illich's argument that the institution of school was itself a means of perpetuating and enforcing social divisions and power structures. In *Freedom and Beyond* (1972) Holt wrote, "...people, even children, are educated much more by the whole society around them and the general quality of life in it than they are by what happened in schools." Abandoning the idea of reform, Holt advocated in *Growing without Schooling* (1977) and *Teach Your Own* (1981) that parents withdraw their children from schools altogether to let them learn at home.

Criticism

As Holt's ideas developed, they also seemed to some observers to become increasingly more harsh and less flexible. Holt, for example, began to believe that teaching itself prevented learning, since in his view only knowledge that resulted from the child's own curiosity was beneficial. Critics questioned how a child might become curious about a subject it did not even know existed unless someone was allowed to instruct him or her about it first. Some educationists and parents, among others, also worried that Holt's view of all peer-group relationships at school as being "competitive and snobbish and status-oriented, and so full of meanness and teasing and ganging up," ignored any positive aspects of that relationship, such as friendship and camaraderie; they were worried that homeschooled children might suffer from loneliness, isolation, and problems in relationships later on in life. Holt was also criticized for advocating an elitist form of education, since many parents believed homeschooling was only possible if at least one parent was at home. Holt, however, argued that working parents could homeschool their children, since from the age of eight they could usefully occupy themselves and learn on their own if left alone during the day by a working parent or parents.

addition, he says, since the homeschoolers were selected by sending out a questionnaire, they constitute a self-selected group, not a representative sample of the entire home-schooling population.

And there's the rub. In order to assess homeschooling's effectiveness, researchers need full access to homeschooled children. Unfortunately, many homeschooling parents— particularly those in the religious right, who are also the most organized group within the movement—are vehemently opposed to any outside interference. They even have a lobby, part of the 50,000-member Home School Legal Defense Association, dedicated to blocking the logical next step that would follow further studies: the creation of national standards that would ensure all homeschooled kids are getting at least a rudimentary education.

Why do you think such groups are unwilling to take part in research?

Turning a blind eye—the forgotten children

Not that the homeschoolers need to worry about a serious challenge to their autonomy. The Department of Education has traditionally left the administration of compulsory education to local government, and it shows no inclination to get involved now. As for the press, it has been too busy touting homeschooling miracles to look at the movement critically. But, instead of glowing descriptions of seven-year-old prodigies, the public needs to hear about the overextended mothers, like the one I interviewed, while she juggled a telephone, a toddler screaming for a piece of string cheese, and a second-grader she was supposed to be homeschooling. And the public needs to hear about the public school teachers, like several in the Missouri school, who, Carole Kennedy says, are struggling to reeducate a student who fell several grades behind during the two years his mother taught him at home. This child's remedial education will cost the taxpayers money. That, if nothing else, should get the public's attention.

Do you agree that media coverage is biased in favor of homeschooling? If so, why do you think that is?

Summary

Homeschooled children are on the increase in the United States, leading parents, educationists, and government officials to question why that is. Does this method of education provide an acceptable alternative to school? Or is it an example of how some antisocial parents seek to isolate their children from contact with the rest of society? The two preceding articles discuss various aspects of the issue.

The first is an extract from an interview with home education proponent John Holt, originally published in *Mother Earth News*. He argues that homeschooling has a positive influence on children by teaching them to be nicer and more inquisitive human beings. He asserts that for many it is a "family-saving movement." He also claims it is possible to homeschool a child and have a full-time job. Holt claims that the "society" of a school—which he characterizes as one of teasing, bullying, and competitiveness—would be reason enough on its own to keep a child out of school.

Katherine Pfleger, in the second article, disagrees. She cites the case of a young boy pulled out of school by his parents in Missouri who now sits at home doing nothing. Missouri homeschooling law does not dictate a curriculum for students, and it is easy for many young people to fall through the cracks. She claims that homeschooling has gone from being something associated with the religious right to a more mainstream movement, claiming that fears about the standard of education in public schools are a big factor. But Pfleger points out that it is difficult to judge how effective homeschooling is, because homeschooling parents are not held accountable to any objective standards. It is the state that suffers when they have to reeducate a homeschooled child who comes back into the system.

FURTHER INFORMATION:

Books:

Henke, Robin R., *Issues Relating to Estimating the Home-Schooled Population in the United States with National Household Survey Data*, Washington, D.C.: U.S. Department of Education, 2000.

Stevens, Mitchell L., *Kingdom of Children: Culture and Controversy in the Homeschooling Movement*, Princeton, NJ: Princeton University Press, 2001.

Useful websites:

http://nces.ed.gov/pubs2001/HomeSchool/index.asp
"Homeschooling in the United States, 1999."
http://epaa.asu.edu/epaa/v7n27.html/
"Homeschooling and the Redefinition of Citizenship."

The following debates in the Pro/Con series may also be of interest:

In this volume:

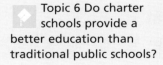

Topic 6 Do charter schools provide a better education than traditional public schools?

Topic 12 Should religion be taught in schools?

IS HOME EDUCATION AN ACCEPTABLE ALTERNATIVE TO PUBLIC EDUCATION?

YES: Fears of violence, drugs, and other social problems are even leading some teachers to take their children out of school to educate them

YES: Students receive, if anything, a better constructed, more thoughtful education in a loving environment. Some homeschoolers are leading members of the community.

FAILURE
Has the failure of the public school system led to the increase in home education?

COMPREHENSIVE EDUCATION
Can homeschooling really give the student as comprehensive an education as the normal school system?

NO: The strength of the movement lies in a variety of factors related to religious and cultural belief systems, not in failing public schools

NO: In 2001 Resolution B-29 clearly stated that home education programs "cannot provide the student with a comprehensive education experience"

IS HOME EDUCATION AN ACCEPTABLE ALTERNATIVE TO PUBLIC EDUCATION?

KEY POINTS

YES: Studies have shown that homeschooled children often achieve better academically

YES: Students and parents work together in close proximity, according to established procedures. That inevitably will bring them closer.

ACADEMIC EXCELLENCE
Does homeschooling produce better-educated students?

FAMILY VALUES
Do people who educate their children at home have stronger family relationships?

NO: Subjects outside parents' experience or knowledge inevitably get less attention or are ignored altogether, closing off children's options for their future

NO: Homeschooling can lead to conflict, since if any problems arise, the student has nowhere to go to for advice—his parent and teacher are one and the same person.

Topic 8
SHOULD ILLEGAL IMMIGRANT CHILDREN GET PUBLIC EDUCATION?

YES
FROM "RESPONDING TO UNDOCUMENTED CHILDREN IN THE SCHOOLS"
ERIC CLEARINGHOUSE ON RURAL EDUCATION AND SMALL SCHOOLS
EDO-RC-99-1, SEPTEMBER 1999
SUSAN C. MORSE AND FRANK S. LUDOVINA

NO
FROM "WE ARE OVERWHELMED"
PART 2 OF *BORDER WARS*
THE WASHINGTON TIMES, SEPTEMBER 24, 2002
JERRY SEPER

INTRODUCTION

In 2002 an estimated eight million illegal immigrants lived in the United States, including a high percentage of children. According to some estimates, the total increases by between 350,000 and 450,000 each year. Many are Hispanic, especially Mexicans drawn by increased economic opportunity in the United States, but there are also large numbers of other groups. The problem is most acute in the Southwestern states along the Mexican border, where there are large Hispanic communities among which illegal immigrants can lose themselves relatively easily.

Although some illegal immigrants come to the United States alone, planning to work temporarily in order to send money to their families at home, many others arrive with their families. Current U.S. law, as established by a landmark Supreme Court ruling in *Plyler v. Doe* (1982), allows the children of illegal immigrants free education in public schools throughout the United States. The ruling has many opponents, however: The judgment was made over 20 years ago, they argue, and sharp increases in the rate of illegal immigration mean it is now outdated.

The *Plyler* decision effectively guaranteed education to all children living in any state under the Fourteenth Amendment to the Constitution. That amendment does not actually refer to education specifically, but it clearly stipulates that "no State shall ... deprive any person of life, liberty, or property, without due process of law; nor deny to any person within its jurisdiction the equal protection of the laws." The court ruled that an illegal immigrant is a "person" as described in the amendment, and that withholding education from any group of people infringed its Equal Protection Clause.

There has been much opposition to that argument. One of its clearest expressions came in 1994, when California voters approved Proposition 187. The proposition excluded illegal immigrants from welfare benefits, banned their children from public schools, and prevented health providers from giving them any but emergency treatment. Supporters claimed that would both preserve the state's finite resources and discourage further illegal immigration. Although Proposition 187 passed, it was ruled unconstitutional and has never been applied.

> *"We cannot ignore the significant social costs borne by our nation when select groups are denied the means to absorb the values and skills upon which our social order rests."*
>
> —*PLYLER V. DOE,*
>
> 457 U.S. 202 (1982)

Those in favor of educating immigrant children argue that all children are entitled to an education: They have little or no say in where their parents choose to live, and it is unfair to penalize them for their parents' choices. In practical terms they argue that the failure to educate illegal immigrant children will only create an illiterate underclass that may be drawn into crime and antisocial behavior. Their inability to read, write, or speak English would prevent them from ever being able to fulfill a useful role as adults in U.S. society.

Those who argue against the public education of illegal immigrants believe it is unfair to the legal citizens of a state for its resources to be diverted to people who make no contribution to society. While they agree that all children are entitled to an education, they argue that it is better provided in the child's country of origin.

In practical terms opponents of educating illegal immigrants argue that it puts a serious strain on the finances of border states such as California, Texas, and Arizona. They dismiss the idea that excluding children will result in gang culture: Gangs are already prevalent, they point out, so it is impossible to blame their creation on a particular cause. They also suggest that withdrawing the provision of free education for illegal immigrants might actually discourage immigration.

Supporters of providing education counter that immigrants arrive in the country seeking economic opportunity, not free schooling, and would keep arriving anyway. They also claim there are fewer illegal immigrant children in schools than their opponents suggest, and that—because school funding from both state and federal authorities is adjusted to match the number of children in a school—no U.S. child is disadvantaged by the presence of illegal immigrants in a school.

In the first of the articles that follow, education consultants Susan C. Morse and Frank S. Ludovina analyze the *Plyler v. Doe* judgment and argue that schools should not act as agencies of the U.S. government. In the second journalist Jerry Seper argues that the provision of education for illegal immigrants puts an unfair burden on U.S. taxpayers.

RESPONDING TO UNDOCUMENTED CHILDREN IN THE SCHOOLS
Susan C. Morse and Frank S. Ludovina

The metaphor of the "melting pot" has often been used to describe the United States' long history of immigration. The term became popular after Israel Zangwill (1864–1926) wrote a play of the same name in 1906, in which one of the characters says, "America is God's Crucible, the great Melting-Pot where all the races of Europe are melting and reforming."

…Despite the United States' historical image as a "melting pot," immigration has long evoked fears in the parts of the country most affected by it. In recent years, such fears have been propagated once again by factions in those states most apt to receive immigrants. Part of the argument turns around allegations that immigrants, and especially undocumented immigrants, cause the cost of providing social services, including education, to increase beyond reason. Acting on such fears, citizens have sometimes supported anti-immigrant provisions (e.g.,California's Proposition 187).

The actual cost of schooling undocumented children is, however, unclear. Because of the ways schools are funded, state and federal aid tend to keep pace with enrollment increases. Hence, local taxpayers are not likely to suffer an increased tax burden from the mandate to serve undocumented children. In fact, studies suggest that taxes withheld from the pay of undocumented workers (who seldom file for refunds) provide a *net gain* to local, state, and federal governments. One study found that undocumented immigrants used public services at a lower rate than other U.S. residents. Like filing for tax refunds, accessing public services (including schooling) is potentially dangerous for undocumented residents.

Theory and practice of the common school

The term "common school" is usually associated with the public elementary schools established in the first half of the 19th century, the forerunners of today's public school system.

Only within the past 50 years has the United States begun to realize the ideal of a high school education for *all* students. For most of their existence, U.S. public schools have been exclusive, and the "common school" has been more theory than practice. This long history means that the tendency to exclude, track, and marginalize some students (e.g., impoverished students, students of color, language minorities) remains a force both in society at large and throughout educational practice. As recently as the 1940s, most children in rural areas did not attend school beyond the eighth grade. Truancy laws were not enforced, and educators actively encouraged "difficult" students (including those who spoke languages other than English) to quit. Only a privileged few had access to the best schooling. The 1954 Supreme Court decision *Brown v. Board of Education* changed all of this, giving … African American children the right to more equitable access to public education. *Brown* brought us closer to a school system we all could hold in common.

In the early 1960s, when new programs began to assist the children of migrant farmworkers, fewer than 50% of migrant children at second-grade level attended school. Farmworkers needed their children to help in the fields or care for younger siblings. Improving attendance became a major goal of the Federal Migrant Education Program. In the 1960s and 1970s, pressure increased to enforce child labor laws, due in part to accidents among children working in the fields.

In the 1980s and 1990s, however, anti-immigrant sentiment has urged the reestablishment of policies of exclusion.… California's Proposition 187, passed in 1996, "would have excluded approximately 308,000 children from the schools, and required public schools to verify the legal status of students and their parents." The education provisions of Proposition 187 were found unconstitutional because they so blatantly contradicted *Plyler v. Doe*.

Complying with *Plyler*

The 1982 U.S. Supreme Court ruling *Plyler v. Doe* stands as the federal law regarding the admission of undocumented children to public schools. *Plyler* guarantees undocumented children the right to a free public education. The Court believed that denying … [them] access to education unfairly punished … [them] for their parents' undocumented status. As a result of the ruling, schools may not

- deny admission to a student on the basis of [their] undocumented status
- treat a student fundamentally different from others to determine [their] residency
- engage in practices to "chill" [their] access to school
- require students or parents to disclose or document [their] immigration status
- make inquiries of students or parents that may expose their undocumented status
- require Social Security numbers from all students

Chilling. Chilling refers to actions (of affected individuals or agencies—for instance, teachers, principals, schools, and school districts) that create fear among undocumented

In Plessy v. Ferguson (1896) the Supreme Court ruled that racial segregation was consistent with the Constitution as long as facilities provided for blacks —including schools —were not inferior to those provided for whites. In Brown v. Board of Education of Topeka, Kansas (1954), however, it later ruled segregated public education a contravention of the Constitution's Fourteenth Amendment. See http://brownvboard. org/ for more about that landmark case.

Go to www. tourolaw.edu/ patch/Plyler/ for the full text of Plyler v. Doe. Do you think that access to education is a basic right?

The government agency responsible for enforcing immigration law was formerly the Immigration and Naturalization Service (INS), part of the Department of Justice. On March 1, 2003, however, the INS was replaced by the Bureau of Citizenship and Immigration Services (BCIS), which is part of the newly created Department of Homeland Security.

Go to www.ed. gov/offices/OMI/ fpco/ferpa for a brief summary of FERPA's provisions.

students or their families. Many families are understandably fearful of completing forms such as vaccination records. They know their residency in this country is precarious and are generally unclear about how U.S. institutions function. For example, the free-lunch application requests Social Security numbers but does not require them. Indeed, the completion of enrollment forms can dissuade many parents from enrolling their children in school in the first place.

Exposure. Educators are required not to "expose" children and families to the Immigration and Naturalization Service. Fear of exposure, however, leads parents to keep their children from school, and it causes children to worry about being arrested, separated from their parents, or kicked out of school. Firm leadership and clearly stated rules are required in an arena of such simultaneous controversy and clearly articulated legal principles. The Family Educational Rights and Privacy Act (FERPA) also prohibits schools from providing information to outside agencies that would expose students' citizenship status.

Disparity. Disparity refers to the imposition of different rules according to individual or group characteristics. An example would be a clerk who demands original documents of "suspicious" students but accepts copies from all others. Such procedures, whether gratuitous or a matter of written policy, can jeopardize the already fragile security of undocumented children....

States' policies. Guidelines do not allow schools to ask students about their legal status, but staff can verify residence for purposes of district attendance.

Serving undocumented children well

Schools that serve undocumented children well attend to staff attitudes, admission and school procedures, organization, and (more generally) good educational practices.

Attitudes. School staff expect immigrant children to be motivated and hardworking. Indeed, many families that immigrate to the United States are motivated by the opportunity to send their children to good schools. Economic survival, however, generally figures as a high family priority, possibly limiting school attendance and participation. It helps if school staff realize that newly arrived and non-English-speaking parents, although educated in their own country, will have difficulty dealing with the U.S. education system.... Staff should receive training about cultural and experiential expectations of the populations they serve.

Admission procedures. A courteous, welcoming environment and bilingual staffing make it likely that parents and children will feel comfortable. Clear maps of the school, well-marked rooms, color coding, bilingual signs, and escorts or "buddies" for new students send a welcoming message. Classroom placements should be made by someone especially familiar with bilingual and immigrant children and the programs available to help them.

School procedures. School administrators need to lead the ongoing effort to explain (to both parents and staff) the procedures (including those relating to *Plyler*) that particularly affect immigrant, bilingual, and undocumented children. School rules should be made available in the language of the parents; the purposes of applications, forms, and questionnaires should be clearly explained to parents. ...

Education practices. The characteristics of good schools in general include many that can enhance the education of undocumented children. Parents are involved and welcomed; staff works as a team on the clear behalf of students. The school values students, their families, and their experiences and cultures. Good practices include effective assessment of academic needs and language proficiency; appropriate class and course placement, including consultation with parents and teachers; and instruction geared to students' prior knowledge and experience. Limited English proficient students should be included in classes with English-speaking students, but should also receive instruction or support in their first language.... Also important are social and academic multicultural programs, drop-out prevention efforts, college and career counseling, and "second-chance" opportunities for education and training.

The challenge

Teachers and administrators who work hard to understand the strengths, the lives, and the cultures of undocumented immigrant children help to create a school environment that benefits all students. At the state, district, and local levels, educators and educational institutions must ... [uphold] the law. They must ensure that undocumented children have access to the services to which their legal rights entitle them.

> Do you think it would be practical and affordable to provide teachers with the extra training that the authors recommend?

> Do you agree that bilingual education is essential? See Volume 1, Individual and Society, Topic 7 Should English be the official language in the United States?

> The authors argue that illegal immigrant children contribute to a a multicultural environment that is beneficial to all students. Do you agree?

WE ARE OVERWHELMED
Jerry Seper

NO

School overcrowding

…[A]crisis exists in public education, where illegal immigration has had a major effect on elementary and secondary school enrollments, particularly among the four border states. Schools … are prohibited under federal law from denying immigrant students access to a free public education. As a result, the annual cost to taxpayers … is estimated in the billions of dollars.

A report last month by the Federation for American Immigration Reform (FAIR) said that rising immigration numbers were to blame for school overcrowding, adding that if the flow of immigrants was not cut, they would account for 96 percent of the future increase in the school-age population over the next 50 years.

The report said the numbers included a massive flow of illegal aliens into U.S. schools and predicted that the quality of education would not improve if the government did not stop illegal immigration.

The effects of *Plyler v. Doe*

In 1982, the U.S. Supreme Court, in a 5-4 decision, said children of illegal immigrants have a constitutional right to a free public education. [It] prohibited schools from adopting policies or taking actions that would deny illegal aliens access to education based on their immigration status.

The ruling, in a case known as *Plyler v. Doe*, overturned a Texas law that at the time allowed school districts to bar illegal immigrants or require them to pay tuition. "By denying these children a basic education," the court said, "we deny them the ability to live within the structure of our civic institutions, and foreclose any realistic possibility that they will contribute in even the smallest way to the progress of our nation." "It is difficult to understand precisely what the state hopes to achieve by promoting the perpetuation of a subclass of illiterates within our boundaries, surely adding to the problems and costs of unemployment, welfare and crime," the majority opinion said.

The court said school officials could not require children to prove they were in the country legally by asking for

Founded in 1979, FAIR is a nonprofit public interest group that advocates reform of immigration law to reduce overall immigration and stamp out illegal immigration. Go to www.fairus.org for more information. Do you think illegal immigration is the main reason for overcrowding in schools?

Do you agree with the court that education will allow the children of illegal immigrants to contribute to society?

A teacher instructs nonnative English-speaking students, using cards.

documents such as citizenship papers, but could require proof the child of illegal aliens lived within school district attendance zones, as they might for any other child. But the high court warned the schools to be "careful of unintentional attempts to document students' legal status," which could lead to the "chilling" of their rights. The court said schools could not inquire about a student's immigration status, make inquiries that could expose the students' legal status … [nor] require the students to supply a Social Security number.

The court also prohibited any communication with the U.S. Immigration and Naturalization Service [INS] concerning a student's immigration status and said the schools should not cooperate with the INS in any manner that "jeopardizes immigrant students and their right of access."

The Urban Institute and others have estimated that 15 percent of all kindergarten through high school children in California are illegal immigrants, who cost the taxpayers $1.6 billion annually. Elected officials and education and immigration experts do not have specific numbers for New Mexico, Arizona and Texas, but believe that between 10 percent and 15 percent of the total enrollment in those states are illegal aliens.

The high cost of educating illegal immigrants is one reason California voters passed Proposition 187 in 1994, which called for the state's schools not to admit illegal aliens. The courts, so far, have blocked implementation of Proposition 187 and schools in that state still provide a free public education for school-age children regardless of their immigration status.

"Every child is an individual of great worth," said Lowell Billings, assistant superintendent of the Chula Vista, Calif., Elementary School District. "We're not the immigration cops and that is not a function of our public school system."

Mr. Billings, who takes over as superintendent on Oct. 1, said Chula Vista officials make "every effort" to find out if the 25,000 children attending the district's 39 schools actually live in the city, including a proof of residency and home visits, but that the law requires him to educate those children who show up for class.

"I would be a bald-faced liar if I told you that 100 percent of the children enrolled in the district's schools are legal residents," Mr. Billings said. "But we are not the INS. Our job is education and we are focused on teaching and learning."

The predominantly Hispanic school district, located just three miles north of the U.S.-Mexico border, has built six schools since 1998 and is adding 600 to 800 students a year.

The Urban Institute, a social and economic policy research think tank, was founded in 1968. Go to www.urban.org for more information.

Proposition 187, which sought to prevent illegal aliens in the State of California from receiving benefits and public services, was passed by California voters on November 8, 1994. Several lawsuits were immediately filed, including one by the American Civil Liberties Union (ACLU), and a district judge struck down parts of the measure as unconstitutional. California's attorney general appealed, and five years of legal arguments ensued between supporters and opponents of the proposition. In 1999 they reached a federally mediated settlement, and the measure was effectively killed.

The costs of illegal immigration

The cost of providing federally mandated health care and education to illegal immigrants has been estimated at more than $5 billion a year, although Congress lacks any accurate assessment of the actual costs borne by the states.

Those expenses do not include other mandated costs, including funds required by the states, cities, and counties to prosecute illegal aliens who commit crimes. One study in 2001 said the 28 border counties spend $125 million a year to process and prosecute illegal aliens. It also costs more than $500 million annually to incarcerate illegal immigrants. Much of that financial burden is being borne by California, where one in every seven inmates is an illegal alien.

"Not much attention is being paid to the tremendous costs of mandates imposed on states and local governments that must provide care to a swelling number of noncitizens within their borders," said Sen. Jon Kyl, Arizona Republican. "Yet those costs ultimately take a human toll, too. Every tax dollar spent on emergency care or criminal justice for an illegal immigrant has to be paid by American taxpayers," Mr. Kyl said, noting that at the same time, indigent [poor] U.S. citizens "must abide by stricter limits, fewer choices and rising prices under their government health care coverage." "We are a generous people, but more and more of my constituents are saying this is unfair," he said.

But we need a more commonsense approach to dealing with [the] costs and problems of illegal immigration. A compassionate people must act to help those in need, but the needs of American citizens and taxpayers must also be considered....

The author uses statistics to make his argument. Does he do so effectively? Why does Congress lack an accurate assessment of the costs caused by illegal immigrants?

Do you think illegal immigrants are more likely to commit crimes than those residing in the country legally? If so, why do you think that is?

Do you agree that the costs to the taxpayer of providing for illegal immigrants may constitute a "human toll" comparable to that of denying education and health care to illegal immigrants?

Summary

Recent increases in the numbers of illegal immigrants in the United States have led to a fierce debate about whether illegal immigrant children should continue to be entitled to a free public education.

In their digest for the Clearinghouse on Rural Education and Small Schools Susan C. Morse and Frank S. Ludovina argue that despite a tradition of fear of immigrants and resentment of the financial burden illegal immigrants create, the additional cost of educating the children of illegal immigrants is actually relatively small. They also argue that in the last 60 years the United States has begun to realize the creation of an education system that provides for all students, thus overcoming a history of exclusion and deprivation for students from marginalized parts of society. Efforts to exclude the children of illegal immigrants from public schools are unconstitutional, they argue, as underlined by the Supreme Court judgment in *Plyler v. Doe*. They itemize the ruling's main points to support their argument.

In the second article journalist Jerry Seper of *The Washington Times* argues that illegal immigrants—mainly Hispanics—are overwhelming border states such as California. He argues that the large number of illegal immigrants in school costs California taxpayers $1.6 billion per year. While it is all very well for educators to support principles such as the equal treatment of all students, he argues, in practice the system needs to be reconsidered. This is largely because of the unreasonable cost of supplying education to non-taxpayers. He claims that more and more U. S. citizens are beginning to feel that it is unfair that they have to support illegal immigration.

FURTHER INFORMATION:

Books:

Dudley, William (ed.), *Illegal Immigration: Opposing Viewpoints*. San Diego, CA: Greenhaven Press, 1997.

Olson, Laurie, *Made In America: Immigrant Students in Our Public Schools*. New York: The New Press, 1998.

Squyres, Suzanne B., Cornelia Blair, and Margaret A. Mitchell (eds.), *Immigration and Illegal Aliens: Burden or Blessing?* Wylie, TX: Information Plus, 1997.

Useful websites:

www.aclumontana.org/rights/plyler.html
American Civil Liberties Union of Montana page on *Plyler v. Doe*, with some useful links.

http://ericweb.tc.columbia.edu/pathways/immigrant_issues/impol.asp
Educational Resources and Information Center/ Clearinghouse on Urban Education (ERIC/CUE) site, with links to articles on immigration and education issues.

www.facts.com/icof/i00053.htm
Facts on File site. Section on immigration controversies.

www.wcl.american.edu/hrbrief/v2i2/point.htm
"Proposition 187: An Important Approach to Prevent Illegal Immigration," Alan C. Nelson.

The following debates in the Pro/Con series may also be of interest:

In *Individual and Society*:
Topic 7 Should English be the official language in the United States?

SHOULD ILLEGAL IMMIGRANT CHILDREN GET PUBLIC EDUCATION?

YES: Illegal immigrants cost the country $5 billion a year. One way or another that money comes from ordinary taxpayers.

YES: A compassionate society has a moral duty to care for the needy whether or not they are legal citizens

COST
Does providing services for illegal immigrants put a financial burden on taxpayers?

OBLIGATION
Does the United States have a duty to look after illegal immigrants?

NO: The cost is minuscule compared to other government expenditure, and federal funding means that it does not fall unfairly on citizens in the worst-affected states

NO: U.S. citizens have no duty to care for illegal immigrants who choose to come to the United States. Fewer would come if they did not receive health and education support.

SHOULD ILLEGAL IMMIGRANT CHILDREN GET PUBLIC EDUCATION?

KEY POINTS

YES: A child should not suffer because of parental choices over which it has no control

YES: Fewer families would come if parents knew that their children would not receive free education and health care

FAIRNESS
Is it fair to punish children for the decisions of their parents?

ATTRACTION
Does free education attract illegal immigrants to the United States?

NO: It is fairer in the long run to withhold education so that parents will be encouraged to take their children back to their country of origin

NO: It is a myth that illegal immigrants are attracted by welfare provision. In virtually all cases they are attracted by the availability of jobs, not welfare.

PART 3
TEACHERS, TEACHING METHODS, AND THE CURRICULUM

INTRODUCTION

For many years critics have argued that the U.S. education system has been in difficulty. Some commentators believe that the education system's problems lie in the fact that there is no national school system. Individual states have ultimate power over education policy, in accordance with the Constitution, and most states have delegated the administration of schools to local government level. This has created great diversity in the kind of education students receive across the United States. There is no consensus or legislation to enforce other factors that would make education policy more consistent, such as a national curriculum, the universal establishment and recognition of institutions, the recognition of degrees or professions, the governance of constitutions, or the legal status of students or faculty.

The teacher problem
Some critics think the problem is far more basic; they believe it can be laid at the door of badly trained, inefficient, or incompetent teachers. Others argue that there are simply not enough teachers, that classes are too full, and that students do not receive enough attention, leading to both academic and social disorder problems.

But advocates of educational reform claim that the initiatives launched by President George W. Bush in 2001 to improve education standards are already changing the situation. They argue that the United States will soon be at the top of any tables comparing international educational systems, instead of near the bottom.

More vs. better teachers
In 2001 President George W. Bush introduced the No Child Left Behind Act. It proposed to make the education system accountable and flexible. By 2002 federal expenditure on elementary and secondary education had risen by almost 27 percent in a year. The extra funding was to be used for improving teaching quality and adult literacy, and for assessing school performance.

The initiatives seemed to have some early effects. Whereas in 1999 the National Center for Education Statistics reported there were around 3.1 million teachers working in elementary and secondary schools, in 2003 there were around 6.3 million teachers in the United States. Critics, however, argue that it is not the quantity of teachers that matters but the quality of those employed. They assert that powerful teaching unions and tenure make it difficult to fire incompetent teachers or even to retrain them. Advocates of unions argue that they help to maintain teaching standards and promote much-needed reform. They claim that unions are a convenient scapegoat for the real problems hounding education. This issue is examined in Topic 9.

Teaching methods

Advances in technology, changes in demographics, and debates over the best ways to teach subjects have all revolutionized the way people teach. In 1995, 50 percent of schools had access to the Internet, but by 2003 this figure had risen to 98 percent. Most students are computer literate,

Some commentators counter that teachers already have overly heavy workloads, and the pressure of having to teach in two languages would be too much for most people to take on. They also state that the United States has enough of a literacy problem without complicating the issue further. Some educationalists promote phonics teaching as the best way to teach students to read, in contrast to whole-word teaching. This issue is considered in Topic 10.

Difficult subjects

For many educationalists the lack of a national curriculum creates all kinds of problems. Each state has its own

---

"The curriculum is so much necessary raw material, but warmth is a vital element for the growing plant and for the soul of the child."
—CARL JUNG (1865–1961), SWISS PSYCHIATRIST

---

and educationalists are now investing more time and money in using the Internet to teach difficult subjects such as science or math with varying degrees of success. Both science and math were targeted by Bush's administration as particular problem areas.

The change in demographics over the 20th century has also brought new challenges to teaching. In 2003, according to *The Washington Post*, around 10 million of the 53 million students at elementary and secondary school spoke a language other than English at home—for more than two-thirds it was Spanish—leading some people to argue that schooling in the United States should be bilingual.

political, social, cultural, and religious agendas. In some states the idea of sex education is abhorred, and abstinence education is taught instead. Other states teach character education to instill a sense of ethics and morals. Similarly, studies in citizenship are becoming more popular.

Religion, however, is an area where schools increasingly come into conflict. Some have ended up in court defending their stance against students, parents, and even teachers, who object to Bible instruction or the banning of creationism on the grounds that it is in violation of the Establishment clause of the First Amendment. These issues are studied further in Topics 11 and 12.

Topic 9
DO TEACHERS' UNIONS HINDER EDUCATIONAL PERFORMANCE?

YES
FROM "TEACHERS' UNIONS: ARE THE SCHOOLS RUN FOR THEM?"
WWW.LIBERTYHAVEN.COM
JAMES BOVARD

NO
"HOW UNIONS BENEFIT KIDS: NEW RESEARCH DISPELS MYTHS ABOUT UNIONS"
NEW YORK TEACHER, MARCH 28, 2001
NEW YORK STATE UNITED TEACHERS

INTRODUCTION

For many years the standard of education in the United States has been the subject of serious discussion. For some critics the issues of whether teachers are performing adequately, and what factors, if any, influence their performance are central to the debate. While class sizes, funding, and pay are factors often mentioned, some government officials, educationists, and parents claim that the strength of teachers' unions has hindered the education system.

Historically, teachers' unions (organizations of workers formed to advance the interests of their members, normally through collective bargaining) have served to protect the rights of their members, including the number of hours teachers are required to work, conditions of employment, and their salary.

Teachers are primarily protected by two unions, the National Education Association (NEA) and the American Federation of Teachers (AFT). Educationists and parent groups have, however, become increasingly concerned that the NEA and AFT have too much power. They assert that far from working for the interests of their students, unions have, in fact, stood in the way of change, opposing the introduction of systems that might lead to an improved education system or give parents a better choice about where and how to school their children—school vouchers and homeschooling among them. This has led critics to question if the interests of teachers' unions actually clash with the rights of students.

Supporters, however, claim that unions are among the strongest advocates of students rights. They assert that from the beginning unions have fought to improve the conditions under which students are taught. The NEA website, for example, lists school safety, health (including teenage pregnancy and sexually transmitted diseases), reading, and George W. Bush's No Child Left Behind Act among the issues that need to be dealt with. It is also a member of Educational International (EI), an organization connected to over 300 unions in 160 different countries, that "promotes every child's right to a quality public education and advocates for human and trade union rights within the profession."

> *"When school children start paying union dues, that's when I'll start representing the interests of school children."*
> —ALBERT SHANKER, FORMER PRESIDENT, AMERICAN FEDERATION OF TEACHERS (1985)

Those factors, advocates argue, show that teachers' unions are committed to helping promote change in education. They claim that business and government antagonism to strong unions has led them to be used as scapegoats for the failing education system when, in fact, unionization and the power of collective bargaining have enabled teachers to voice concerns about the education system that the government and their employers have to listen to.

Critics, such as 1996 Republican presidential candidate Bob Dole, disagree. Dole, in his acceptance speech at the Republican National Convention (1996), stated, "When I am president, I will disregard your [union] political power for the sake of the children, the schools, and the nation. I plan to enrich your vocabulary with those words you fear—school choice, competition, and opportunity scholarships—so that you will join the rest of us in accountability, while others compete with you for the commendable privilege of giving our children a real education." Bob Dole was not elected president, but he raised some key issues in the debate—such as "choice" and "competition."

Critics argue that some of the proposals that the teachers' unions are blocking are in actual fact reforms that will improve the education system. They point to the lack of union support for George W. Bush's No Child Left Behind Act, which promised to improve U.S. education by focusing on problem areas such as literacy, teacher quality, and making schools and teachers accountable if certain standards are not met. Unions like the NEA claim, though, that they are not criticizing the act; they are highlighting areas that need further government commitment, such as teacher investment, dealing with problem schools and students, and funding.

Teachers' unions have not avoided controversy, and that has fueled the opposition they often encounter. For example, taking the view that many students are already sexually active, the unions support the availability of contraception on school premises. That has brought them into conflict with right-wing and religious groups that consider these to be antifamily values.

The following two articles examine the debate further.

TEACHERS' UNIONS: ARE THE SCHOOLS RUN FOR THEM?
James Bovard

Opening with a strong statement that gets straight to the point gives your argument a powerful start.

✓ …Government schools are increasingly run by the unions and for the unions. Former U.S. Secretary of Education Lamar Alexander observed, "After the post office, schools are the most unionized activity in America. [Teachers' unions] collect a lot of money in dues, they are often the largest lobby in the state, they are very, very powerful." Teachers' unions are especially powerful in inner cities, where teacher pay is often highest and teacher performance is usually the worst. Mario Fantini, in his book *What's Best for Children*, declared, "For many black and Puerto Rican parents, the teachers' unions now represent the 'enemy.'" Reverend Jesse Jackson has questioned teachers' "right to strike for more money when the employer—a taxpaying parent—holds tax receipts in one hand and test results in the other that prove he's paying more and more for less and less."

Do you think teachers deserve the pay they get? Why should they be paid more?

Teacher monopoly-bargaining laws (laws that permit unions to claim to represent and speak for all teachers, and to force school boards to deal with unions) in 34 states cover 67 percent of the nation's teachers. Teachers' unions have worked to destroy local control of education, subvert standards, prevent teacher accountability, and deny parents a significant voice in their children's education. Unions have launched strikes to prevent and restrict "parental interference" in public education. Thanks to a strong union, New York school janitors are paid an average of $57,000 a year, yet are required to mop the schools' floors only three times a year. As a result, New York City public schools are sometimes filthier than New York City streets.…

Rush Limbaugh has a highly successful national radio talk show. He is controversial because of the conservative views he expresses to his millions of listeners.

The New York Times noted last year that teachers' unions have been "for decades the most conspicuous voice in American education." Teachers' unions do not hesitate to use their clout blatantly. The NEA announced a boycott of Florida orange juice after the Florida citrus department advertised on the Rush Limbaugh radio show. As Barbara Phillips reported in the *Wall Street Journal* in January, the local teachers' union in Jersey City, New Jersey, threatened a statewide boycott against Pepsi if PepsiCo did not withdraw from its support of Mayor Bret Schundler's school voucher proposal. There is no limit to the brazen demands of some unions: the West Virginia teachers' union sparked controversy in February by demanding that teachers be permitted to retire at age 50 with full benefits—even though the teacher pension fund was far in hock.

See Topic 4 Do school vouchers work? *for more on this issue.*

Policy dictators

Teachers' unions are increasingly dictating policy to the schools. The NEA has denounced back-to-basics programs as "irrelevant and reactionary." The union is the leading advocate of "no-fault" teaching—whatever happens, don't blame the teacher. The *Chicago Tribune* concluded in 1988 that the Chicago Teachers Association has "as much control over operations of the public schools as the Chicago Board of Education" and "more control than is available to principals, parents, taxpayers, and voters." The *Tribune* noted that "even curriculum matters, such as the program for teaching children to read, are written into the [union] contract, requiring the board to bring any proposed changes to the bargaining table."

As Richard Mitchell noted in his classic *The Graves of Academe*, the NEA has played a crucial role in mentally debasing American public schools. In 1918 it authored a federal government report known as "Cardinal Principles of Secondary Education." Mitchell summarized the principles:

Richard Mitchell (1929–2002) was a professor of English at Glassboro State College, NJ. His book, published in 1981, attacked the educational establishment.

> *It is a thematic illusion of our educational enterprise that understanding can be had without knowledge, that the discretion can be informed without information, that judgment need not wait on evidence.... The self-interest of a massive educationists' trade union is evident on every page of Cardinal Principles.... They wanted to be not teachers but preachers, and prophets too, charging themselves with the cure of the soul of democracy and the raising up in the faith of true believers.*

In 1971 the NEA issued a "Call to Action" that renewed its commitment to the Cardinal Principles. It declared, "We have overemphasized the intellectual development of students at the expense of other capacities." Thanks to the NEA's success in rewriting school curricula, student knowledge of history has nose-dived, student reading and comprehension have plummeted, and college remedial classes have thrived.

What might the "other capacities" be that the NEA refers to? Do you think there are aspects of education that are more important than students' intellectual development?

"Solidarity forever"

…Teachers' unions blatantly exploit their power over school children. In Montgomery County, Maryland, union teachers refused to write letters of recommendations to colleges for students unless the students first wrote to the county council urging an increase in government spending for education (and, naturally, higher salaries for teachers). One high school senior told the *Washington Post*, "The consensus among students seems to be it may be blackmail, but students are going to go along with it anyway." …

> *Do you think that the examples Bovard quotes are typical or extreme?*

At Wilson High School in Washington, D.C., teachers gave parents a formal notice that they would not write letters of recommendation for students unless parents wrote three letters demanding higher pay for teachers: "Please submit to each teacher from whom your child is requesting a college recommendation your letters to your city council member, the superintendent and your school board member along with three addressed and stamped envelopes." Parents thus had to grovel in front of a teacher—to surrender their right to their own opinion on public education policy—in order for their children to receive consideration from the teachers.

Teachers have stronger legal rights to tax dollars than the taxpayers have to a quality education for their children. School systems face vastly more repercussions from firing an incompetent teacher than from totally neglecting school children.… A 1992 Detroit Free Press investigation entitled "Shielding Bad Teachers" concluded that it takes a school district seven years and costs an average of $100,000 to fire a single incompetent public school teacher. Seven years is over half of the schooling time of the average pupil. *The Free 1992 Detroit Press* concluded, "No protections are built in for the state's 1.5 million public school students, who can suffer physical, sexual or educational abuse." The American Association of School Administrators conducted an audit of District of Columbia public schools and concluded that an "astonishingly low" number of teachers receive unsatisfactory ratings and that it is "nearly impossible" to fire bad teachers.

> *Public school teachers have tenure that protects them from arbitrary dismissal. Historically, tenure was established to stop schools from basing decisions to hire or fire on favoritism and politics. However, tenure does not give teachers lifetime appointments to their jobs.*

Potent political power

Many politicians have claimed that the problems of public education can be resolved by rigorous new teacher evaluation programs. But teachers' unions often politically dominate state legislatures, and the legislators protect the teachers against their own incompetence. In 1991 the Louisiana legislature voted to suspend teacher evaluations for one year. That evaluation had originally been introduced as part of a joint package with large pay raises for teachers; after the legislature enacted the pay raises, the teachers' unions then launched a successful attack on the evaluation program.

Homeschooling is one of the fastest growing triumphs in family rights in the country. Naturally, teachers' unions have been fiercely opposed to permitting parents to teach their own children to read and write. Annette Cootes of the Texas State Teachers Association declared that "home schooling is a form of child abuse." …

See Topic 7 Is home education an acceptable alternative to public education? *for more on this issue.*

School vouchers

One measure of the coerciveness of the government school monopoly is the percentage of parents who would remove their kids from government schools if they could. If Americans could choose—if they had not already paid for public education through taxes—there would likely be a wholesale exodus from government schools in many cities. A 1992 poll of black residents of Milwaukee revealed that 83 percent favored a voucher system that would allow parents to choose their children's school. A 1991 Gallup poll found that 71 percent of people 18 to 29 favored educational vouchers and 62 percent of people 30 to 39 favored vouchers. The Gallup survey found that "by a 10-to-1 margin, respondents said private schools do a better job of … giving students individual attention and maintaining discipline.

Teachers' unions and school officials have repeatedly sabotaged parents' efforts to defect from the public school monopoly. In 1992 in California, a coalition sought to put on the state ballot a proposal to provide a $2,500 state scholarship to children attending private schools. (Since the state of California was then spending over $6,000 per public school student, taxpayers would save over $3,000 for each additional student transferring from public to private schools). Though organizers got almost one million signatures to put the measure on the ballot, the effort was bushwhacked by the California Teachers Association and public school officials.…

"Bushwhack" means to attack suddenly.

The power of the teachers' unions is one of the best reasons to pursue the separation of school and state. There is no simple reform, no fancy political trick that will break the power of the teachers' unions over the day-to-day activities of public schools. Given the realities of campaign contributions and organized greed, it will always be easier for teachers' unions to exploit the education system for their own benefit than for parents to fight the eternal bureaucratic and political wars necessary to protect their children.

Do teachers and parents share the fight to protect children's interests?

HOW UNIONS BENEFIT KIDS: NEW RESEARCH DISPELS MYTHS ABOUT UNIONS
New York State United Teachers

NO

The Harvard Educational Review *is a scholarly journal known for its well-balanced approach to educational research. It is read by educators and researchers around the world.*

The stereotypes about unions are all too familiar. Anyone who works in public schools has heard an oft-repeated litany that blame unions for public education's woes.

New research published in the *Harvard Educational Review* blows those stereotypes out of the water and backs up what teachers have known all along: there's a strong positive link between teacher unions and higher academic achievement among students.

A team of researchers from Indiana University in Bloomington and the University of South Carolina in Columbia examined rates of teacher unionization in each state and compared them with interstate variation in SAT and ACT scores. The researchers, led by sociologist Brian Powell of Indiana University, found that the presence of teacher unions appears to be linked to stronger state performance on these two standardized tests.

The study, "Do Teacher Unions Hinder Educational Performance? Lessons Learned from State SAT and ACT Scores," was published in the *Harvard Educational Review* Winter 2000 issue. It found that, on average, a state in which all teachers are covered by collective bargaining has an average SAT score that is 51.6 points higher than its unorganized counterpart. States with higher rates of unionization also appear to have higher ACT scores.

Do the researchers' comments have any effect on the way you view the findings of their research?

The researchers, [Brian] Powell and Robert Carini of Indiana, and Lala Carr Steelman of South Carolina, were actually quite surprised by their findings. "When we began this project, we thought that our results would discount both anti- and pro-teacher union positions," said Powell. "That is, we anticipated that there would be at best a minimal link between teacher unionizations and state scores."

Carini added, "The robustness of the positive impact of teacher unions, across a variety of student outcomes, using different measures of unionization, was quite startling."

In the study, the researchers wrote, "That we found such a strongly consistent positive relationship across so many permutations of analysis should give pause to those who characterize teacher unions as adversaries to educational success and accountability."

Tom Hobart, president of New York State United Teachers [NYSUT] isn't at all surprised by the study's findings.

The study "confirms what all of us who believe so strongly in the teacher union movement inherently know: the presence of teachers' unions in schools plays a positive role in improving student achievement," Hobart said.

"From now on," he added, "it's going to be harder for our opponents to demonize teachers' unions and accuse us of being an obstacle to real education reform."

Dispelling the myths

Hobart said the study reinforces earlier research, such as a 1988 Rand study that found a strong contract is the best route to greater teacher professionalism. The Rand study found that, contrary to the myth that unions are a roadblock to change, strong unions can more easily win support for new policy directions and education reform.

Rand is a nonprofit institution that attempts to improve policy and decisionmaking through research and analysis.

The newest research did not explore the reasons why unions correlate so positively with student achievement, but Powell offered a theory: "Teachers' unions are going to push for things like preparation time, a reasonable teaching load, and smaller classes—which benefit students, not just teachers."

Does everything that benefits teachers also benefit students?

Teacher leaders agreed. NYSUT Executive Vice President Alan Lubin noted that the statewide union's strength in numbers makes it a successful advocate for kids. "NYSUT lobbies on behalf of our students every day at the state Capitol," said Lubin, ticking off a list of achievements over the years, including extra funding for remedial help, smaller class-size initiatives, and funds for computers and technology. NYSUT's membership now tops 450,000 statewide.

NYSUT and its national affiliate, the American Federation of Teachers, are outspoken advocates for high academic standards. NYSUT First Vice President Antonia Cortese, who oversees the union's Division of Research and Educational Services, admits that it's tiresome to see unions portrayed in the media as "naysayers" when "in fact we have led the way in encouraging our students to reach for the stars."

NYSUT's support for high standards in the teaching profession has been evidenced by an exponential growth in its educational offerings, which include graduate courses through its Effective Teaching Program; inservice conferences; and regional workshops and seminars. The union regularly publishes information helpful for parents and teachers on helping students succeed.

Helping our students

Just as NYSUT advocates for students at the state level, so too do local affiliates make a difference for their students in a myriad of ways.

"Teachers' unions are the ones who have fought for better education for years," said Steve Frey, president of the Yonkers Federation of Teachers [YFT].

"We're the ones who push the issues that benefit students either directly or indirectly."

The YFT, one of the first unions involved in NYSUT's Local Action Project (a community outreach initiative), has worked hard over the years to raise the union's profile in the community. In return, the union received strong community support during its successful three-day strike in October 1999, which was primarily about educational, not pocketbook issues.

A "pocketbook issue" is one that relates to economic interests.

One of Yonkers' most successful outreach programs has been its annual Story Book Bonanza, said Arline Frey, who heads the local's public relations committee. The union gives away as many as 1,000 free storybooks at a shopping mall. Teachers also dress up as popular storybook characters and pose for free photographs with the children.

The local also publishes two community newsletters with tips for parents, and gives away $9,000 in scholarships every year. All of these activities are "a continual reminder that teachers are here for students," said Arline Frey.

The voice for the students

The Utica Teachers Association has also worked hard to promote both the issues of unionism and better education.

Utica TA President Al Martorella said his local fought early on for the establishment of a districtwide discipline code and the creation of an alternative academic program for troubled students.

Both initiatives helped reduce a high dropout rate, improve attendance and get the high school taken off the list of low-performing schools.

"We're organized to bring the best quality of service to the students," Martorella said. "The demands we make are to provide what's necessary for schools and students to perform at high levels. We're the voice for the students."

The researchers who conducted the study on teachers' unions and educational performance said they were motivated in part by the vitriolic nature of public attacks made against teachers' unions. "If you do any work at all in the field of education, it is difficult to miss the anti-union rhetoric over the past decade in the school reform discussion," Carini said.

Powell said that attacking teachers' unions "serves as political capital" for some individuals and organizations, but it does not further the cause of education reform. "I think it's time for people to stop thinking in such adversarial ways," he said. "This idea that teachers' union are opposed to education reform is a really dangerous idea."

Does the existence of unions mean that the system is inevitably "adversarial"?

Underestimating our impact

The trio that conducted a recent study on the link between teacher unions and educational performance say a key part of their research was to make statistical adjustments for state differences in the characteristics and percentage of students who take the SAT or ACT. "The impact of teacher unions remains hidden if no adjustment is made," said Robert Carini, a doctoral student at Indiana University and a research analyst for the National Survey of Student Engagement. "The effect of unions is underestimated because heavily unionized states tend to have larger percentages of the eligible students completing the exams," Carini said. That means students with a wide range of abilities, not just the top few students, are taking the tests, pulling down a state's average.

Brian Powell, the lead researcher and a sociologist at Indiana University, noted that in 2000 the average SAT score in Mississippi was higher (scores of 562/verbal and 549/math) than scores in many other states including New York (494/verbal and 506/math), New Jersey (498/verbal and 513/math), and Connecticut (508/verbal and 509/math).

Quoting statistics can add strength to your argument; but use them carefully, and make sure that your audience understands their significance.

However, in Mississippi, most high school students who plan to attend college take the ACT instead of the SAT. Only 4 percent of graduating seniors in Mississippi—typically those top-ranked students aiming to get into an Ivy League school—take the SAT, Powell said.

In contrast, 77 percent of students in New York take the SAT, and 81 percent in both New Jersey and Connecticut take the SAT, said Powell, himself a product of the New York state public school system, having graduated from Liberty High in Sullivan County. When the test scores are adjusted to take this into account, New York, New Jersey and Connecticut have considerably higher scores than Mississippi, Powell said.

Summary

In the first article James Bovard argues that the rights of teachers' unions rank above the expectations of both students and parents in the current school system. He says that Americans are paying more money for a poorer quality of teaching because schools are run for and by the unions. Bovard points out that restricting what unions call "parental interference" has eroded the rights of parents and their children. He sees many demands made by unions as unjust and thinks that unions should not be able to dictate policy. He blames the unions directly for poor student performance and the increase in remedial classes. He views the unions' actions as little more than blackmail and sabotage of student and parental rights. Bovard concludes that the only solution is a complete separation of school and state.

In the second article the New York State United Teachers (NYSUT) attack what they call stereotypes and myths about teachers' unions. They cite evidence published in the *Harvard Educational Review* that there is a direct correlation between teachers' unions and higher academic achievement. Results examined from the Scholastic Assessment Test (SAT) and the American College Test (ACT) scores have shown that the presence of teachers' unions helped produce better results. This reinforces earlier research, such as that conducted by Rand in 1988, which indicated that, contrary to popular belief, unions are not a barrier to education reform. By arguing for benefits such as smaller classes, it is the students who ultimately benefit, say NYSUT. The unions do not deserve to be demonized because they are often the only voice for the students themselves.

FURTHER INFORMATION:

Books:
Loveless, Tom (ed.), *Conflicting Missions? Teachers' Unions and Educational Reform*. Washington, D.C.: Brookings Press, 2000.

Articles:
Stern, Sol, "How Teachers' Unions Handcuff Schools." *City Journal*, 7: 2 (Spring 1997).

Useful websites:
www.edexcellence.net/topics/teachers.html
Guide to reports and articles on teacher quality by the Thomas B. Fordham Foundation, an educational reform organization.
www.educationpolicy.org/files/insitoct.htm
"Q: Do Teachers' Unions Have a Positive Influence on the Educational System?" by Dr. Myron Lieberman.

www.nea.org/presscenter/NYTimes/Reprint.html
"Conservatives, Teachers' Unions, and Poisoned Debate" by Richard Rothstein, *New York Times* 2002.

The following debates in the Pro/Con series may also be of interest:

In this volume:

Topic 5 Should private businesses run public schools?

In *Commerce and Trade*:

Topic 4 Do unions adversely affect economic growth?

DO TEACHERS' UNIONS HINDER EDUCATIONAL PERFORMANCE?

YES: Teachers' unions are far too powerful and demand pay over performance. This is unfair.

YES: Union protection makes it very difficult to fire incompetent teachers

TOO MUCH UNIONIZATION?
Is the education system too unionized?

PERFORMANCE
Do unions help bad teachers keep their jobs?

NO: Unions only grow in areas where they are needed. Teachers are not treated fairly; they do a tough job and should be rewarded adequately.

NO: It is not in the unions' interest to protect incompetent teachers. It just ruins the reputation of the union itself and that of teachers in general. Unions protect teachers from wrongful dismissal.

DO TEACHERS' UNIONS HINDER EDUCATIONAL PERFORMANCE?
KEY POINTS

YES: There have been several cases of teachers coercing children into supporting union action. That is wrong.

YES: There is evidence that unions have prevented schools from endorsing policies that might help their students

MANIPULATING CHILDREN
Do unions use children to increase their bargaining position?

POLICY
Do unions have too much influence over school policy?

NO: That is a myth. Teachers always have the best interests of their students at heart.

NO: It is in the interest of unions to work within school policy, but they have the right to disagree with policies that they believe do not work

Topic 10
IS PHONICS INSTRUCTION THE BEST WAY OF TEACHING STUDENTS TO READ?

YES
"PHONICS TEACHING GETS TOP GRADE"
THE BALTIMORE SUN, APRIL 14, 2000
MIKE BOWLER

NO
FROM "THE READING DEBATE: HAS PHONICS WON?"
ORIGINALLY PUBLISHED IN *SUBSTANCE*, 27 (2): 24, 21, 2001
STEPHEN KRASHEN

INTRODUCTION

In the late 1960s the federal government established the National Assessment of Educational Progress (NAEP) tests to find out how students were doing in a variety of school subjects. Analysis of the results over a number of years revealed some rather worrying statistics about the reading skills of young students.

The first set of test results, released in 1971, suggested that nearly 40 percent of students across the nation were unable to read at a basic level, with this figure rising to 70 percent of fourth-grade students from low-income families. Students living in urban areas were also at a disadvantage, with almost half unable to perform basic reading skills such as understanding and summarizing a simple story.

The statistics provoked widespread concern among educationists and parents alike. It is generally accepted that sound reading skills lay the foundation for future academic success.

Indeed, studies have shown that able young readers are more likely to do well in other subjects, such as math and science. But a high percentage of students who cannot read well drop out of the education system and therefore limit their employment opportunities later in life.

Consequently, raising the reading standards of all students in schools became a top priority for national and state educators. But there is much disagreement over the best way to achieve this improvement. The debate centers around two main teaching methods. Some educationists think that systematic phonics is the best way to teach young students how to read, while others favor the whole-language approach to reading instruction.

Phonics is a method of teaching beginners to read and pronounce words as a combination of distinct speech sounds, called phonemes, each one representing a letter, letter group, or a syllable. In much the same way as musicians may learn to read a piece of music by first identifying a set of symbols that represent musical notes, students learn to read a book by first mastering the combinations of speech symbols that represent words.

"The best evidence we have on the reading crisis indicates that no crisis exists on average in United States reading."
—JEFF MCQUILLAN, EDUCATIONAL RESOURCES INFORMATION CENTER (1998)

The whole-language system takes a very different approach to reading. Proponents of this method believe that learning to read and write English is much like learning how to speak the language. For most young children, learning to speak comes naturally and unconsciously as they are immersed in the spoken words around them. By choosing to read a range of simple books, and by reading the stories aloud, young students string together letters of the alphabet and start to read printed words as whole symbols. If the young reader does not understand a word, he or she can leave it out, guess, or pick it up from the context of the story.

The debate about reading instruction has raged throughout most of the 20th century, with both phonics and whole-language approaches falling in and out of favor. The whole-language system gained momentum in the early 1920s and was consolidated with the

publication of texts such as Dr. Seuss's *The Cat in the Hat* (1957). But the tide turned back toward phonics instruction in the 1960s, following the success of publications such as Rudolf Flesch's *Why Johnny Can't Read* (1955).

By the 1980s the tide had turned again with the development of a public-education program called Reading Recovery, devised by a teacher from New Zealand called Marie Clay. While Clay's program in New Zealand draws on both methods of instruction, in the United States Reading Recovery became a vehicle for proponents of the whole-language approach. The first set of results of the long-standing NAEP tests were released soon after the whole-language system gained momentum, throwing the debate wide open again.

Proponents of phonics instruction were quick to blame the poor NAEP test results on a failed whole-language system of reading instruction. Many state education departments now only fund teachers in phonics instruction for grades four through eight. Those on both sides of the divide must now await the next NAEP test results to see if the argument can finally be laid to rest.

The following articles present the argument for and against the two methods of reading instruction. In the first article Mike Bowler cites research from the National Reading Panel, which concludes that phonics instruction is the most effective way of teaching younger students to read.

In the second article Stephen Krashen argues that although systematic phonics is dominant at present, there is serious evidence to suggest that it is not the best method of reading instruction.

PHONICS TEACHING GETS TOP GRADE
Mike Bowler

YES

Using quotations and evidence from research by recognized experts in moderation may add weight to your argument.

A phoneme refers to the unit of significant sound in language. For example, the sound of "c" in "cat" is different than the sound of "b" in "bat" and distinguishes the two words.

Phonics theory holds that learning to read is like learning music notation or Morse code. Children therefore first need to learn the letters and letter combinations that convey the English language's 44 sounds. That is often accomplished through drills.

WASHINGTON—National experts who sifted through 34 years of research on reading reported to Congress yesterday that instruction in systematic phonics is "significantly more effective"—across all grade levels and student abilities—than instruction that doesn't emphasize phonics or neglects it.

The National Reading Panel, ordered by Congress two years ago to cull from thousands of studies the most effective teaching methods, concluded that systematic phonics instruction "is a valuable and essential part of a successful classroom reading program," makes better spellers of children, and is especially valuable for disabled readers.

The panel said research also confirmed the effectiveness of early instruction in phonemic awareness, the ability to recognize and manipulate the sounds of language. Kindergarten isn't too early to start instruction in phonemic awareness and phonics—knowledge of the relationships between letters and sounds—the report said. Educators said yesterday's findings are bound to hasten the recent national and local swing. from the whole language approach to reading instruction—which stresses literature and often neglects phonics—to systematic phonics. The two contrasting methods have long been the subject of an internal war among the nation's educators.

The latest research says a balanced approach that begins with phonics and then stresses good literature is generally best, and the panel took care to note that reading isn't—and can't be—all phonics all the time. It also stressed that phonics, often viewed as involving too much dull drill, can be taught "in an entertaining, vibrant and creative manner."

Phonics instruction "is a means to an end," the report said, and "programs that focus too much on the teaching of letter-sound relations and not enough on putting them to use are unlikely to be very effective."

Maryland steps

Two years ago, Maryland increased the required number of courses in reading instruction for teachers as a first step toward encouraging widespread improvement in the state's

Phonics instruction centers on teaching young children to recognize letter shapes as well as sounds when learning to read.

stagnant reading test scores. Nancy S. Grasmick, Maryland schools superintendent, said, "This report should force another step with its implications for both higher education and our instructional programs." Maryland reading test scores stagnated last year after slow but steady improvements for several years. Marylanders showed a modest gain from 1994 in the 1998 National Assessment of Educational Progress. Grasmick praised recent improvements in the reading programs of Anne Arundel, Cecil, Charles, and Montgomery counties: In Montgomery, officials have lowered reading class sizes and have fashioned their instructional program around the latest research findings, which also stress the primary role of phonics.

Word Masters is a national program that helps develop vocabulary, analogy sense, and analytical reading.

This school year, Arundel began a similar program called Word Masters, which provides teachers a month-by-month plan for teaching phonics. "We are unifying our teachers in beginning reading instruction," said reading coordinator Ruth Bowman.

The Three R's refer to the fundamental areas of education: reading, writing, and arithmetic.

Charles and Cecil also are placing increased emphasis on beginning reading. This summer, Charles will hold a summer camp for 1,000 first- and second-graders who need help in mastering the first R.

First-time effort

The 14-member national panel on reading research of the past three decades—the first time such an effort has been made—was headed by Donald N. Langenberg, chancellor of the University System of Maryland.

Langenberg, who oversees all public teacher education in Maryland, except at Morgan State University and St. Mary's College, said he would try to apply the panel's findings to the state university system—where training in the teaching of systematic phonics and phonemic awareness is spotty at best.

The panel's charge was to sift through more than 100,000 studies of reading since 1966 and narrow them to those that meet rigorous standards similar to those applied in medical and behavioral research. A few hundred met those criteria. In phonics, 38 of 1,373 studies since 1970 qualified. The panel found almost no reliable studies of how the education of teachers affects reading comprehension, as well as a "dearth" of research on comprehension among very young children.

"Dearth" means a lack or scarcity.

A lot of work to do

"It's fair to say we have a lot of work to do," said Sally Shaywitz, a neuroscientist and professor of pediatrics at Yale University, the panel's only medical representative. She has been using magnetic resonance imagery to conduct research on the brain functions of problem readers.

Shaywitz said many in educational research aren't familiar with the scientific rigor of medical studies, "but now we know what areas need more work."

The panel—a mix of higher education specialists, scientists and reading teachers—was chosen jointly by the two federal agencies that sponsor most school research, the Department of Education and the National Institute of Child Health and Human Development. Duane Alexander, NICHD director, said members were chosen who had not "taken strong stands" in the reading wars and who had no commercial interest in reading programs or materials.

"The panel was asked to deal in science, not ideology, and we did our level best to do that," said Langenberg, a physicist who Alexander said was chosen to head the panel because he had no direct interest in the ideologically charged reading controversies.

> *"Magnetic resonance imagery"* is a technique that produces computerized images of internal body tissues, which are then used to make medical diagnoses.

> Why do you think the issue is so controversial? What are the implications of the debate?

Internet applications

The panel also found little research on Internet applications or other uses of computers in reading. But it said recent developments in computers' speech-recognition capabilities might make it possible for them to "hear" children reading and "talk" back to them.

In addition to research on phonemic awareness, phonics and technology, the panel looked at vocabulary, reading comprehension, and the ability to read aloud.

One finding that surprised several experts was that silent reading has neither a positive nor a negative effect on achievement.

A minority report from Joanne Yatvin, a school principal in Boring, Ore., said the panel viewed the reading field too narrowly, excluding inquiry into language and literature, the chief emphases of whole language.

"The claims of whole language were not addressed by this panel," Yatvin said at a news conference in the Capitol.

> In adulthood most people usually read silently. Why might reading aloud be thought to be so important?

THE READING DEBATE:
HAS PHONICS WON?
Stephen Krashen

Guide your audience at the start by clearly defining the main points of the debate.

NO

There are two factions in the current reading debate. Those in the skill building or "phonics" camp believe that we learn to read by first learning a large number of sound-spelling correspondences, the rules relating letters and sounds. They believe that in order to learn to read, one first has to learn to read outloud. These rules range from very simple ones (the letter "b" is pronounced "bee") to complex rules (when there are two vowels side by side, the long sound of the first vowel is heard and the second vowel is silent, e.g. in the word "bead", the E-sound of the first vowel is heard—this rule is quite famous and is often referred to as "when two vowels go walking the first does the talking.") These rules are learned consciously, and practiced until they become "automatic." Children first apply these rules to individual words, and gradually work up to larger units. The faction of the skills camp that is dominant at this time is systematic phonics, a step-by-step approach in which children learn rules of phonics in a prescribed sequence.

The primary opposition to the skill-building camp is the whole language camp. Whole language advocates hold that literacy is developed when we understand what we read. (I have referred to this position as the "comprehension hypothesis.") For reading, this is the view that we "learn to read by reading." As we read, and as we understand text, we subconsciously absorb (or "acquire") the principles of phonics, as well as vocabulary and grammar. Thus, for advocates of whole language, "skills" are largely the result of reading, not the cause.

Krashen articulates a crucial point for supporters of whole reading. They believe that reading skills, including phonics, are a result of the reading process rather than a cause of it.

(It is important to mention that whole language supporters do not dismiss the value of teaching some rules of phonics; some conscious knowledge of sound-spelling correspondences can occasionally help children understand texts. For example, if a child is unable to read the final word in "The man was riding on the h___," but knows how "h" is pronounced, the combination of context and this phonics rule will help the child determine what the unknown word is; there are a limited number of possibilities (horse, mule, donkey) and knowledge of this phonics rule will eliminate all but one (this example is from Frank Smith's book, *Reading Without Nonsense*.) Whole language advocates have never advocated a strict "no phonics" approach. They argue, however, that there are severe limits on how much phonics can be consciously learned (see below) and that most of our knowledge of phonics is a result of reading. Whole language supporters also argue that knowledge of phonics is only one of the ways we understand text. Readers are also helped [by] other means of assistance, such as their background knowledge and pictures.)

Evidence and counterevidence

Skill builders point to reports of panels such as the recent National Reading Panel to support their view. Members of these panels claim that their approach is "scientific" and that whole language advocates are unscientific. They claim that whole language advocates rely on intuitions, ethnographic descriptions, and correlational studies. The panels, it is asserted, have reviewed studies that follow scientific guidelines, such as randomization or other methods of insuring that subjects are equivalent before the treatment begins, a well described treatment, a control group, and posttests. They claim that according to the research children who learn to read with systematic phonics-based methods do better on reading tests than do children who learn to read with less intensive phonics-based methods and with whole language methods.

> *Why is the way in which research and testing is done on reading so important to the debate? Krashen argues against the findings of the National Reading Panel, which were used as the basis of the opposing argument. In your opinion which argument is more convincing?*

Whole language advocates respond to these criticisms by pointing out that so-called non-scientific studies are very valuable and provide insights not available in controlled studies. Also, whole language advocates argue that the panel reviews were done incorrectly. The reviews omitted crucial studies and misinterpreted the studies they did include. This is an important criticism, because it accepts the same scientific principles that skills advocates accept. Specifically, many of the studies reviewed tested children only on the ability to read phonetically regular words presented in isolation. It is no surprise that children drilled on phonics do well on such tests. When tests of reading comprehension are used, tests that ask children to read meaningful passages in which not all the words are phonetically regular, the impact of phonics training is much less impressive....

> *Krashen identifies a fundamental flaw in the research into phonic reading instruction.*

In addition, I have argued that when whole language appears to fail in the studies, very often the group labeled "whole language" did not really do whole language. When whole language is defined correctly, as involving a great deal of real reading for meaning, children in whole language classes actually do better on tests of reading comprehension, and do just as well on tests of skills.

The complexity argument

Whole language supporters advocate some instruction in basic phonics, but argue that there are severe limitations on how much phonics can be consciously learned. Many phonics rules are extremely complicated and have numerous exceptions. Consider the example given above, "when two vowels go walking the first does the talking." In 1963, Clymer reported that nearly 50% of the words in basal stories with two vowels back to back were exceptions to this rule.

Theodore Clymer is the author of an old but influential study that suggested phonic generalizations commonly taught to young children are not very useful.

Frank Smith provides an excellent example of the complexity of phonics, pointing out that the "ho" spelling combination has many different pronunciations, including hope, hoot, hook, hour, honest, house, honey, hoist, horse and horizon. A child dependent on the rules of phonics not only needs to learn this complex rule but must also look at the entire word, at what comes after "ho" in order to pronounce it correctly. In addition, it has been documented that different phonics programs teach different rules.

Can you think of other examples of phonics that might prove difficult for children to learn or understand?

The assault on alternative views

The skills camp is clearly dominant today. The report of the National Reading Panel is the basis for the Bush plan for reading. What is odd is the skills faction continues what can only be described as an all-out assault on alternative views:
—Panels of experts have been assembled several times to proclaim the superiority of phonics and skills instruction, repeating the claims of previous panels.
—The results of the National Reading Panel have been widely distributed, parts have been republished (although the original is easily available free of charge), a video tape version has been made and distributed, and the NRP has even hired a public relations firm to publicize its results.
—Eligibility for grants have been made contingent on accepting the skills position. In effect, other approaches have been outlawed.

A well-chosen metaphor can give the language of your argument more force, but use them carefully.

The skills camp has not only won, it is killing the prisoners of war. One wonders why…. [T]he heavy and aggressive PR campaign for skills and the demonization of critics is unprecedented. Skills supporters are making sure that this is not a swing of the pendulum. The pendulum is being nailed to the wall.

Proponents of skills claim that after whole language was introduced in California in 1987 test scores immediately "plummeted" to the point where California fourth graders came in last in the country in 1992 on the NAEP reading test (National Assessment of Educational Progress).

Before 1992, however, NAEP scores for individual states were not calculated. There was no previous score to compare to. In addition, there is no evidence that reading scores have declined in California. McQuillan, in his book *The Literacy Crisis: False Claims and Real Solutions*, examined CAP (California Achievement Program) reading scores in California from 1984 to 1990 and found no significant drops or increases.

To be sure, California did poorly on the NAEP test, but as McQuillan has pointed out, performing poorly is not the same thing as declining. There is strong evidence that California's poor performance is related to its print-poor environment....

McQuillan calculated that California ranked 40th out of 42 states in access to print. California ranked last in the country in the quality of its public libraries, and ranked near the bottom in public libraries. In addition, its children do not have reading material at home. California ranked ninth in the country in the number of children ages 5–17 living in poverty in 1995, and near the bottom of the country in the percentage of homes containing more than 25 books. This data, and the clear relationship between access to print and NAEP scores, points to the conclusion that California's problem is not whole language but a lack of reading material. In addition, there has been no significant increase in fourth grade NAEP reading scores since 1992, no evidence that the increased emphasis on phonics has done any good.

Can you think of ways to encourage children to read more? Are computers a good development in this respect?

Conclusions

The skills camp has the upper hand politically, but there is serious counterevidence to their position. In addition, the unprecedented attack on opponents and the aggressive public relations campaign mounted by the skills group makes one suspect that they are not fully confident of their position.

What are the possible dangers of the reading debate being such a political issue?

Summary

Two contrasting methods of teaching reading—phonics instruction and the whole-language approach—have long been the subject of controversy among national and state educators. In the first article, "Phonics Teaching Gets Top Grade," Mike Bowler presents evidence from a National Reading Panel study published in 2000. The study, which points to a large body of research over 34 years, suggests that teachers should place greater emphasis on phonics instruction than on any other method of reading instruction. However, the panel notes that teachers should adopt a balanced approach, starting with phonics from an early age and then moving on to language and literature once the early skills have been mastered. The author suggests that the results of the study should go some way to improve reading test scores in states such as Maryland, where results have stagnated after steady improvements over several years. Bowler concludes his article with the views of a critic, Joanne Yatvin, who suggests that the panel viewed the reading field too narrowly.

In the second article, "The Reading Debate: Has Phonics Won?" Stephen Krashen, professor of education at the University of Southern California, argues that while advocates of whole-language reading value phonics, they recognize that there is a limit to how many phonics can be learned because the rules are complicated and have many exceptions. Krashen contends that the findings of the National Reading Panel are biased toward phonics because the tests focused on the ability of children to read words in isolation rather than for general comprehension. He claims that the fall in California's reading test scores reflects a lack of reading material in the home rather than the fact that whole reading was introduced. Krashen concludes that although phonics is politically dominant at present, it is being so aggressively defended by its supporters that it seems they are not fully certain of their position.

FURTHER INFORMATION:

Books:

Coles, G., *Misreading Reading: The Bad Science That Hurts Children*. Portsmouth, NH: Heinemann, 2000.

Articles:

Lemann, Nicholas, "The Reading Wars." *The Atlantic Monthly*, November 1997.

Useful websites:

www.nationalreadingpanel.org/
Website of the panel created to assess the effectiveness of different approaches to teaching children to read.
www.ncrel.org/sdrs/timely/brires.htm
Guide to Internet resources on balanced reading.

www.nrrf.org/features.htm
Topical essays on the reading instruction debate.

The following debates in the Pro/Con series may also be of interest:

In this volume:

Topic 7 Is home education an acceptable alternative to public education?

IS PHONICS INSTRUCTION THE BEST WAY OF TEACHING STUDENTS TO READ?

YES: Some educationists have jumped on the bandwagon and made this method of teaching the only way to teach reading

YES: Some students learn through a combination of hands-on teaching, reading, and peer interaction. They suffer if taught purely by phonics instruction.

A FAD?
Is phonics instruction just the latest fad in education?

SUITABLE FOR ALL LEARNERS?
Does phonics education work with some students and not others?

NO: Literacy is a problem in the United States, and this method has proved to be effective in helping reduce illiteracy

NO: Studies show that everyone benefits from phonics education, otherwise why would educators endorse the method?

IS PHONICS INSTRUCTION THE BEST WAY OF TEACHING STUDENTS TO READ?

KEY POINTS

YES: The importance of phonics instruction has been exaggerated; it cannot stand alone as an effective method

YES: Whole-language instruction and other reading methods are very important and need to be taught alongside phonics

PART OF A WIDER PROGRAM
Would phonics instruction be more effective if it were part of a more balanced reading program?

NO: Statistics support the fact that phonics has helped teach more children to read successfully than any other program

NO: Other reading programs, such as whole language, have failed; this is the best method

135

Topic 11
SHOULD PUBLIC SCHOOLS TEACH CREATIONIST THEORY?

YES
FROM "CREATIONISM V. EVOLUTIONISM IN AMERICA'S SCHOOLS"
TRINCOLL JOURNAL, 1997
ALEX RAINERT

NO
FROM "THE CREATIONISM CONTROVERSY"
WWW.ADL.ORG, 2000
ANTI-DEFAMATION LEAGUE

INTRODUCTION

The question of whether creationism should be taught in U.S. public schools has raged in courtrooms, schools, and universities for years. Creationism is the belief that humankind was created by a divine being separately from all other animals and according to a literal interpretation of the Judeo-Christian creation story in the Book of Genesis.

At the heart of the debate lies the issue of whether such teaching is in violation of the Establishment Clause of the First Amendment, which forbids the government from endorsing any particular religious belief. Many advocates of creationism, however, argue that it should be on school biology curricula alongside evolution—the scientific theory that today's life forms gradually developed through billions of years of natural processes.

According to creationists, the Earth and all living things on it were created in the process detailed in Genesis. While some people still accept this version of how life was created, several converging strands of thought began to challenge it many centuries ago.

Astronomy in the 17th century showed that the Earth was just one of many planets orbiting the sun, while geology and paleontology in the 19th century began to indicate the great age of the Earth. In the field of biology Jean-Baptiste Lamarck (1744–1829) advocated a theory of evolution that included the idea that traits that had been acquired by their parents could be passed along to offspring.

It was, however, Charles Darwin (1809–1882) who really challenged the theory outlined by Genesis with the publication of *The Origin of Species* in 1859. The book put forward Darwin's theory of evolution by natural selection—the process by which random variations among individuals of a species (such as the length of beak of a bird) give some of them an advantage in surviving and so passing on those traits to their offspring (an idea summed up in the phrase "survival of the fittest").

Darwin's theory received a mixed reception. The Christian churches were initially hostile, since they considered species as unchanging. Other critics viewed evolution as difficult to prove, especially since it made predictions based on scientific knowledge that had not yet been discovered. Subsequent advances in biochemistry, paleontology, and zoology have given a wealth of supporting evidence to the theory, while in the second half of the 20th century the discovery of DNA and subsequent research in genetics has revealed the mechanisms through which natural selection works.

> *"[W]hen two opposite points of view are expressed with equal intensity, the truth does not necessarily lie exactly halfway between them. It is possible for one side to be simply wrong."*
> —RICHARD DAWKINS,
> BRITISH ZOOLOGIST (1996)

By the early decades of the 20th century the major Christian churches had accepted evolution; and in most parts of the world where science is taught at all, Darwin's theory is no longer regarded as being in dispute. In the United States, however—where small communities can control educational curricula at the local level—some parts of the country resisted this change. A number of laws were introduced in various states, particularly in the South and Midwest, outlawing the teaching of evolution, and this legislation remained in several states until the 1960s. In 1968, however, the Supreme Court in *Epperson v. Arkansas* invalidated the Arkansas statute prohibiting the teaching of evolution. It stated that the statute was in violation of the First Amendment. That led some anti-evolutionists to mount a rearguard action, claiming that evolution is also a religion, so teaching it is also unconstitutional. In court rulings such as *Peloza v. Capistrano* (1994) the Supreme Court ruled that evolution is not a religious belief.

In spite of that, creationism has its adherents, and organizations such as the Institute for Creation Research were set up in support of it. Some states began to remove evolution from their curriculum—Kansas did so in 1999, although the move was reversed two years later after an international outcry.

The survey conducted by the civil liberties organization People for the American Way in 1999 found that 60 percent of those interviewed rejected the Kansas Board of Education's decision to drop the teaching of evolution. A further 83 percent of those surveyed supported teaching evolution in schools, and about seven out of ten of them believed that evolution was not incompatible with religious belief.

For many people, teaching creationism alongside evolution seemed the most viable political compromise— George W. Bush campaigned for that during his presidential campaign. To others the issue is a constitutional one. The following two articles look at the debate further.

CREATIONISM V. EVOLUTIONISM IN AMERICA'S PUBLIC SCHOOLS
Alex Rainert

YES

For many people, the debate surrounding the issue of creationism and evolution involves believing the impossible, regardless of which side one finds oneself on. Presently in America, there is much debate as to the validity of the respective theories in deciding which is appropriate to teach to children in public schools. It is an age-old debate that began between scientists and the Christian Church over a century ago concerning the theories proposed by scientists such as Darwin, Lyell, Wallace, and others.... In this article, I will outline the two positions and then address the current debate over which view should be taught to the children who attend American public schools....

The creationist view maintains the dignity of humankind—we are created in God's image as the summit of creation, and are the only beings to possess a Divine soul, that is to say, we can consider ourselves to be God's masterpiece. It is the infringement on these values which adherents to creation-science abhor in the theory of evolution presented by Darwin....

The author suggests that creationists reject evolution because they dislike its implications rather than because it is untrue. Do you think this is good reasoning?

Darwin's theory

Charles Darwin authored two books that are the focal point of his theory of evolution and which address the most controversial issues from the point of view of the Christian Church. In *The Origin of Species* [1859], he puts forth the theory of natural selection which can be summed up in the following manner: 1. There are random variations among the species [the author means "among individuals of the same species"], 2. There is a struggle for survival, and 3. The fittest members of a society survive. In *The Descent of Man* [1871], Darwin proposes the idea that man is directly descended from the apes and that our seemingly superior intelligence is merely a difference in degree, not in kind, from that of the primates. The Christian Church was unable to accept such a theory because it eliminated the sacredness of a soul created and ascribed specifically by God. If we, in fact, are descended from apes, then we too are merely creatures of the animal

More information about Darwin's life and work can be found at www.aboutdarwin.com/ (including the full texts of The Origin of Species *and* The Descent of Man).

kingdom, without a soul that is particular to humans. And if we were created in God's image, God would have to be an animal as well. The assurance that the Bible provided that man had control over nature was seriously threatened....

The reason that Darwin's theory was not well received is that his evidence was indirect. His theory offered a new explanation for phenomena that, until then, were unexplainable by science. The problem was that it rested ... upon many things that had yet to be proven by science. It was not until Mendel's work on genetics was uncovered that Darwin's theory began to gain concrete scientific support. Mendel's work provided "a reliable basis for evolutionary inheritance."... By 1930, Sir Ronald Fisher had paved the way for Neo-Darwinism by showing how "genetic mutations function in the process of natural selection."

In fact, Darwin gave a wealth of direct evidence of species changing over an observable period, using the examples of dogs and pigeons that had been bred to emphasize characteristics such as speed, endurance, or sense of smell.

Evolution: a natural law?

At the turn of the century, Herbert Spencer pioneered a discipline known as Social Darwinism, which combined biology, physics, sociology and philosophy and used Darwinian thought to analyze society's structure. Essentially, it stated things were the way they were because it was "natural" for them to be that way. The rich were rich and the poor were poor all because of "natural law." ... It spawned a new order that was ... based on the old principle of the divine right of kings. People who wanted to escape this had to turn to the churches that were not caught up in this phenomena.

The author describes one way in which evolution has been used to justify questionable social outlooks. Do you think this is relevant in discussing the scientific evidence for evolution?

Recently, there has been much debate over which of the two theories of human origin is appropriate and should be taught to America's public school students. Many of the current legal battles can be traced back to the Scopes trial of 1925 during which John Scopes, a science professor in Dayton, Tennessee, was convicted for illegally teaching Darwin's theory of evolution.

The lawyer responsible for prosecuting Scopes was William Jennings Bryan, an avid supporter of the Bible's account of creation.... Although Bryan won the case, Scopes's defendant [the author means "attorney"; Scopes himself was the defendant], Clarence Darrow, managed to humiliate Bryan in court and seemed to have gained a victory nonetheless. ...

See "The Scopes 'monkey trial' (1925)," pages 148–149, for further information on the trial of John Scopes.

The Scopes trial marked the beginning of the debate that is still heated in America. In order to address it properly, it is inevitable that the dichotomy of Church and State, and their relative powers over society, [must] be once again reconsidered. The debate centers around the fact that teaching creation-science in public schools might infringe upon one of the most important freedoms provided by the U.S. Constitution, the freedom of religion. The main motivation behind the creationist movement is to show that "our species was singled out for a special creation in God's own image." ...

Theory or hypothesis?

As of November 1989, California's public schools no longer present Darwin's theory of evolution as fact, but as both fact and theory. This is an "equivocation pleasing to the religious right because few understand that to scientists, 'theory' is not synonym for mere 'hypothesis'." Philip Dunne, a writer for *Time* magazine, brings up an interesting point in that, to most people (non-scientists), the term 'theory' implies something that is debatable, which essentially the theory of evolution is, but as many scientists would argue: "It's true that evolution is 'just a theory.' So is Einstein's theory of relativity, the theory of plate tectonics, and the theory of subatomic particles. Yet no one argues that teachers should present alternatives, because no other alternatives exist. All these theories have unanswered questions, and any of them might someday be overturned by a new idea that explains its facts better. But at the moment, no other is even close." This seems to be the strongest argument in favour of the evolutionary theorists who hold that the theory of evolution should be taught to children in public schools as more than "just a theory."

Creationists, though, tend to feel that if evolution is in fact a theory, then why can we not see creation-science as an alternate theory that should be accorded the same amount of importance in places such as schools. The problem arises in that if the U.S. were to institute a mandate that required creationism to be given the same weight as evolution and in some case taught as the sole theory ... one could see it as a subversive way of imposing religion on students. Scientist John Cole feels that "attacking evolutionism may stem from a simple desire to attack the establishment and to express general discontent rather than from a straightforward disagreement with a biological theory."

The Fundamentalists represent the most extreme believers in the creationist movement when it comes to teaching the origin of life to children in U.S. public schools. They want to re-institute prayer in the classroom (the Gallup Polls show that 69% of Americans are in agreement with that particular suggestion), and to censor school libraries and textbooks in

The author makes a distinction between "fact" and "theory," as if one implies greater certainty than the other. See www.talkorigins. org/faqs/evolution-fact.html for an explanation of what scientists actually mean when they use these terms.

If the creation story in the Book of Genesis is given equal importance with evolution, do you think creation stories of other cultures (such as the ancient Greeks or Native Americans) should also be given equal importance?

accordance with their tenets.... It is apparent that the Fundamentalists do not have a problem with forcing religion on students. One must note, though, that this particular group represents the extreme right on the issue and shouldn't be seen as a representation of the creationist movement as a whole. Polls consistently show that nearly half of the American population do not subscribe to Darwin's theory of evolution which explains the inability to secure one of the theories as the one to be taught in schools. They both display a practically equal amount of supporters.

> In virtually the whole of the Western world evolution is no longer seriously questioned. What do you think such poll results reveal about Americans?

A middle way?

It is difficult to see a way that these two seemingly polar opposite theories can coexist if one is to take the two theories in their strictest sense. If one is to take the Biblical account of creation literally, it is impossible to, at the same time, believe that we also evolved from single-celled organisms. But if one were able to reach a compromise between these two theories without compromising one's own respect for scientific knowledge or religious belief, then I believe the two can be compatible. It is definitely a possibility that a Divine Force set the universe in motion with the Big Bang and provided all of the laws for the universe, including evolution—perhaps we can accept "evolution as the process the Creator may have used to bring life and mind into being."

> This is the position of the churches representing the majority of the world's Christians, including the Catholic Church and the Anglican Communion. See www.biology.ttu. edu/courses/ 1402_Porter/ evolution.htm for a listing of various doctrinal statements.

Dunne concludes his article by pointing out that, in a sense, we are all creationists because "to some extent, we may learn how it happened, when it happened, but never why, any more than we can bound infinity or clock eternity." Once again, we are shown that science and religion are engaged in the same project, to discover the origin of life, but will forever, as far as we can see, be unable to find the final piece of the puzzle, the meaning of life. Dunne also says that "we [creationists and evolution-theorists] differ! Only on the specifics. The idea of linear time is so embedded in our consciousness that we instinctively believe there must have been a beginning, a creation, a genesis. But on what impulse, whose design? That we can never know." I feel that Dunne has located the issue central to the debate at hand. As far as we can see, there will never be a definite answer as to which theory is correct. We should be able to remain open to different possibilities—we should be able to credit both Science and Religion for their respective accomplishments and in teaching them to the American youth, refrain from over-imposing either of them on the youth.

> Does the fact that there is no definite answer to the question mean that all possible theories are equally likely?

THE CREATIONISM CONTROVERSY
Anti-Defamation League

What are the differences between a scientific theory and a pseudoscientific one? See http://skepdic.com/pseudosc.html for some pointers on definitions.

NO

X "Creationism"—the belief that humankind was created by a divine being according to a literal interpretation of the Book of Genesis—is a pseudoscientific collection of religious ideas based on varying interpretations of the Bible. Any attempt to supplant or supplement the teaching of evolution in public schools in order to promote creationism would have a religious purpose....

The pseudoscience of creationism

Scientists have long recognized that evolution accounts for the diversity of life on earth. Using the methods of scientific inquiry and analysis, biologists have established that human beings and other species evolved over time by a process of natural selection. It is entirely appropriate, therefore, for public schools to make evolution a significant part of their biology curriculum.

See www.bbc.co.uk/education/darwin/leghist/dawkins.htm for a more detailed but straightforward description of how evolution by natural selection works.

While the role of evolution in shaping the biological world is accepted as a fact in the scientific community, some religious people—from a variety of faiths—reject its veracity because they believe that it is irreconcilable with the Biblical story of creation. In their view, the teaching of evolution in public schools represents an anti-religious bias against those Christians, Jews and others who believe in a literal interpretation of the Bible. Many opponents of the teaching of evolution believe that it is merely one example of the "secular-humanist" religion that government favors in place of traditional Judeo-Christian beliefs. They argue that evolution remains unproven and that schools should give equal time to "creationism"—the belief that humankind was created by a divine being according to a literal interpretation of the Book of Genesis. This idea—which cannot be proved or disproved scientifically—is plainly a religious doctrine and should not be taught as fact in public schools.

Is the Bible meant to be taken literally?

Teaching creationism as science

The Establishment Clause of the First Amendment prohibits the government from endorsing any particular religious belief. This prohibition ensures that our public schools remain places in which students of all faiths—or no faith—

may learn in an atmosphere free from divisive theological debates and sectarianism. In banning organized prayer in the public schools in 1962, for example, the U.S. Supreme Court said that "[w]hen the power, prestige and financial support of government is placed behind a particular religious belief, the indirect coercive pressure upon religious minorities to conform to the prevailing officially approved religion is plain." Our public schools must fulfill the First Amendment's mandate of separation of church and state and remain free from the influence of religious dogma in order for students of all faiths to attend school without fear of coercion.

Do you agree that the influence of religious dogma in public schools might lead to fear and coercion? Give some examples to back up your answer.

Proponents of teaching creationism in public schools share a distinctly religion-based view of the world's origin and believe that the public schools should modify their curricula to take that view into account or even to teach that view alone. However, any such modification would plainly violate the First Amendment's prohibition against state action designed to advance a religious belief.

In 1968, in *Epperson v. Arkansas*, 393 U.S. 97 (1968), the Supreme Court held unambiguously that it is unconstitutional to restrict a public school teacher's right to teach evolution. More recently, in *Aguillard v. Edwards*, 482 U.S. 595 (1987), the high court decisively held that it is unconstitutional to require educators who teach evolution to also teach creationism. These two important rulings form the basis for a fair and sensible approach to the teaching of science in our public schools. While the Biblical story of creation may constitutionally be taught as part of a class on religion or religious literature, in science classes teachers must present only scientific explanations for life on earth. Further, science teachers may not teach as fact the theory that humankind was created by a divine being or that the Book of Genesis presents an accurate version of the world's creation. The Supreme Court's approach is beneficial not only to science teaching, but also to an atmosphere which allows diverse religious beliefs to co-exist in the classroom.

The full texts of these judgments can be seen at www.bc.edu/bc_org/ avp/cas/comm/free_ speech/epperson. html (Epperson v. Arkansas) and http://cns-web.bu. edu/pub/dorman/ edwards_v_ aguillard.html (Aguillard v. Edwards).

Recent efforts to promote creationism in schools

Since any attempt to ban evolution or to include creationism in a school curriculum would run counter to the Supreme Court's rulings, creationists have developed new tactics to promote their goal of undermining the way biology is taught in the public schools. For example, in 1999 the Oklahoma State Textbook Committee mandated that publishers doing business with the state be required to place a disclaimer in all biology books. The disclaimer states, among other things, that

Cartoon of Darwin as an ape inviting a fellow ape to note their family resemblance in a mirror, published in the London Sketch Book in 1874.

evolution is "a controversial theory which some scientists present as a scientific explanation for the origin of living things, such as plants and humans." It goes on to say that evolution is "the unproven belief that random, undirected forces produced a world of living things." ... [S]ome supporters of the disclaimer have openly stated that its purpose is to give creationism an equal chance in the schools. In 1999, the Kansas Board of Education took a different approach by simply removing evolution from the required biology curriculum of the state's high schools. While teachers in the state may still choose to teach the subject, they are no longer required to do so. Whether the decision will survive constitutional scrutiny remains to be seen, but it is difficult to imagine a secular purpose behind the elimination of a subject that forms the very backbone of the entire discipline of biology.

The Kansas statute did not remain in place long enough to be challenged constitutionally. It was reversed by the Kansas Board of Education in February 2001, following an election in which some of those who had sponsored the original statute lost their seats.

Teaching creationism harms religion

... Both public school educators and religious leaders should be concerned about the prospect of biology lessons degenerating into debates on Biblical interpretation. Our history has been largely free of the kind of sectarian discord that has plagued other countries precisely because we have kept government out of religion and religion free from government control. Many religious people, of course, are able to reconcile the teachings of the Bible with those of modern science. But this task should be left to families and their clergy based upon a full understanding of the scientific basis of evolutionary biology. To deny students an adequate education in biology for fear of insulting their religious sensibilities underestimates the ability of believers to distinguish between scientific facts and matters of personal faith.

Do you agree that it is worth the risk of offending students in order to teach them about scientific ideas?

Conclusion

Evolution is one of the fundamental bases for the study of biology at even the most elementary level and it is supported by the overwhelming weight of scientific evidence.... Creationism is a collection of religious ideas based on varying interpretations of the Bible.

Consequently, any attempt to supplant or supplement the teaching of evolution in public schools in order to promote creationism would have a religious purpose. By protecting the right of students to learn science uninfluenced by religious doctrine, we best fulfill the purpose and the promise of the First Amendment.

Summary

The debate about where humankind and other life forms originated has been heated for many years in some parts of the United States, although in the rest of the Western world it is no longer seriously considered to be in dispute. While creationism, based on the teachings of Genesis, holds that God created humankind separately from other animals, other theories have evolved to explain how life was formed. For many people creationism should not be taught in schools since it endorses one religion. Others disagree. The preceding articles examine the debate in greater detail.

In the first journalist Alex Rainert looks at the history of the debate. Drawing on arguments by *Time* writer Philip Dunne, Rainert argues that it may be possible for creationism and evolution to be taught in schools side by side. He concludes: "We should be able to remain open to different possibilities—we should be able to credit both Science and Religion for their respective accomplishments and in teaching them to the American youth, refrain from over-imposing either of them on the youth." However, the definition of creationism that Dunne proposes and Rainert endorses would be unlikely to satisfy most people who identify themselves as creationists.

The extract from "The Creationism Controversy" by the Anti-Defamation League (ADL) looks at the reasons why creationism should not be taught in schools. It argues that creationism is a "pseudoscientific collection of religious ideas based on varying interpretations of the Bible," and therefore that any attempt to promote creationism in public schools could only have a "religious purpose." For that reason the ADL article argues that the Establishment Clause of the First Amendment prohibits teaching creationism in schools.

FURTHER INFORMATION:

Books:

Mayr, Ernst, and Jared Diamond, *What Evolution Is*. New York: Basic Books, 2001.

Moore, Randy, *Evolution in the Courtroom: A Reference Guide*. Santa Barbara, CA: ABC-CLIO, 2002.

Skehan, James W., and Craig Nelson, *The Creation Controversy and the Science Classroom*. Arlington, VA: NSTA Press, 2000.

Useful websites:

http://physics.syr.edu/courses/modules/ORIGINS/origins.html
An "Evolution vs. Creationism" page based at Syracuse University, with links to other resources and sites.
www.talkorigins.org/
Online articles on evolutionary and creationist ideas.

The following debates in the Pro/Con series may also be of interest:

In this volume:
The Scopes "monkey trial" (1925), pages 148–149

In *The Constitution*:
Topic 9 Does the Constitution protect religious freedom?

In *Individual and Society*:
Topic 9 Should there be a right to violate laws for religious reasons?

SHOULD PUBLIC SCHOOLS TEACH CREATIONIST THEORY?

YES: Creationism is an important explanation of how life began, and teachers should be free to teach it as part of the curriculum

YES: Every theory, including intelligent design, should be taught as part of the curriculum

FREEDOM
Should schools be free to teach different theories as part of their curricula?

FAIRNESS
Would teaching creationism give students a more complete background to the development of humankind and other life forms?

NO: Freedom does not mean that anyone is free to use science classes to promote religiously motivated, untestable theories that have no scientific basis

NO: Creationism is based in religion and is not a science. It has nothing to do with the development of humankind.

SHOULD PUBLIC SCHOOLS TEACH CREATIONIST THEORY?
KEY POINTS

YES: Since creationist propositions are not valid scientific theory; their only purpose is religious, so they must violate the Establishment Clause of the First Amendment

YES: The Constitution says that governments cannot endorse any particular religion in schools, and allowing creationism to be taught violates that principle

CONSTITUTION
Is teaching creationism unconstitutional?

NO: Creationist science is not a religious-based theory and so does not violate the Constitution

NO: Evolution is as much a religion as creationism

THE SCOPES "MONKEY TRIAL" (1925)

"[I]f the Darwinian hypothesis should irritate any one it should only be the monkey.... [W]hen science definitely recognizes him as the father of the human race the monkey will have no occasion to be proud of his descendants."

—*PARIS SOIR*, JULY 13, 1925

In 1925 John Scopes, a high school biology teacher in Dayton, Tennessee, was accused of illegally teaching Charles Darwin's theory of evolution in school in violation of the recently passed, controversial antievolution statute known as the Butler Act. The bill made it unlawful to "teach any theory that denies the story of divine creation as taught by the Bible, and to teach instead that man was descended from a lower order of animal." Scopes's subsequent trial, held from July 10 to 25, 1925, attracted world media attention and divided U.S. society on issues concerning the Constitution, religion, and educational theory. The trial highlighted the conflict of social and intellectual values in the United States in the 1920s. Some commentators regard the trial as the greatest in U.S. legal history. The debate about creationism and evolutionism still rages in U.S courts and schools today.

Background to the trial

At the end of World War I (1914-1918) many Americans were concerned that in the changing world traditional social and moral values were becoming irrelevant to the younger generation. The Jazz Age, Freudian theories, and a backlash against the Prohibition policies of the 1920s resulted in greater social and cultural freedom and experimentation for some young people. Fired by what many saw as a loss of moral, religious, and cultural values, religious fundamentalism, stressing a literal interpretation of the Bible, began to flourish, particularly in the American South and Midwest. Critics focused their wrath on the views of Charles Darwin (1809-1882) and the theory of evolution. *The Origin of Species* (1859) articulated Darwin's belief that the diversity of species lay not with God but in natural selection. Scandalized, the fundamentalists sought to remove evolutionism from every sector of society beginning with schools. By 1925 several states had passed antievolution laws banning the teaching of Darwin's theory in the classroom. In response to the passing of Tennessee's antievolution statute, the Butler Act, the American Civil Liberties Union (ACLU), concerned about what it saw as an infringement of basic constitutional rights and academic freedom, published a press release in a Tennessee newspaper offering legal support to any teacher who was willing to challenge the law.

George W. Rappalyea and John Scopes

George W. Rappalyea, a coal company manager, saw the ACLU's press release and, along with other like-minded locals, decided to test the law by finding a teacher who had taught evolutionary theory. They found John Scopes, a 24-year-old football coach and science teacher. Rappalyea explained that they thought "nobody could teach biology without teaching evolution." Scopes agreed and confirmed that he had been using George W. Hunter's *Civic Biology* (1914)—the state-approved textbook, which mentioned Darwin. Scopes was at first reluctant but eventually agreed to participate; his friends subsequently arranged to have him arrested for teaching the forbidden doctrine, contacting the ACLU to provide his defense.

A "duel to the death"

The ACLU assembled their defense team, which included Clarence Darrow (1857–1938), a 70-year-old attorney, arguably one of the greatest orators of the time and a religious agnostic. William Jennings Bryan (1860–1925), three-time presidential candidate (for the Democratic Party) and a prominent Presbyterian layman, volunteered his services to present the case for the state.

The trial attracted attention from the media both at home and abroad. The town was swamped with reporters and the courtroom packed with photographers and radio broadcasters. The issues were, after all, important and controversial: Among them were the academic freedom of teachers, free speech vs. parental rights, governmental authority vs. individual rights, and crucially the constitutional separation of church and state, and religion vs. science.

For Darrow the main purpose of the case was to test the Butler Act; he wanted the jury to find Scopes guilty so that they could appeal the decision in a higher court—preferably the Supreme Court—and to obtain a declaration that laws forbidding the teaching of evolution were unconstitutional.

The trial itself was eventful. In the opening remarks Darrow argued, "Scopes isn't on trial, civilization is on trial," and Bryan stated, "if evolution wins, Christianity goes." Darrow maintained that evolutionary theory was consistent with certain interpretations of the Bible, and in what the *New York Times* called the "most amazing courtroom scene in Anglo-Saxon history" he called Bryan to the stand and asked relentless questions designed to disprove a literal view of the Bible. Some observers felt that Bryan acquitted himself ably; others felt he stumbled badly and was unable to answer questions about the Bible's accuracy and consistency.

After eight days the trial ended: The jury returned a verdict of guilty. The judge fined Scopes $100, the minimum the law allowed. Five days after the trial Bryan died in his sleep, many claimed a broken man humiliated by Darrow's interrogation of him on the stand.

In January 1927, almost a year later, the state supreme court in Nashville reversed the decision on a technicality—by Tennessee law the jury, not the judge, had to set the fine if it was above $50. The case was dismissed, and the court remarked "nothing is to be gained by prolonging the life of this bizarre case."

The Butler Act remained, and laws forbidding the teaching of evolution were not ruled unconstitutional until the case of *Epperson v. Arkansas*, almost 43 years later.

Topic 12
SHOULD RELIGION BE TAUGHT IN SCHOOLS?

YES
FROM "THE BIBLE & PUBLIC SCHOOLS: A FIRST AMENDMENT GUIDE"
WWW.TEACHABOUTTHEBIBLE.ORG, NOVEMBER 1999
NATIONAL BIBLE ASSOCIATION AND FIRST AMENDMENT CENTER

NO
"ELEVEN-YEAR-OLD MUSLIM GIRL HARASSED AFTER DECLINING BIBLE FROM SCHOOL PRINCIPAL, ACLU OF LA CHARGES"
WWW.ACLU.ORG, APRIL 10, 2001
AMERICAN CIVIL LIBERTIES UNION

INTRODUCTION

The First Amendment to the Constitution states that "Congress shall make no law respecting an establishment of religion, or prohibiting the free exercise thereof." Religious freedom is among the most fundamental of the liberties enjoyed by citizens of free societies, so it is fitting that it had pride of place in the Bill of Rights of 1791.

The idea of religious freedom includes both freedom to practice one's own religion without the supervision of the state ("free exercise") and freedom from the tyranny of those who would impose an orthodoxy on all citizens (no "establishment of religion"). Those two aspects of religious freedom are, in many cases, reverse sides of the same coin: Free exercise is perhaps only possible when there is no establishment of a favored religion.

This topic considers one of the most hotly debated issues concerning religious freedom: the study of religion in public schools. Is it constitutionally appropriate for religion to be taught in public schools? Does the First Amendment require a "wall of separation" between church and state that would preclude the study of religion in public schools? Or does it require simply that the study of religion be academic and not devotional? Even if the study of religion in public schools is constitutional, is it educationally worthwhile? After all, religion is an intensely personal matter; and even if we should be informed about our own religion, should the religion of others be of any concern to us?

Debate about the teaching of religion in public schools grew more intense after the September 11, 2001, terrorist attacks on the United States by Islamic extremists. This was shown by the public uproar over a decision by the University of North Carolina at Chapel

Hill in 2002 to require all new students to read a book about Islam. According to university officials, the book was chosen not to promote any one religion but because of interest in Islam since the September 11 attacks. "What more timely subject could there be?" asked the university chancellor.

> *"It might be said that one's education is not complete without a study of comparative religion … and its relationship to the advancement of civilization. It certainly may be said that the Bible is worthy of study for its literary and historic qualities."*
> —SUPREME COURT JUSTICE TOM CLARK, *ABINGTON TOWNSHIP V. SCHEMPP* (1963)

The author of the book, for his part, has insisted that teaching about Islam is not the same as trying to convert people to that religion. "The point of this book," he said, "is to … ask, 'What is it in the religion that makes 1.2 billion people see it as meaningful?' And present that just as you would present what it is in the Christian story of the death and resurrection of Jesus that is meaningful to Christians."

But not everyone sees the issue in this way. A conservative Christian educational organization filed a lawsuit against the university contending that it is unconstitutional for a publicly funded university to force students to study a specific religion and, moreover, to assign a book that is not neutral about the religion. According to the group that filed the lawsuit, the book presents a biased view of Islam by leaving out any consideration of those passages from the Koran that contain exhortations to kill infidels and that have served as inspiration or justification for some Islamic terrorists. The great controversy surrounding this case illustrates that just as interest in Islam is greater than ever, so is the sensitivity of the issue. Indeed, could a concern to avoid controversy force many educators in the nation's public schools to shy away from teaching about religion altogether?

The following articles provide opposing answers to the question of whether religion should be taught in school. The National Bible Association and First Amendment Center argue that teaching about religion is not only constitutional but is an essential part of a well-rounded education. The authors argue that teaching about religion "promotes cross-cultural understanding in our increasingly diverse society."

In the opposing article the American Civil Liberties Union (ACLU) argues that this is not the case. Joe Cook, executive director of the ACLU Louisiana, states that the teaching of religion belongs in the home and places of religious worship, not in public schools. According to the ACLU, the experience of an 11-year-old Muslim girl who was humiliated by her peers when she refused to accept a Bible offered by a school principal underscores the need to keep religion out of the classroom.

THE BIBLE & PUBLIC SCHOOLS
National Bible Association and First Amendment Center

The common school movement was a social and political effort, starting in the early 1800s, from which the common school—today's public school—evolved. A core belief of the movement was that a good education was essential to the democracy of the new nation.

YES

☑ Ending the confusion and conflict about the Bible and public schools would be good for public education and for our nation. But finding common ground will not be easy because Americans have been divided about this issue since the early days of the common school movement. "Bible wars" broke out in the 19th century between Protestants and Catholics over whose version of the Bible would be read in the classroom. Lawsuits in the 1960s led to Supreme Court decisions striking down devotional Bible-reading by school officials. Recent conflicts have involved differences about the limits of student religious expression and the constitutionality of Bible courses offered in the curriculum....

The Bible and the public-school curriculum

Educators widely agree that study about religion, where appropriate, is an important part of a complete education. Part of that study includes learning about the Bible in courses such as literature and history. Knowledge of biblical stories and concepts contributes to our understanding of literature, history, law, art, and contemporary society.

The Supreme Court has held that public schools may teach students about the Bible as long as such teaching is "presented objectively as part of a secular program of education." The Court has also held that religious groups may not teach religious courses on school premises during the school day. The Department of Education guidelines reiterate that public schools "may not provide religious instruction, but they may teach about religion, including the Bible or other scripture." In keeping with the First Amendment's mandate of governmental neutrality toward religion, any study of religion in a public school must be educational, not devotional....

What is the difference between educational and devotional study of religion? Can you think of specific examples of how the Bible adds to our understanding of other subjects such as history and law?

A relatively small number of lower court decisions have dealt directly with the constitutionality of Bible classes in public schools. These rulings show that the constitutionality of such classes is highly dependent on such factors as how the class is taught, who teaches it, and which instructional materials and lessons are used.

How the class is taught: Any class about the Bible must be taught in an objective, academic manner. The class should neither promote nor disparage religion, nor should it be taught from a particular sectarian point of view.

Who teaches the class: A superintendent or school board should select teachers for a class about the Bible in the same manner all other teachers are selected…. Teachers should be selected based upon their academic qualifications, rather than their religious beliefs or nonbeliefs….

Teaching "about" the Bible

If teachers are to understand clearly how to teach about the Bible—and to feel safe doing so—then local school boards should adopt policies on the role of study about religion in the curriculum. The policy should reflect constitutional principles and current law, and should be developed with the full involvement of parents and other community members. Parents need to be assured that the goals of the school in teaching about religion, including teaching about the Bible, are academic and not devotional, and that academic teaching about the Bible is not intended to either undermine or reinforce the beliefs of those who accept the Bible as sacred scripture or of those who do not. Faith formation is the responsibility of parents and religious communities, not the public schools….

> *Do you agree that faith is the sole responsibility of parents and religious leaders? If not, why not?*

Which Bible?

Selecting a Bible for use in literature, history, or elective Bible courses is important, since there is no single Bible. There is a Jewish Bible (the Hebrew Scriptures, or Tanakh), and there are various Christian Bibles—such as Catholic, Protestant, and Orthodox—some with additional books, arranged in a different order. These differences are significant. For example, Judaism does not include the Christian New Testament in its Bible, and the Catholic Old Testament has 46 books while the Protestant has 39. There are also various English translations within each of these traditions…. [T]eachers should remind students about the differences between the various Bibles and discuss some of the major views concerning authorship and compilation of the books of the Bible….

Which interpretation?

The Bible is interpreted in many different ways, religious and secular. For example: In Judaism, the Hebrew Bible is typically read through the eyes of various rabbinic commentators. For Roman Catholics, the authoritative interpretation of the church is crucial for understanding the Bible. Some Christians and Jews use the findings of modern scholarship to interpret the Bible, while others reject some or all scholarship....

Teaching about the Bible, either in literature and history or in Bible electives, requires considerable preparation. School districts and universities should offer in-service workshops and summer institutes for teachers who are teaching about the Bible in literature and history courses....

The Bible and literature

Academic study of the Bible in a public secondary school may appropriately take place in literature courses. Students might study the Bible as literature. They would examine the Bible as they would other literature in terms of aesthetic categories, as an anthology of narratives and poetry, exploring its language, symbolism, and motifs. Students might also study the Bible in literature, the ways in which later writers have used Bible literature, language, and symbols. Much drama, poetry, and fiction contains material from the Bible....

Why do you think the Bible has been so influential on other forms of literature?

The Bible and history

See Topic 11 Should public schools teach creationist theory? for a debate about this issue.

The study of history offers a number of opportunities to study about the Bible. When studying the origins of Judaism, for example, students may learn different theories of how the Bible came to be. In a study of the history of the ancient world, students may learn how the content of the Bible sheds light on the history and beliefs of Jews and Christians— adherents of the religions that affirm the Bible as scripture....

In U.S. history, there are natural opportunities for students to learn about the role of religion and the Bible in American life and society. For example, many historical documents— including many presidential addresses and congressional debates—contain biblical references. Throughout American history, the Bible has been invoked on various sides of many public-policy debates and in conjunction with social movements such as abolition, temperance, and the civil rights movement. A government or civics course may include some discussion of the biblical sources for parts of our legal system....

The Bible and world religions

Given the importance and influence of religion, public schools should include study about religion in some depth on the secondary level. As we have suggested, such study may include study about the Bible, where appropriate, in history and literature courses as well as in elective courses that deal with the Bible. However, a course that includes study about the Bible and its influence will not educate students about religion generally. Just as there is more to history than American history, so there is more to religion than the Bible, Judaism, and Christianity.

Public schools should also include study about other religious faiths in the core curriculum and offer electives in world religions. Because religion plays a significant role in history and society, study about religion is essential to understanding both the nation and the world. Moreover, knowledge of the roles of religion in the past and present promotes cross-cultural understanding in our increasingly diverse society....

Do you think that some parents would be unhappy about their children learning about different religious faiths? Why is it important to learn about world religions?

Elementary education

The study of family, community, various cultures, the nation, and other themes and topics important in elementary education may involve some discussion of religion. Elementary students are introduced to the basic ideas and practices of the world's major religions in a number of textbooks and curriculums used in public schools. These discussions of religion focus on the generally agreed-upon meanings of religious faiths—the core beliefs and symbols, as well as important figures and events. Such discussions may include an introduction to biblical literature as students learn something about the various biblical faiths.

This early exposure to study about religion builds a foundation for later, more complex discussions in secondary school literature and history courses. Such teaching is introductory in nature; elementary education is not the place for in-depth treatment of religion. Stories drawn from various religious faiths may be included among the wide variety of stories read by students. But the material selected must always be presented in the context of learning about religion.

One court has permitted elective Bible courses at the elementary level. But if such instruction is undertaken, it must be done academically and objectively by a qualified teacher. Children would need to understand that they are studying about what the people of a particular religious tradition believe and practice. Devotional books intended for faith formation or religious education may not be used in a public-school classroom.

If students elect to study the Bible, should there be the chance to do so in school?

As in secondary schools, a balanced and fair curriculum in the elementary grades would not limit study about religion to Judaism and Christianity, but would include a variety of the world's major religious faiths.

ELEVEN-YEAR-OLD MUSLIM GIRL HARASSED AFTER DECLINING BIBLE FROM SCHOOL PRINCIPAL...
American Civil Liberties Union

NO

Think back to the arguments in the first article. How does this school contravene the approach it advocates?

ALEXANDRIA, LA—The American Civil Liberties Union of Louisiana filed a lawsuit here today on behalf of an 11-year-old Muslim girl who was humiliated when she refused to accept a Bible handed out by her public school principal. Later, a teacher forced her to participate in a classroom quiz game about Jesus.

"The teaching of religion belongs in the home, the church, the synagogue, the temple, and the mosque but not in public schools," said Joe Cook, Executive Director of the American Civil Liberties Union of Louisiana.

"This little girl has been the target of severe persecution and harassment by her schoolmates because of her religious beliefs," Cook added. "Principal John Cotton and other school officials prompted this cruelty with their actions and statements of religious intolerance."

The target of harassment

If only two children in the school are Muslim, should the school be more concerned with the majority of students?

Yazied and Fatima Jabr, whose two children are the only Muslims who attend Paradise Elementary school in Pineville, filed a complaint with the ACLU after their daughter, Hesen, was made to accept a Bible and became the target of harassment at her school because she told classmates that her family does not read the Bible.

"You cannot imagine the heartbreak and the anguish of dealing with your children's doubt about their own faith, especially when they are still too young and immature to completely understand the differences between the faiths and what makes us all different," said Hesen's mother. "All we can hope is that others will treat our children in the way that we have taught them to treat others—with respect."

According to the ACLU complaint, on December 14, 2000, Hesen and the rest of her fifth-grade class were each presented with a Bible from Principal John Cotton. Hesen politely declined the offering, but Cotton told her to "just take it." Feeling pressured, she accepted the Bible.

COMMENTARY: Religious schools

A religious school is one that is associated with or part of a religious institution. The curriculum includes teaching and devotional worship of the particular religion it promotes, for example, Catholicism, Islam, or Judaism.

The funding issue

Religious schools by their nature as private schools are self-funding. Under the principle of separation of church and state as set down in the Constitution, religious schools have not been able to receive government funding. However, in recent years school vouchers have been promoted as a way of giving parents part of the fees for enrolling their children in a private school, either religious or secular. For the school year 1999–2000 the Sixth Circuit Court of Appeals found that around 96 percent of students enrolled in the school voucher program attended sectarian institutions. The voucher program is therefore indirectly financing religious schools with government money.

School vouchers are a controversial issue. Supporters of school vouchers see them as a way of taking poor children out of bad public schools into private institutions where they can truly achieve. However, critics believe that this will ruin public schools, leaving them with the nation's most unwanted school children. According to a report in *Time Magazine* in 1999, "Voucher programs, especially ones that include religious schools, will Balkanize America by abandoning its common core of teachings and traditions." Some people think that public schools have united diverse groups of children from different races, classes, and religions in ways that private schools, including religious schools, cannot. As Princeton Professor Amy Gutmann has said, children in public schools "are taught as much by the mixing of students as they are by the curriculum."

Historic ruling

In 2002 the Supreme Court ruled in favor of a Cleveland program that allowed public money to be used to send children to private schools, including religious schools. The court found that the Cleveland program did not violate the constitutional separation of church and state because, although the vouchers can be used at religious schools, it also allows nonreligious schools to participate, although in reality few have. Education Secretary Rod Paige said the decision "will open the doors of opportunity to thousands of children who need and deserve the best possible education." The Supreme Court ruling added fuel to the flames of the separation of church and state debate, especially as it came the day after an appeals court decision that the Pledge of Allegiance is unconstitutional because it mentions "under God" (see pages 34–45). The debate appears likely to continue as other states seek to follow the Cleveland example.

Mandatory prayers in public schools are unconstitutional. But students can legally pray in many school situations, such as in the corridors and in the classroom before and after lessons.

Afterwards in her classroom, students called Hesen a "Jesus-hater" and told her that she would burn in hell. In an apparent attempt to quiet the students, Hesen's teacher told them that Hesen believed in Jesus, just "not the same Jesus."

The next day, Mrs. Jabr and her mother, Mona Odetalla, called Principal Cotton to discuss the incident. Cotton informed the two women that he had been distributing Bibles for 35 years, that no one had ever complained before, and that he saw no reason to stop.

Furthermore, according to the complaint, five days after the Bible incident Hesen's teacher led her students in a quiz game about Jesus and asked Hesen to be the scorekeeper because she would not know many of the answers.

> What do you think about the way Hesen's teacher dealt with the situation? What is his position from a legal point of view?

The ACLU said that a majority of Supreme Court justices have recognized that a student in a classroom or other school setting has relatively little choice but to go along with school officials in such situations. Hesen had already learned that lesson with Mr. Cotton.

"The issue here is not whether one religion or faith is better than another, but about forcing one's faith on another person with no respect for that other person's right to practice their own beliefs," said Fatima Jabr.

"As practicing Muslims, we turn in prayer to God not once, but five times a day," she added. "We believe in Jesus Christ and the miracle of his birth, which is why, when she came home that day in tears and told us what had happened, my husband and I were devastated."

"We always taught our children to respect others' beliefs, and now our children were ridiculed because of theirs. Our daughter lost her best friends because of this incident, and suffered nightmares of burning in hell … " she said.

Not an isolated incident

In a similar incident last year, a school district in Beauregard Parish settled a case after ACLU attorneys advised them of their obligations under the Constitution.

"Superintendent Patsy Jenkins and the Rapides Parish School Board can put an end to the Jabr family nightmare by confessing the error of their ways and conveying to their employees and the community that the law of the land must be obeyed," said the ACLU's Cook.

> The "Golden Rule," or the ethic of reciprocity, is the belief shared by nearly all religions that people should treat others in a decent manner. It has been summed up as "Do unto others as you would wish them do unto you."

"We ask the law-abiding citizens of Rapides Parish to speak up by encouraging their public officials to follow the Constitution and the Golden Rule. That would be a blessing for the Jabr family and save the taxpayers' money for education instead of lawyers' fees," he said.

Summary

The issue of whether religion should be taught in schools is a controversial one, leading to much heated debate and a number of related questions. What kind of religion should be taught? Should schools be multifaith? What is the best method to represent the multicultural nature of our society?

The preceding two articles examine the debate in more detail, illustrating opposing views on the issues of the constitutionality and educational worth of teaching about religion in schools. The National Bible Association and First Amendment Center argue that studying religion is "an important part of a complete education." Knowledge about the Bible, for example, "contributes to our understanding of literature, history, law, art, and contemporary society." So long as such study is "academic and not devotional," it is perfectly consistent with the constitutional protections of the First Amendment.

The American Civil Liberties Union, however, strongly disagrees with that idea. The second article, which looks at the case of an 11-year-old Muslim girl, confirms that in the ACLU's view, religious instruction in schools is in sharp conflict with the right to free exercise of religion protected by the Constitution. The American Civil Liberties Union argues, contrary to the National Bible Association, that the best way to promote religious freedom, tolerance, and respect is to keep religion out of the public school system.

FURTHER INFORMATION:

Books:

Dwyer, James G., *Religious Schools vs. Children's Rights*. Ithaca, NY: Cornell University Press, 1998.

Useful websites:

www.aclu.org/ReligiousLiberty/
ReligiousLibertylist.cfm?c=139
Press releases and news items on the issue of religion in schools on the American Civil Liberties Union site.
www.atheism.about.com/library/decisions/indexes/
bl_l_schoolsindex.htm
List of Supreme Court decisions on religious liberty.
www.teachingaboutreligion.org/
Educational site encouraging a consideration of world views when teaching religion.
www.ed.gov/speeches104_1995/prayer.html
Statement on religion in public schools drafted by 35 different groups trying to find common ground.
www.facsnet.org/issues/faith/haynes_pittsburgh.php
Historical background article "Religious Liberty and Public Schools" by Fielding Buck.

www.pta.org/ptawashington/issues/religion.asp
National PTA website provides background to the issue.

The following debates in the Pro/Con series may also be of interest:

In this volume:

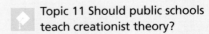

Topic 11 Should public schools teach creationist theory?

The Scopes "monkey trial" (1925), pages 148–149

In *The Constitution*:

Topic 9 Does the Constitution protect religious freedom?

SHOULD RELIGION BE TAUGHT IN SCHOOLS?

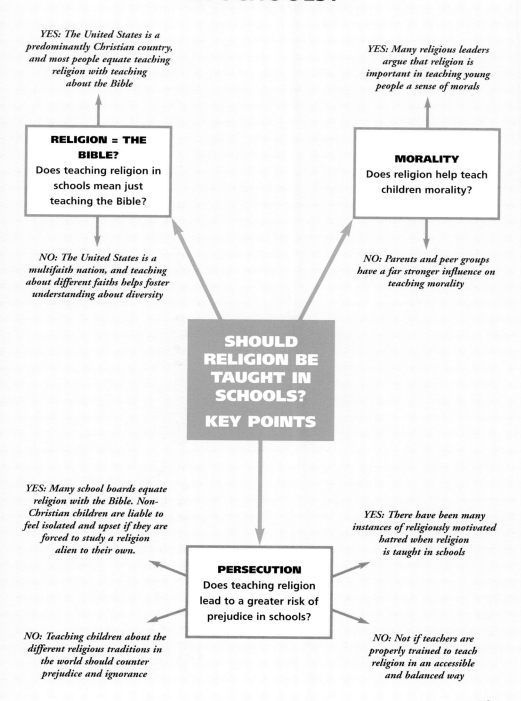

YES: The United States is a predominantly Christian country, and most people equate teaching religion with teaching about the Bible

RELIGION = THE BIBLE?
Does teaching religion in schools mean just teaching the Bible?

NO: The United States is a multifaith nation, and teaching about different faiths helps foster understanding about diversity

YES: Many religious leaders argue that religion is important in teaching young people a sense of morals

MORALITY
Does religion help teach children morality?

NO: Parents and peer groups have a far stronger influence on teaching morality

SHOULD RELIGION BE TAUGHT IN SCHOOLS? KEY POINTS

YES: Many school boards equate religion with the Bible. Non-Christian children are liable to feel isolated and upset if they are forced to study a religion alien to their own.

YES: There have been many instances of religiously motivated hatred when religion is taught in schools

PERSECUTION
Does teaching religion lead to a greater risk of prejudice in schools?

NO: Teaching children about the different religious traditions in the world should counter prejudice and ignorance

NO: Not if teachers are properly trained to teach religion in an accessible and balanced way

PART 4
HIGHER EDUCATION

In 1828 the Yale Report stated, "We are aware that … [our present plan of education] is imperfect; and we cherish the hope that some of its defects may ere long be remedied." This statement, made 175 years ago, was made in the hope that the U.S. higher education system would improve. Many commentators, however, still believe that higher education is in crisis, providing degrees not worth the money they cost and of low academic standard.

A value for money system?

Figures indicate that around 59 percent of the population think that higher education is worth the cost, which in 2000–2001 was just over $8,000 for a public university and $22,520 for a private university (an increase of 21 and 26 percent respectively between 1991 and 2001). However, some commentators argue that high tuition fees are making it impossible for the average parent to send his or her son or daughter to college.

The number of international students studying in higher education increased by 4.8 percent between 1999 and 2000, prompting some critics to argue that educational institutions are more concerned with generating income than providing native students with a cost-effective and comprehensive education. This has led to an emphasis on "value for money" education, a fact that has been picked up by journalists abroad. The British national newspaper *The Guardian* reported in September 2003 on *Paying for College*, a U.S. magazine that offers guidance to prospective students on the best deals in higher education. The rankings in it listed the "best" and "worst" value colleges according to factors like graduate debt, financial aid packages, and tuition fees, rather than quality of education, number of students, number of successful degrees, and so on. Issues like this have fuelled the debate on whether higher education is a waste of time, money, and resources, especially since the Digest for Education Statistics, 2002, reported that America also spent approximately $19,220 in public funds per student, ranking it among the highest spenders internationally, along with Switzerland, Canada, and Sweden.

But is this money well spent? The statistics seem to suggest that people believe that this is the case since more Americans in the 21st century are completing degrees: between 1990–1991 and 2000–2001 associate degrees increased by 20 percent, bachelor's degrees by 14 percent, master's degrees by 39 percent, and doctor's degrees by 14 percent. With such demand surely a degree is worth having?

Some commentators, on the other hand, feel that the standard of faculty in colleges and universities is the problem.

In 1999 around 2.9 million people were employed in universities and colleges, including 2 million professional staff. About 44 percent of staff were faculty or teaching assistants. Although colleges have different practices in employing staff, it is estimated that in the fall of 1999, 50 percent of the employees in public two-year colleges were full time, compared with 70 and 71 percent in four-year public and private universities

people claim are nothing more than a group of hierarchical clubs that encourage young people to behave inappropriately and to believe that they are superior to nonfraternity students. Advocates claim that such clubs are a rich part of the country's heritage and that that many key figures have belonged to them, including several presidents. The incidence of deaths during "hazing" or initiation rituals into

> *"On many American campuses the only qualification for admission was the ability actually to find the campus and then discover a parking space."*
> — MALCOLM BRADBURY (1932–2000), NOVELIST

and colleges. The proportion of full-time faculty with tenure (a permanent position at a college or university) was around 62 percent in 1999. The system of tenure has been the cause of much debate and criticism. Originally introduced to protect academic freedom, today many people argue that it only serves to keep inefficient, fusty professors in jobs rather than those who actually deserve it. The proportion of women and nonwhites who hold tenure in universities is also much lower than that of white, Anglo-Saxon men, leading some critics to argue that tenure is used to keep unwanted elements out of higher education. The issue of tenure is explored in Topic 13.

An elitest system?

Another area that critics perceive as problematic is the existence of fraternities and sororities, which many

these clubs has led several universities to phase them out. The question of whether fraternities and sororities should be banned and the problem of hazing are examined in Topic 14 and on pages 188–189.

Some people argue that the existence of separate colleges and universities for minority groups promotes division. While recognizing, for example, the reasons behind the formation of black universities, many people think that they should, in the current multicultural climate, be disbanded. Topic 15 discusses whether black universities should be phased out.

Plagiarism is another problem in higher education today. Critics argue that the Internet has made copying information, whether by accident or design, easy. The last topic in the book looks at whether universities are taking this problem seriously enough.

Topic 13

DOES TENURE PROTECT INCOMPETENT TEACHERS?

YES

"PROFS DO BETTER ON SHORTER LEASH, STUDY CONCLUDES"

NEWSMAX.COM WIRES, MARCH 12, 2002

NEWSMAX.COM

NO

FROM "TENURE AND ACADEMIC EXCELLENCE"

ACADEME, THE MAGAZINE OF THE AMERICAN

ASSOCIATION OF UNIVERSITY PROFESSORS, MAY–JUNE 2000

LINDA L. CARROLL

INTRODUCTION

"Tenure" derives from the Latin word meaning "to have or hold in possession." Receiving tenure in a modern context means being given a permanent job as a university or college professor. Originally introduced to protect academic freedom, tenure is one of the most hotly debated issues in higher education today. Opponents argue that it is an outdated system that allows incompetent, often older teachers to remain in work at the expense of younger, better ones. Critics also blame tenure for rising costs and falling standards. Supporters argue that it creates better teachers by ensuring that the best teachers have the best jobs. Also, they assert, it preserves the integrity of educational institutions and promotes academic excellence.

A form of tenure existed as early as 1820, when tutors at Harvard University had to complete a lengthy probation period before being appointed as lifetime professors or being asked to leave. In 1940 the Association of American University Professors (AAUP) reissued an earlier statement, which came to be known as the 1940 Principles on Academic Freedom and Tenure. It not only protected the freedom of professors to take risks or hold challenging opinions but stated that tenure made "the profession attractive to men and women of ability" since it offered economic security.

Today the issue of tenure is a battleground. Many critics argue that because there is no universal standard of tenure, it is very difficult to judge exactly how effective tenure is for universities. Some universities give it as a reward for academic distinction. In others it is simply awarded for years of service or age.

In most cases, however, tenure is granted after a probationary period of up to seven years, during which time an academic's peers evaluate his or her ability. In all educational institutions competition for "tenure track" jobs is intense, and the standards for obtaining tenure are tougher than ever. Fewer colleges offer it as an option, and staff on renewable contracts often replace retiring professors on tenure.

Part of the reason that tenure has come under fire is that education cuts have put pressure on universities to generate more revenue. Critics such as Harvard Professor Peter Chait claim that tenure is out of step with modern economic reality. Chait argues that corporations make money by adapting to market forces and, if necessary, downsizing, and colleges must do the same. Tenure, he asserts, prevents colleges from being flexible.

> *"Tenure is a much-maligned and misunderstood concept in today's world."*
> —JAMES T. RICHARDSON, PRESIDENT, AAUP (1999)

For many academics tenure upholds certain rights. They argue that competition for top-flight staff is tougher than ever. Unless academia can offer tenure, they say, highly skilled candidates will seek better-paid jobs elsewhere. Academics do their best work when they are not worried about job security. The probation period allows only top candidates to receive tenure, and reports show that tenured staff publish more research, sit on more academic committees, and get better results.

Critics, however, claim the system is sheltering "deadwood"—academics who have lost interest in teaching or have no incentive to do their best. Tenured professors can be fired, but only in extreme circumstances. Accountability is at stake, some critics state. The tenure system is open to abuse since it is decided by peer review. And how accountable are professors once they have tenure?

Colleges that have tenure, however, say their institutions have many other systems in place to ensure that their teaching staff remain accountable. Some colleges have adopted "posttenure review," evaluating tenured academics later on in their career with the understanding that they may be fired if found to be failing.

Another key argument of critics centers on the notion of academic freedom. They question why tenure is necessary if freedom of speech is protected by the First Amendment? Supporters of tenure counter that the First Amendment does not protect the right of the speaker to keep his or her job while exercising that freedom.

In recent years courts have heard dozens of tenure-related lawsuits, many relating to alleged discrimination on the grounds of gender or race. Many critics argue that tenure was introduced by white males for white males, and that all it has done is keep minority groups out of secure jobs.

The first article reports on a study by the Fraser Institute that claims tenured professors lose the incentive to do the best for their students. In the second piece Linda L. Carroll argues that tenure promotes academic excellence, and that putting financial considerations first can ruin the quality of education.

PROFS DO BETTER ON SHORTER LEASH, STUDY CONCLUDES
Newsmax.com

The Fraser Institute's mission statement is to provide "competitive market solutions for public policy problems." Given the institute's belief in the effectiveness of market forces, why would it not be likely to support tenure?

Go to the website oldfraser.lexi.net/ publications/ digital/collegial models.pdf to download a copy of this report.

YES

☑ Tenured college professors might be bad teachers and even worse scholars, but their institutions and peers have little ability to influence their conduct, according to a recent study by the Fraser Institute, a libertarian think tank in Vancouver, British Columbia.

To improve the quality of their teaching, professors need incentives, something radically nonexistent in the individualistic culture of the North American university, write Rodney Clifton and Hymie Rubenstein in "Collegial Models for Enhancing the Performance of University Professors."

Tenured professors neglect students

Often when professors receive tenure they neglect their students and focus on research or outside assignments like consulting businesses, Clifton and Rubenstein write. The sheer number of extraneous commitments may cause professors to view students as nuisances rather than the paying consumers they are, according to the authors.

"At many institutions, professors often teach out of necessity, not because they love teaching or because they are inspiring teachers, sometimes taking delight in repeating the tired aphorism 'this would be a great job if it weren't for the students,'" Clifton and Rubenstein write.

Professorial nonchalance has led to graduate students conducting a significant amount of university teaching, and is one of the reasons behind declining academic standards, the authors [Clifton and Rubenstein] claim.

Undergraduate students are often short-changed by poor teaching, huge classes, poorly designed examinations, grade inflation, ideological indoctrination, political correctness, and "Mickey-mouse" courses.

To change the prevailing culture of neglect, the authors argue that professors should be evaluated and rewarded for the collective achievement of all the professors within their

Many teachers are concerned about their tenure position.

academic departments. If professors are judged on a departmental basis, they will be more inclined to be involved in and aware of the activities of their peers, they say.

Penalizing poorly performing departments

One incentive the authors suggest is withholding financial and staffing resources from departments that receive, on average, poor reviews from student evaluations. Departments that receive the highest ratings from students would obtain increased money and staff. Departments that have neither superior nor dismal ratings would retain their resources.

Group evaluation, with some variations, also would apply to scholarship. Rather than increasing performance, a group rewards system would only exacerbate the current situation, says David Salisbury, director of the Center for Educational Freedom at the libertarian Cato Institute in Washington, D.C.

Teaching and scholarly activity is an individual activity and achievements are made as individuals, not as groups [Salisbury says]. It would make people who are not really productive and effective look better than they really are and it would make people who are extremely productive and effective look worse than they really are.

Despite flaws in the current university evaluation system, viable alternatives to the system of peer review don't exist, according to Herbert London, president of Hudson Institute, a conservative think tank in Indianapolis.

While I think there are abuses and I'm very much concerned about those abuses, and I would like to see the university system sanitized to some degree so that ideology plays less of a role in these matters, by and large I think peer review is the most effective way of evaluating one's colleagues [London says].

Peer review occurs when a university committee judges the merit of a professor's work and research. It is often a prerequisite for achieving tenure.

Although student evaluations are an important indicator of performance, London cautions against inflating their significance.

Students are more inclined to support professors they regard as popular or entertaining, not necessarily those

---

Do you think removing resources from bad departments would just make them worse?

In its mission statement the Hudson Institute says it "demonstrates commitment to free markets and individual responsibility." See its website at www.hudson.org to learn more about the institute.

Do you agree that students are more likely to support popular teachers over more effective ones? Does this tell us anything about the writer's opinion of students?

who exhibit the greatest scholarship [London says]. So to rely on students to make judgments of this kind is sometimes, I think, a very problematic matter.

London does not think, however, that student evaluations are worthless. For example, many university pay increases are directly tied to such reports.

Using market initiatives in higher education

The Fraser Institute report is an example of a growing movement in North America to use performance standards when assessing professors, according to Robert Benjamin, president of the RAND Council for Aid to Education. Benjamin agrees with Fraser's contention that it is often difficult to assess how well a professor is doing at his job because education is continuous, completed a little at a time.

Quality standards are an example of the introduction of market initiatives within universities, Benjamin says.

Reassessing tenure is an important step, introducing the same incentives that work in other parts of the marketplace, says Salisbury.

What does the author mean here by "market initiatives"? Do you think market initiatives have a place in higher education?

Tenure protects the less productive [he says]. There is not a job in any other sector that I know of where you're guaranteed a job for the rest of your life no matter what you do, unless you do something extremely unethical or illegal. Why should we have such a system in education?

Do academics need more job protection than other people? What additional threats and pressures might affect them?

Short-term contracts that can be extended are [a] viable alternative to tenure cited by the authors of the Fraser report. The reasoning is that professors would be held to and therefore act in accordance with higher standards, because their jobs could otherwise be in jeopardy.

Benjamin, however, does not advocate abolishing tenure and does not believe the system will be dismantled anytime soon.

"I think you do need a critical mass of full-time faculty to develop curriculum and to attend the running of a college or university," he says. "You just can't do it only on a part-time basis."

TENURE AND ACADEMIC EXCELLENCE
Linda L. Carroll

Defenders of tenure have traditionally focused on its ability to protect academic freedom. But a close look at its functions shows that it actually does much more: it provides the foundation for academic excellence. To be effective, the work of the university—the objective discovery and dissemination of knowledge—must be protected from outside influence.

By vesting the faculty with wide autonomy in pedagogy, research, and institutional governance, tenure serves this function. In addition, faculties confer tenure to recognize the mature professional status of colleagues who have given sustained evidence of an ability to work independently. The American university system's leadership in research and its ability to attract first-rate faculty members and students from all over the world prove the excellence of this combination of academic freedom and professionalism.

The case of Galileo

History's most famous academic freedom case is instructive. After teaching for several years at the University of Padua, Galileo was offered a tenured position there by the Venetian Republic. The republic wanted to reward him for having developed the telescope that would help Venice's efforts to regain maritime preeminence as a link between the Mediterranean and northern Europe and between Europe and the East. But Galileo, tempted by the prospect of a higher salary and the desire to return to his home state of Tuscany, turned down the offer and became the court mathematician of the Medici.

What he failed to realize was the extent to which the Catholic Church and Aristotelian philosophers would react adversely to the information about the heavens that his telescope revealed. Stung by blame for the Protestant Reformation heaped on earlier popes, especially Leo X and Clement VII, and fearing the challenges that Galileo's discoveries posed to the authority of the Bible and the scientific texts of Aristotle, Popes Paul V and Urban VIII, together with the Inquisition, twice silenced him. If Galileo had remained in Padua, the Venetian Republic could have

The term "pedagogy" can mean both the profession of teaching and the methods used to teach.

The Polish astronomer Nicolaus Copernicus (1473–1543) first put forward the theory that the planets, including the Earth, revolved around the sun. In 1632 Galileo (1564–1642) was able to prove this theory using a telescope. It went against the teaching of the Catholic Church, which said that the Earth was the center of the universe. Galileo was placed under house arrest for the rest of his life for heresy.

protected him. At the time, it was the only state on the Italian peninsula independent enough to resist the church, having been vigorously defended by Galileo's friend, the political theoretician Paolo Sarpi, during a recent papal interdict. The Medici could not, and Galileo's work was lost to the University of Padua and to the world.

Like similar cases before and since, Galileo's experience shows that systems of oversight are often imposed in times of contraction and weakness, not in those of expansion and strength. In the United States, the recent trend toward accountability—which is the chief characteristic of what I call the "managerial university"—appears to result from a period of weakness.

Managerial university

In an article in the January–February 2000 issue of *Academe*, Richard Ohmann traces the rise of the accountability movement to the conservative reaction against the success of the left in the 1960s and to the economic crisis that began in the 1970s and lasted two decades. Its supporters claim that the managerial university brings many improvements. But instead, with its restriction of faculty autonomy and obsession with short-term financial considerations, it severely damages educational quality.

In the managerial university, top-down control, short-term contracts, and limits on faculty governance effectively curb the scope of faculty research and the range of faculty professionalism. These practices suppress precisely those features of the American university system that have produced the excellence for which it is known throughout the world.

One way in which the managerial university erodes educational quality is by driving away talented faculty. The relative independence of academic work is one of its greatest attractions for potential faculty members. Many accept considerable financial sacrifice in exchange for the freedom to accomplish their work in the manner they deem best and to act together with colleagues to build an educational community. If academic life ceases to offer this breadth of action, its attractiveness to the most creative and responsible individuals will decline, and the obstacles blocking good work by those who continue in the academy will increase. And if, as expected, faculty salaries remain low compared with those of other professionals, not to mention those in the business world, academic life will lose much of its appeal.

> The Medici were a rich and influential family who ruled Florence and Tuscany in Italy in the 14th, 15th, and 16th centuries. They were important patrons of the arts, sciences, and literature.

> Richard Ohmann is professor emeritus of English at Wesleyan University in Middletown, Connecticut. He is the author of several books and articles written from a leftist perspective. Why are people on the left more likely to support tenure? See www.aaup.org/publications/Academe/00jf/JF00Ohma.htm for a copy of Ohmann's article.

> Why do academics need to be independent?

Managerial universities weaken tenure and erode faculty autonomy in several ways; one of the most important is post-tenure review. Under post-tenure review, faculty members may not feel free to undertake lengthy projects that cannot be completed in time for a periodic evaluation....

By imposing collective, external oversight structures, such as department- and college-level review committees, universities nullify the two core activities of faculty members: thinking autonomously and teaching others to think autonomously. Further, the universities thus declare that professors cannot be trusted with their own work and imply that it is suspect or valueless. Some universities that have instituted post-tenure review or other means of restricting the protections of tenure have inadvertently shown how loss of autonomy decreases the attractiveness of academic life: excellent faculty members have left their institutions for others offering the full protections of tenure and a strong faculty role in governance, which the professors see as ensuring their academic freedom against such incursions.

> *Will independent-thinking teachers produce independent-thinking students?*

Encouraging conformity

Another feature of the managerial university is excessive use of adjunct or multiyear contracts. A university that views its faculty as short-term or part-time employees, gives them little or no say in governance, and subjects them to continuous outcome checks blunts its competitive edge by encouraging timidity and conformity among its faculty. Although short-term and part-time faculty as a group are dedicated to their profession, their institutions provide them with few tools for achieving excellence, in comparison with those available to tenured and tenure-track faculty. The role of the classroom laborer imposed on contingent faculty by their institutions precludes long-term, committed service, sustained contributions to programs, and a role in university governance. Instead, those working under such conditions must focus their attention on securing their next contract or job.

Constant turnover robs programs of stability and direction, as a parade of short-term faculty members with different academic backgrounds alters course selection and content. It also damages the relationship between faculty members and students that is critical to the quality of higher education....

Recent research refutes the charge that the absence of oversight results in poor faculty performance. The Faculty Work Project of the Associated New American Colleges recently conducted a national study with support from the Pew Charitable Trusts. The study found that faculty members

> *The Associated New American Colleges is a consortium of 22 small and midsized universities and colleges. One of the findings of the study was that many faculty members feel they are not rewarded with incentives, and that governance structures and service obligations to the institution do not make good use of their time.*

work an average of 53.6 hours a week, with 34 of these hours devoted to student-connected activities (teaching, advising, and the like), 10 to research, and 9 to institutional service.

Does the small amount of time spent on research inspire you?

Barriers to creativity

Indeed, the shoe is often on the other foot: it is often not faculty members who fail in their obligations to their institutions, but the institutions that fail in their responsibilities to the faculty.

Post-tenure review and other incursions on tenure often occur at institutions that underemploy the positive incentive of raises. Some institutions, after creating nontenured positions, find that they can make the positions attractive only by increasing pay, an ironic reversal of the original intent to decrease costs. Declarations that institutions need more flexibility than the tenure system permits also curiously invert the facts. Managerial universities lacking in tenure do not achieve excellence; instead, they condemn themselves to passivity and susceptibility to fads....

Recent studies have shown that tenure and faculty governance are strongest at large, private research universities, which also tend to have great prestige. Not coincidentally, these institutions are the most in demand by prospective students and their parents. As other colleges and universities have undercut the role of the faculty member, interest in the kind of education that these prestigious universities offer has increased.

Here the author is repeating a point she has made earlier in the article. Does repetition weaken or strengthen her argument?

The weakening of tenure also threatens the quality of research. Good research requires much time and some risk taking. Obsessive checks on outcomes will favor small, safe projects with predictable results over the daring, conceptually complex projects that have produced cutting-edge research...

Unsatisfactory substitutes

Some people argue that tenure is unnecessary because courts protect free speech. This argument is flawed; the guarantee provided by tenure is not the right to free speech but the protection of one's job in the exercise of it. Moreover, it is dangerous to transfer the authority over academic issues to outside parties affected by the political process....

To protect the traditional excellence of the American academic system, faculty members must fight to preserve academic freedom, the professional status of the faculty, and the faculty role in university governance. Doing so means safeguarding tenure. The tenure system is like democracy: it is not perfect, but it is light years ahead of any alternative.

Summary

The first article reports on a study by the Fraser Institute, a libertarian think tank in Canada. The study argues that tenured professors, once they have received tenure, lack incentives to improve the quality of their teaching, and that many academics neglect their teaching because of other commitments. According to the study, students are powerless to do anything about the poor teaching they receive. It discusses whether tenured professors would perform better if departmental staff were evaluated on a group basis by students and rewarded or penalized accordingly. Under this system the resources of poorly rated departments would be frozen, and poorly performing tenured professors would face pressure to improve. However, the article also notes that there is some skepticism about this approach, saying that student evaluations should be used with caution.

In the second article Linda L. Carroll argues that tenure promotes academic excellence by vesting the faculty with autonomy. She says the recent shift toward what she calls the "managerial university" is eroding educational quality by curbing faculty autonomy and driving away talented academics. An obsession with financial considerations is harmful to education, she says, adding that academic life will become progressively less attractive to talented, creative individuals if such trends prevail. Carroll specifically criticizes the trend toward employing staff on short-term contracts, saying that this could prevent them undertaking important longer-term research. She also takes issue with posttenure review, which, she says, leaves faculty members feeling insecure about their work and gives them little say in governance of the faculty. She concludes by saying that academics must fight to preserve tenure, which is not a perfect system but is still better than any alternatives on offer.

FURTHER INFORMATION:

Books:

Baldwin, Roger G., and Jay L. Chronister, *Teaching without Tenure: Policies and Practices for a New Era*. Baltimore, MD: Johns Hopkins University Press, 2002.

Articles:

Richardson, James T., "Tenure in the New Millennium: Still a Valuable Concept," *National Forum*, Vol. 79, No. 1, 1999.

Useful websites:

www.aaup./Issues/tenure
The American Association of University Professors website contains links to several articles and reports on tenure.

www.aaup.org/publications/Academe/00mj/MJ00TOC.htm
Academe Online, "Tenure, Will It Survive?" Vol. 86, No. 3, May–June 2000. This online edition of *Academe* contains six articles of interest to the debate on tenure.

The following debates in the Pro/Con series may also be of interest:

In this volume:

Topic 9 Do teachers' unions hinder educational performance?

DOES TENURE PROTECT INCOMPETENT TEACHERS?

YES: Tenure makes people compete for jobs and thus makes them perform better

YES: A probationary period, after which tenure would be taken away from incompetent teachers, would be more effective

BEST TEACHERS
Does tenure ensure that the best teachers get the best jobs?

PROBATION
Should tenure be dependent on performance?

NO: People are often awarded jobs on the grounds of age or length of service, not because of their teaching skills

NO: Academic research is too difficult to evaluate in terms of "performance"

DOES TENURE PROTECT INCOMPETENT TEACHERS?
KEY POINTS

YES: Tenure protects academics from outside influences, and academics tend to be more productive if they have job security

YES: Academics have the intellectual freedom to experiment with their theories without fear of losing their jobs

ACADEMIC EXCELLENCE
Does the tenure system promote academic excellence?

NO: Tenured academics are often lazy because universities are unlikely to get rid of them if they fail to perform

NO: People are more likely to be competitive in a free market system

Topic 14

SHOULD FRATERNITIES AND SORORITIES BE BANNED?

YES

"WITHOUT REFORM, THE GREEK SYSTEM SHOULD GO"
THE MINNESOTA DAILY, OCTOBER 14, 1996
EMMANUEL ORTIZ

NO

"WHAT IS 'TENS OF MILLIONS' GOOD FOR?"
THE DARTMOUTH REVIEW, FEBRUARY 17, 1999
ALEXANDER WILSON

INTRODUCTION

In 2003 there were approximately 20,000 fraternities (for men) and sororities (for women) in the United States and Canada. To many people fraternities and sororities, collectively known as "Greek letter societies," are an essential part of university and college life. Many students, including 80 percent of U.S. presidents since 1900, have belonged to such a society during college or university.

While advocates believe that the system helps both promote community values and produce successful and confident individuals, critics think that the system should be banned. They argue that the Greek system is outdated, elitist, and often discriminatory. But is that the case?

The first fraternity—Phi Beta Kappa— was established in 1776 at the College of William and Mary in Williamsburg, Virginia. Its members originally met in secret, largely because the college administration was anxious that students who met to discuss topical issues might challenge accepted views. Phi Beta Kappa later renounced its secrecy and became a scholarship honor society, giving recognition to scholarship in various fields. A number of other social fraternities were established in the first decades of the 19th century, and the first sororities appeared in the 1850s.

Fraternities and sororities have developed over the years, and today many of them are organized at national and even at international level, with chapters (or branches) at many different colleges.

Advocates of the Greek system claim that it gives students a valuable sense of identity and community on campus and beyond. They argue that the societies became essential once universities and colleges grew large and impersonal. Fraternities and sororities became a focal point for like-minded students.

Supporters also claim that many successful citizens have belonged to either a fraternity or a sorority—including 76 percent of congressmen and senators in 2003.

Some also argue that Greek societies actually help academic achievement. Many Greek society websites claim that the graduation success rate is 20 percent higher for students who belong to a fraternity or sorority; critics claim that figure is unreliable.

Opposition to the Greek system has grown over the years. Some people think it creates exclusive groups with restrictive membership policies that discriminate against some students on the basis of sex and ethnicity. Others associate frat house culture with the scenes of binge drinking and juvenile mayhem depicted in the notorious *Animal House* movies.

"The forces that have been greatest in my life have been God and the college fraternity that molded me."

—THOMAS RILEY MARSHALL, FORMER VICE PRESIDENT (1922)

Among the accusations made against the Greek system is that it is too secretive. Using Greek letters in names and adopting secret rituals were features of the very first fraternities, and those traditions have been maintained. Similarly, although some fraternities are now coeducational, the Greek system has been criticized for preserving a mainly single-sex culture within what is now predominantly a coeducational system. For some people Greek-letter societies represent an antiquated, sexist culture.

Possibly the most controversial feature of the system is the practice of "hazing" (see pages 188–189 for more information)—the trial period of a potential fraternity/sorority member, when they are required to carry out tasks as a condition of their acceptance. There have been an increasing number of reports of abuses that have occurred during hazing episodes, including drinking to such excess that it has resulted in alcohol poisoning, rape, beatings, and in a few extreme cases, deaths. That and other criticisms have led some colleges to abolish the Greek system, and some now claim that they have been able to attract higher-quality students since doing so.

Many students believe it is their constitutional right to belong to a Greek society, and some societies have filed lawsuits against colleges trying to ban them. On remote campuses, in particular, Greek societies provide the only social life for students, and even those who are not actually members of a society may not wish to see them disappear. Feelings about fraternities and sororities also run deep among alumni. Colleges with popular Greek societies have the highest alumni giving rates in the country, and in some cases alumni have actually withdrawn their donations from colleges threatening to ban or reform the system.

The following two articles examine the issue further. In the first article student Emmanuel Ortiz argues that the Greek system leads to alcohol abuse and violence. In the second article Alexander Wilson strongly disagrees.

WITHOUT REFORM, THE GREEK SYSTEM SHOULD GO
Emmanuel Ortiz

When this article appeared in The Minnesota Daily, *October 14, 1996, Emmanuel Ortiz was a junior in the College of Liberal Arts at the University of Minnesota. He was cofounder and chair of Men against Rape and Sexism, a former coordinator of the Peer Education Program for the Program against Sexual Violence, and a member of the University's Alcohol, Tobacco, and Other Drug Policy Review Committee.*

YES

If I were to create a "Top Ten List" of things I have a strong distaste for, three things that would appear at the top of my list are: drugs (especially alcohol and tobacco), violence (particularly sexual violence) and silence (or the refusal to communicate). When these vices are perpetrated by institutions, my blood boils. This is because we are a society that hesitates—refuses—to hold institutions accountable not only for wrongdoing, but also for fostering an environment where people find encouragement and coercion to embrace destructive attitudes and behaviors.

The greek system, most notably the fraternal portion, is an institution with insufficient measures in place to deter the abuse of alcohol and drugs and the perpetration of violence, specifically sexual violence, by its members and their allies. University systems, in conjunction with the greek system, perpetrate the third aforementioned vice by ignoring these issues or downplaying their importance and impact in the University community. Therefore, the greek system and the University alike can be found guilty of fostering destructive, oppressive environments. The University should be required to make changes in policy, or be forced to eliminate the greek system from the University community.

Abuse

We can begin our examination of the problematic nature of the greek system with a look at alcohol abuse. The results of a 1993 survey of more than 17,000 students at 140 four-year colleges in 40 states show that 86 percent of students who lived in fraternity houses were binge drinkers. This means that they had consumed at least five or more drinks at a time in the two-week period prior to being surveyed. In comparison, 50 percent of male students overall were classified as binge drinkers. Another finding reveals that students living in greek-system housing drink three times the number of drinks as the average student.

At the University of Minnesota, the fraternity and sorority houses are on property that is not owned by the University.

The author cites statistics from a 1993 survey to support his case, but he gives no specific source. Does that weaken his argument?

The University of Minnesota, which was founded in 1851, has about 60,000 students on four separate campuses. Go to www1.umn.edu for its website.

A fraternity food fight. Do fraternities need to improve their image?

These houses do not fall under the jurisdiction of the University's alcohol policies, which are unclear and easily bypassed. Sororities prohibit alcohol from their premises for insurance purposes, while fraternities, under different insurance regulations, are not required to attain a permit by the University to sell alcohol at parties. In fact, University policy prohibits the sale of alcohol on its premises. Fraternities, with the special privilege of separate land ownership and all the benefits of being immersed in the University, gain financially from the sale of alcohol, quite often to minors. It would be difficult to discuss sexual violence on campus and in the greek system without studying the role of alcohol. Studies have shown that on college campuses, 90 percent of reported rapes involve the

Do you think fraternities and excessive drinking are inherently linked? Go to www.ericfacility. net/ericdigests/ ed436110.html for a 1999 analysis of binge drinking on campus.

Would it make the author's argument more convincing if he cited his source?

COMMENTARY: A history of discrimination?

"Fraternity" means "brotherhood," but despite the egalitarian principles implicit in the name, fraternities have often been accused of fostering a culture of exclusion. Phi Beta Kappa—the first Greek-letter society—was formed in 1776, when higher education was the exclusive preserve of men, so its membership was necessarily limited to males. During the first half of the 19th century many other fraternities modeled on Phi Beta Kappa appeared all over North America; but when women were finally admitted to universities in midcentury, they found themselves excluded from those societies. As a result, they formed their own female fraternities, later called sororities ("sisterhoods"). The first was the Adelphean—later Alpha Delta Pi—which was established at the Wesleyan Female College, Macon, Georgia, in 1851. As more women were accepted in state-supported universities in the second half of the 19th century, more sororities were established.

The exclusion of minorities

Early fraternities tended to discriminate chiefly on the grounds of sex, but that was largely because campuses were predominantly white and Protestant. In the 20th century, as more religious and ethnic minorities began to gain acceptance at universities, some fraternities began to develop further discriminatory policies. As a result, African Americans, Catholics, Jews, and other minorities were excluded from many fraternities. Such discrimination was highlighted in the 1955 book *Fraternities without Brotherhood* by the sociologist Alfred McLung Lee (1907–1992). Although reforms, especially in the 1960s, led to the removal of most discriminatory membership rules, many minority groups had in any case formed their own fraternities and sororities in order to strengthen their own communal identity. Despite the reforms, informal discrimination still exists.

Black Greek-letter societies

The first historically black fraternity, Alpha Phi Alpha, was formed in 1906 at Cornell University in Ithaca, New York. Others soon followed at Howard and Indiana; the former also saw the appearance of the first black sorority in 1908. African Americans also saw fraternities as a means of combating ostracism. Even after graduation black fraternities provided essential civic support in the face of severe racism in many parts of the United States. After World War II (1939–1945) black fraternities and sororities flourished, especially on historically black campuses in the South following the 1964 Civil Rights Act, when more African Americans were admitted to universities. The National Pan-Hellenic Council was established in 1930 as a coordinating body for the nine predominantly African American fraternities and sororities that then existed, and it still functions in a similar role today.

consumption of alcohol or some other drug, and 84 percent of rapes are perpetrated by someone the victim knows.

Although alcohol itself should not be blamed for the occurrence of acquaintance or date rape, it must be recognized as a relevant factor. A quick, informal study of a fraternity party reveals several conditions that make sexual assault highly possible. Men and women are together in a festive mood and a sexually-charged setting. The presence of alcohol in the mix increases male aggression and sexual desire, while simultaneously causing a breakdown in judgment and the ability to communicate effectively. Throw in fraternal peer pressure to "score," and what develops is a situation that promotes rape and rape culture.

Of course, alcohol abuse and sexual violence do not occur in a social vacuum. Nor do they occur solely in the greek system. Athletics and ROTC are other programs that have been targeted as havens of destructive attitudes and behaviors. Residence halls, where young men and women test the waters of social independence for the first time, also have a responsibility to promote healthy lifestyles.

There are many other issues beyond alcohol and sexual violence that foster a desire for change in the greek system. Some of these are in-group superiority, ostracism, the social elitism attributed to membership, misogyny in fraternities and the privilege that can be attained with the pocketbooks of alumni. These factors are cause for policy development that can make the greek system more proactive in promoting healthy living among its members and more accountable for members' actions.

Responsibility

The final responsibility, then, lies with the University to break its silence on the issues facing the greek system. As a single fraternity brother or sister is within the institution of the greek system, so … the individual institution of the University's greek system is within the larger institution of the University. Therefore, it is the University's responsibility (and our responsibility as its constituents), to speak out against destructive behavior and attitudes and to create an atmosphere that fosters respect and responsibility toward ourselves and each other.

If change is not brought about in a collaborative effort by the greek system, or in University offices that are able to adjust policies on alcohol and sexual violence, then I favor the termination of the greek system and an investigation into the shortcomings of University policy as a consequence.

Does the author convince you that fraternity parties might encourage sexual assault? Could his description be applied to any student party?

ROTC stands for Reserve Officers Training Corps, which runs military training programs in many universities across the United States. Go to www-rotc.monroe.army.mill for information.

Merriam-Webster's dictionary defines "ostracism" as "exclusion by general consent from common privileges or social acceptance" and misogyny as "the hatred of women." Do you think these problems would exist even if the Greek system were abolished?

WHAT IS 'TENS OF MILLIONS' GOOD FOR?
Alexander Wilson

NO

"Imagine the possibilities," says President James Wright. "Imagine the possibilities," says Trustee Kate Stith-Cabranes. "Imagine the possibilities," says Trustee William King.

Dreamworld

Dartmouth students are being asked to imagine a new campus, with fundamentally different social and residential options. They are being asked to imagine a campus with new and better facilities and more money for student programming. And they are being asked to imagine a campus without a powerful Greek system.

Their imaginations are to be funded by "tens of millions of dollars" that the Trustees say they will devote to making our dreams come true. Not surprisingly, students are opposed despite their generosity.

While Dartmouth students rally over the freedom of association, the dictatorial nature of the Trustees pronouncements, and the non-social benefits of the Greek system, an important question has yet to be answered: what difference could tens of millions of dollars of Trustee money make on Dartmouth's social life?

Well, I've thought about it. The answer seems obvious at first. Huge changes could be made, great opportunities for a better Dartmouth. That's the kind of thing I've been hearing from enraptured students and Trustee statements. The only problem is that none of it is true.

Reality

The sad fact is that the money the Trustees keep talking about, "whatever it takes to fulfill our goals," etc., can't come close to replacing the Greek system. Whatever funding gets pumped into our community, our community is still Hanover. Hanover isn't a very exciting place. The high school kids hang out at Foodstop. Thirty-somethings go to the Hop to see the Barbary Coast Jazz Orchestra.

The unique ability of Dartmouth to maintain a roaring social life in this remote setting is due to the existence of Greek houses. Amherst and Williams were once highly social places, but once they banned Greeks, the quality of the social life dropped precipitously. Dartmouth is even more remote, and has had the benefit of an even stronger Greek system.

The Trustees say they'll give us "tens of millions" of dollars to re-invent Dartmouth's social life.

Well, what could "tens of millions" buy?

They could build a new student center and pump money into programming. More campus groups could have events. More people could come to those events, and perhaps the events would be of a higher quality. But how many times each week will students show up to see an a cappella group? How many cultural nights per week is too many?

The reality is that while adding these things might provide more social options, and might benefit all segments on the campus, they're strictly marginal gains. They don't deserve comparison with the benefits provided by the Greek system.

Williams College in Massachusetts banned fraternities in 1962. Amherst College, in the same state, abolished its on-campus fraternities in 1984.

Collis

…Collis is a convenient resource for students, but it is severely underutilized. Its four billiards tables are in demand only a few hours a day. I cannot remember the last time I saw the video arcade more than half-full. Dance classes, cultural events, Sheba, the Aires, and everything else that goes on in the Common Ground draw about a quarter as many people as a big fraternity party. The much-touted replacement for Webster Hall is simply a bigger, better Collis, and will mainly be utilized by the same people for the same purposes. This is not to say that a new student center has no worth. It would be immensely valuable to Dartmouth students, especially those who do not patronize Greek parties. But its value is as a supplement to the Greek system, not as a replacement. Yet this is the leading idea to improve student life.

The Aires are an a cappella singing group, and Sheba is a hip-hop dance troupe. Both are well known at Dartmouth.

So what could "tens of millions" really buy?

Dartmouth could build a large concert hall, with sufficient seating for the whole Dartmouth community. But the bands that played there would still be more like Steve Miller than the Rolling Stones. It could build a great theater, but student plays are student plays regardless of the stage they're performed on. They could build an entertainment complex. But ping pong, bowling, and batting cages are not activities that are entertaining if they are done all the time. Without the Greek system these would be the main recreational options, not the occasional pastimes for which they are best suited. They could build a nightclub, or a sports bar, or several of both. At best these could serve only a small

Wilson seems very concerned about recreational facilities. But is the primary function of college to be a place of learning? Are social activities important as well?

183

percentage of the students who currently attend Greek parties. Moreover, the students attending sports bars or nightclubs would be far less diverse than those who interact every weekend at Greek houses. Sports fans would go to sports bars; people who like to dance would go to nightclubs. And only the quarter of Dartmouth students [who are] over 21 would go to either.

Better than the Greek system?

The new co-educational residential experience is even less useful as a replacement of the Greek system. New dorms, no matter what social space they include, will never be cohesive enough to provide a social gathering place. The parties and other events that take place on this campus come exclusively from selective groups, such as DAO and NAD.

The Dartmouth Asian Organization (DAO) and Native Americans at Dartmouth (NAD) are both student organizations.

Students of similar interests or affiliations can gather together to plan events. Random strangers, and even random groups of friends, put under a single roof have never proved capable of the type of organization practiced routinely by Greek houses. Poetry readings and music recitals are the types of events residential communities can provide, just as they do now in the East Wheelock SuperCluster.

At Dartmouth some student residential facilities, like those near East Wheelock Street, are grouped into "clusters" that aim to promote a sense of community by organizing trips and social events. A much improved "cluster" system is one form of social and residential structure that Dartmouth College has proposed as an alternative to the Greek system.

Let us also be realistic about the improvements of residential life made possible by the increase in the number of beds and the construction of new dorms. Rooms may be less crowded, they may be slightly more pleasant, but they will still be dorm rooms — essentially the same as those currently available at Dartmouth and at colleges across the country. There will be no five room doubles, or luxurious bathrooms with Jacuzzis included, just a few less people in a little more space.

At the same time, off-campus living will be "significantly reduced." The hard fact is that off-campus apartments are more attractive, if less convenient, than the dorms. My apartment, which I share with a single roommate, has two bedrooms, a living room, a bathroom, and a fully equipped kitchen, all for the same per person cost as rooming charges at the College. Plus I get cable: 61 glorious channels. Not to mention my own parking space. I will never get as good a deal in a dorm, no matter how much the Trustees spend on residential life.

River and Choates are the names of modern student residences built on Dartmouth's campus in the 1960s and 1950s respectively. Wilson tailors his argument to people familiar with such details.

And lest we forget, the River and the Choates are two of the most recent examples of new residential construction. I think I can safely say that this speaks for itself.

It is especially important to remember just what this amount of money means. "Tens of millions" sounds like a huge sum, but recall that Berry Library is costing the College $30 million all by itself. Great things can be done with the resources being made available, but they are still profoundly limited things, especially with resources split among the many different goals of the trustees.

What can "tens of millions" buy? Not enough.

The Trustees can spend $100 million on student life if they choose, but one thing will always remain the same. Dartmouth College will always be located in Hanover, New Hampshire. Nothing can alter the fact that Dartmouth students will live in a sleepy, backwater town. Social life here is limited by the very nature of its location. This isn't Boston and it certainly isn't New York. For that matter, it's not even Manchester.

The population of Hanover is around 11,000. Manchester, New Hampshire, is about 100 miles away and has a population of around 100,000. How important is it for students to have access to a big city?

Nothing the Trustees can do will provide a vast array of vibrant social options for students. Nor do students attending this institution expect them. When they choose to come here they do so knowing that their social life will be the Greek system and a few lesser options. Those who don't like the Greek option want more choices, and that is both understandable and desirable. But any additional options will inevitably be lesser ones. If the Greek system is abolished, we will be left with minor options masquerading as a campus-wide social life rather than a new type of social life that the majority of students will enjoy.

Only the Greek system can provide what it does in so rural an area as Hanover. Fraternities and local sororities have proved willing to set aside their homes for the use of the campus as a whole; to provide them as places where all students who so choose can interact socially; to allow their homes to be trashed on a weekly basis; to clean up after hundreds of guests; and to do it all for free. It is frankly remarkable that students do this, and have done this, for over 100 years. Short of paying non-Greek students to do what the Greeks do now, the Trustees and their money can never replace such an essential institution.

This is not to say that the Trustees' money is worthless. It can make great things happen for students, especially those who do not enjoy the options provided by the Greek system. But a Dartmouth without the Greeks is a Dartmouth that is irretrievably lessened.

Harvard University, in Cambridge, near Boston, Massachusetts, and Yale, in New Haven, Connecticut, do not encourage fraternities or sororities, although they tolerate them unofficially.

Perhaps Harvard and Yale, located as they are in cities, can afford to abolish their Greek systems without losing social options. But Dartmouth isn't Harvard and Hanover isn't Boston, no matter how much money the Trustees spend.

Summary

In recent years the existence of fraternities and sororities has become increasingly controversial. Should universities ban them?

In the first article University of Minnesota student Emmanuel Ortiz argues that the Greek system institutionalizes a number of vices. He cites research suggesting that over 80 percent of students from fraternity houses—which may not come under the jurisdiction of university alcohol policy—are binge drinkers. Ortiz believes that both the fraternities and the universities are refusing to deal with the problems, including cases of sexual violence, that occur as a result of this. He claims the misogyny and elitism of the Greek system also show that universities must either reform or abolish it.

In the second article Alexander Wilson argues that fraternities and sororities are an essential part of student life. On campuses in backwater towns they often provide the only social option for students. Wilson is a student at Dartmouth College in Hanover, New Hampshire, where college trustees are prepared to invest millions of dollars in building coeducational residences with new social facilities to replace fraternity houses. Wilson contends that such spending can never match the quality and popularity of the social life the Greek system provides for *all* Dartmouth students. He points out that many fraternities now have antihazing policies and argues that fraternities perform a community function. Furthermore, he argues that students have a constitutional right to belong to a fraternity or sorority.

FURTHER INFORMATION:

Books:

Anson, Jack L., and Robert A. Marchesani (eds.), *Baird's Manual of American College Fraternities*. 20th Edition. Indianapolis, IN: Baird's Manual Foundation, 1991.

Nuwer, Hank, *Wrongs of Passage: Fraternities, Sororities, Hazing, and Binge Drinking*. Bloomington, IN: Indiana University Press, 2002.

Whipple, Edward G. (ed.), *New Challenges for Greek Letter Organizations: Transforming Fraternities and Sororities into Learning Communities*. San Francisco, CA: Jossey-Bass, 1998.

Useful websites:

www.indiana.edu/~cscf
Center For the Study of the College Fraternity site.
www.greekpages.com
Site with Greek resources including a database with information about societies across the United States.

www.fraternityadvisors.org
Association of Fraternity Advisors site.
www.lambda10.org
Site of the Lambda 10 Project, an online community for gay, lesbian, and bisexual fraternity issues.
www.nphchq.org
National Pan-Hellenic Council site.
www.stophazing.org
Site dedicated to the elimination of hazing practices through education, with many helpful articles.

The following debates in the Pro/Con series may also be of interest:

In this volume:
Topic 15 Should black universities be phased out?

SHOULD FRATERNITIES AND SORORITIES BE BANNED?

YES: Fraternity members help each other succeed. You are more likely to graduate from college if you belong to a fraternity.

YES: A ban on fraternities denies students their constitutional right to associate with whomever they choose

ACADEMIC SUCCESS
Do students achieve academically if they belong to a fraternity?

CONSTITUTION
Do students have the right to belong to a fraternity/sorority?

NO: Many educationalists argue that students in the Greek system are more likely to binge drink and get low grades

NO: What about the rights of students who want to be educated in a fraternity-free environment? Many students are choosing colleges without Greek organizations for that very reason.

SHOULD FRATERNITIES AND SORORITIES BE BANNED?
KEY POINTS

YES: On college campuses in backwater towns fraternities provide the only social life for all students

YES: Fraternity members are loyal and help each other, but fraternities and sororities offer benefits to all students, not just their members

FUNCTION
Do fraternities and sororities perform a useful function?

NO: Fraternities foster in-group superiority, social elitism, and worst of all, misogyny and other prejudice

NO: The Greek system creates a destructive, unhealthy environment in which alcohol abuse and sexual violence often occur

HAZING IN FRATERNITIES AND SORORITIES

"Hazing is endemic in American schools from junior high through graduate and professional schools."
—HANK NUWER, "EXTERMINATING THE FRAT RATS" (1999)

Hazing is any action taken that intentionally produces injury, embarrassment, distress, or any form of mental or physical discomfort in any person who wishes to become or remain accepted within a group. Hazing can take the form of sexual harassment, ridicule, the coercive use of alcohol, and the application of physical and psychological shocks. Although mainly associated with fraternities and sororities, hazing also occurs in the military, in athletic teams, in high schools, and in many other sectors of U.S. life. In 2003 around 42 states, including Alabama, New York, and Texas, had antihazing laws.

A serious problem?

Most people think of hazing as a harmless, fun activity—nothing more than horsing around, something like a scene from a movie such as *Animal House*. For the victims of hazing incidents, however, the reality is very different.

Hazing can vary from episodes in which the victim suffers only relatively minor embarrassment to much more serious and extreme situations, including even rape and death. From 1970 through 1999 alone at least 56 hazing-associated deaths were reported, and that, according to some experts, may just be the tip of the iceberg. In the May 2002 edition of the *American Journal of Emergency Medicine* Michelle Finkel claimed that, like domestic violence, hazing is seriously underreported because victims are often ashamed to admit what has happened.

Alcohol abuse

According to an article by James C. Arnold entitled "Alcohol, Hazing, and Fraternities as Addictive Organizations," "members of fraternities have a propensity to not only use but abuse alcohol." Certainly alcohol abuse has often appeared in hazing complaints and in inquiries into fraternity and sorority deaths.

Author and journalist Hank Nuwer has spent many years researching the subject. Since 1975, when he experienced the death of a fellow student at the University of Nevada during a fraternity initiation "drinking marathon," he has written many articles and books on the less reputable aspects of fraternity and sorority life in the United States. In 1990 Nuwer drew public attention to the issue of hazing and fraternity alcohol abuse when he published *Broken Pledges: The Deadly Rite of Hazing*, which focused on the death of 20-year-old Chuck Stenzel and his mother's subsequent battle to find out how it happened.

An athlete and honors student at Alfred University in New York, Stenzel pledged to Klan Alpine Fraternity in 1978. One night he and two other pledges were invited to a fraternity party. Hours later Stenzel died of alcohol poisoning. When Eileen Stevens, Stenzel's mother, tried to find out more about how her son had spent his last hours, she was stonewalled by both the fraternity and university.

After months of investigation Stevens discovered that her son and the other pledges had been forced into the trunk of a car and were allegedly forced to drink a pint of Jack Daniels, a six-pack of beer, and a quart of wine before they reached the party. Later, they were given more to drink. When Stenzel passed out, he was carried upstairs and left alone on a mattress, where he stopped breathing.

As a result of Nuwer's book and pressure by Eileen Stevens, Alfred University conducted an extensive study on athlete hazing, and in 1998 it established a council to educate students on "risky behaviors." In 1997 many National Interfraternity Conference (NIC) fraternities, with support from the National Panhellenic Conference (NPC) sororities, who already had alcohol-free house policies, decided to abolish alcohol in chapter houses by 2000. However, some NIC members later voted to delay acceptance until 2003 or beyond.

What are universities and colleges doing about hazing?

Many campuses now have antihazing guidelines. Some have suspended or fined fraternities and sororities that commit offenses. In April 2002, for example, the University of San Diego chapter of Phi Kappa Theta fraternity was indefinitely suspended for hazing and alcohol-related incidents after it had been placed on probation twice for repeated violations. Many argue that this shows that America's campuses are now taking the issue seriously; however, hazing remains a major problem in many colleges and universities.

COMMON MYTHS

Here are some of the many myths that surround hazing:

MYTH A: Hazing is no more than good fun.
FACT: Hazing is an abusive act intended to bully and victimize others. It is usually degrading and humiliating for the victim and often physically harmful. In extreme cases it may even be life threatening.
MYTH B: There is nothing wrong with hazing. It teaches good qualities such as respect for those who are older or more experienced.
FACT: Humiliating and degrading others does not teach respect. Such acts can only breed fear, hatred, and mistrust.
MYTH C: If someone agrees to participate in an activity, it is not hazing.
FACT: Peer pressure and the desire to belong motivate most victims of hazing to agree to participate in potentially dangerous situations. States that have antihazing laws do not accept consent of a victim as a defense in civil suits.

Topic 15
SHOULD BLACK UNIVERSITIES BE PHASED OUT?

YES
"BLACK COLLEGES UNDER PRESSURE TO CHANGE OR CLOSE"
THE ATLANTA JOURNAL-CONSTITUTION, NOVEMBER 14, 2002
JANITA POE

NO
FROM "THE CASE FOR ALL-BLACK COLLEGES"
THE ERIC REVIEW, VOL. 5, ISSUE 3
WILLIAM H. GRAY, III

INTRODUCTION

Historically black colleges and universities (HBCUs) are publicly or privately funded higher educational institutions whose principal mission is the education of African Americans. In 2003 there were more than 100 HBCUs, with an enrollment of around 370,000 students, or around one-third of the total U.S. black student population—this compares to the approximately 17 million students enrolled in U.S. colleges (2000 Census).

While educationalists and black civil rights bodies, among other groups, argue that HBCUs provide much needed education to blacks (and in recent years whites) who might not otherwise attend college or university, others claim that HBCUs are an anomaly in a society that prides itself on rewarding merit regardless of race, color, or sex.

Until the Civil War barely a handful of institutions offered formal education for blacks. Blacks had limited rights and were prevented from having citizenship or basic education. In 1862 the Morrill Act granted federal lands to states to set up universities. However, of the new colleges that were set up, few were willing to admit blacks. In 1890 it became mandatory for states either to admit blacks into white institutions or to allow for black-only institutions to be set up. Sixteen black-only colleges were established as a result.

In 1896 the Supreme Court ruling in *Plessy v. Ferguson* made segregation constitutional in its "separate but equal" ruling. After that, public HBCUs became more common. By 1953 more than 43,000 black students were enrolled in public universities; a further 32,000 were enrolled in private colleges. But in the 1954 *Brown v. Board of Education* ruling overturned the *Plessy* decision.

Despite that ruling, most HBCUs remained segregated, and most black students continued to attend all-black colleges. However, the 1964 Civil Rights

Act and establishment of the U.S. Office of Civil Rights encouraged the enrollment of black students in white colleges, and white students began to attend HBCUs.

The Equal Opportunity Act (1972) further extended the nondiscrimination clauses of Title VI of the Civil Rights Act to educational institutions. As a result, predominantly white colleges have adopted affirmative action policies, which many critics argue have led to falling academic standards in the effort to increase black enrollment. As a result, the number of black students attending non-HBCUs has been increasing.

"Affirmative action really means favoritism for blacks for the sake of racial peace."
—FLORENCE KING (1936–),
HUMORIST AND ESSAYIST

Supporters of HBCUs emphasize that they offer quality education at lower fees to socially and economically disadvantaged students. The nonracial, nonhostile climate in these institutions encourages a nurturing environment for minority groups who may feel alienated in white-dominated universities. The racial composition on campus helps students develop their social and political identities as African Americans. The HBCUs boost the profile of the black communities: Around 35 percent of black lawyers, 50 percent of black engineers, and 65 percent of black physicians graduate from HBCUs each year. But many critics of HBCUs argue that the standards of

education are poorer than in mainstream colleges, the administrative structures weak, and the students who qualify are less well equipped than students from mainstream colleges. They also contend that HBCUs do not give black students exposure to the real world, which is likely to be a handicap.

The fate of HBCUs hinges on changes in the legal and political environment in the United States. The landmark *United States v. Fordice* case (1992), for example, in which the Supreme Court ruled against the state of Mississippi's discriminatory funding for HBCUs, was a directive to both black and white public-funded institutions to increase diversity in student populations. Increasing nonblack enrollment in black institutions is seen to be equally as important to integration as increasing black enrollment in white institutions. In recent years nonblack enrollments in HBCUs have gone up sharply.

Many HBCU advocates argue that despite these changes, black-only colleges are still relevant in today's society. In some states affirmative action is taking a back seat as "race-neutral" policies are increasingly being promoted. In 1996 California banned affirmative action. By 2001 black undergraduate enrollment in the state had dropped by 33 percent. A similar policy by the Texas Law School also affected minority enrollments. However, what is most significant about HBCUs, advocates claim, is that they are a continuing symbol of black heritage whose influence on the political landscape must not be undermined.

In the following articles Janita Poe argues that HBCUs are irrelevant and outdated, while William H. Gray, III, claims they are essential in U.S. society.

BLACK COLLEGES UNDER PRESSURE TO CHANGE OR CLOSE
Janita Poe

YES

Morris Brown College's financial crisis is a wake-up call to the nation's private black colleges, some of which are struggling to keep afloat in a time when students have no memory of the segregation era that produced the schools, black-college leaders say.

Some leaders suggest the most troubled historically black schools need to institute radical change—abandon their single-race mission, or even to go out of business.

I wish Morris Brown good fortune because it is a fine school [said Carolynn Reid-Wallace, president of Fisk University in Nashville]. But there are those schools that may need to merge with sister schools or look at other creative ways to transform their institutions.

If they can't offer quality education, if they can't pay their bills and provide the necessary facilities, they should consider merging or saying: This institution has served its historic mission and now it needs to close.

Reid-Wallace's candid comments reflect the closely held sentiment of many insiders at historically black colleges and universities that Morris Brown's troubles—it may lose accreditation next month—are a tip-of-the-iceberg indicator of financial, academic and management problems at some of the nation's 39 four-year private black colleges. Another 41 four-year HBCUs, as they are known in education circles, operate with state or other government support.

Fully 15 percent of private HBCUs are now on warning or probation status with accreditation agencies.

Many black colleges were founded after the Civil War with funding from philanthropists or religious groups. Atlanta's Spelman College, for example, was started by Baptist missionaries who tapped oil baron John D. Rockefeller for support.

Unlike state colleges, which are part of larger taxpayer-supported systems, private schools have operated without alliances they need to weather difficult times, said

COMMENTARY: Diversity versus equal access

In 1997 Jennifer Gratz and Patrick Hamacher filed a case against the University of Michigan's College of Literature, Science, and the Arts, arguing that the university's preferential treatment of black, Hispanic, and Native American students violated both the Equal Protection Clause of the Fourteenth Amendment and Title VI of the 1964 Civil Rights Act. A year later Barbara Grutter filed a similar suit against the university's law school. The Supreme Court heard the oral arguments on both cases in April 2003. It is due to make its decision in June 2003.

The University of Michigan has defended its policies by saying that they are "essential to assembling a diverse student body." In the meantime affirmative action advocates and critics alike have watched *Gratz v. Bollinger* and *Grutter v. Bollinger* with interest. They believe that they are landmark cases and that the final decision in both cases may revolutionize or change the way that affirmative action policies are applied in the future.

What the evidence says

In January 2003 a report from the American Association of University Professors concluded that 30 years of affirmative action had failed to narrow the education gap for ethnic minorities. The study found that although more black and Hispanic students had gained a college education, the numbers of white college graduates had increased at the same time. Some opponents of affirmative action argue that diversity can be achieved without specifically targeting race; they claim that racial preferences have no place in college admissions.

M. Christopher Brown, a professor of higher education at Penn State University and an HBCU expert.

"The truth is, there are maladies and problems that we've covered up over the years and, like my grandmother used to say, 'Covered wounds don't heal well.'"

Proud histories

Like most private HBCUs, Fisk University has been on a roller coaster ride since its heyday a half-century ago as part of America's black Ivy League.

Established in 1866 for newly freed slaves, the university became known for its traveling Jubilee Singers and respected for competitive programs in music, sociology and pre-med. In 1930, Fisk became the first African-American college to receive accreditation from the Southern Association of Colleges and Schools; in 1953, it was the first black university to earn a charter for Phi Beta Kappa.

The Phi Beta Kappa Society is the oldest and most respected undergraduate honors organization in the United States.

Fisk's enrollment peaked at about 1,500 in the early 1970s. Enrollment began to decline as top "white" colleges and large state schools started luring black students who once sought the Fisk experience.

In 2000, according to the U.S. Department of Education, just 18 percent of all African American college students were enrolled in HBCUs. Over recent decades, Fisk has lost the funding, faculty and esteem associated with being an academic leader. By 1984, enrollment had dropped to 505. The school now has 812 students, according to the 2003 edition of *The Princeton Review*.

Of the undergraduates enrolled at Fisk, 97 percent are African American. The remainder are overseas students.

Taking Fisk in a new direction

Reid-Wallace, a Fisk alumna, took over leadership at Fisk last year. She has had some success in turning the school around financially, raising $18.4 million in the last school year, mostly from private donors—up dramatically from approximately $2.5 million in recent academic years.

Reid-Wallace is also steering Fisk in a new direction, to take into account new racial realities. The school should play up to its historical strength as a good liberal arts school with small classes and talented faculty, she said. Fisk's African American roots are a valuable part of its heritage, she said, but not necessarily the primary focus of its future.

"We can go out and get the best and brightest," Reid-Wallace said. "I don't care what color, what religion or what nationality."

Senior Vashaun Culmer, a native of the Bahamas, said she chose Fisk not only for black history but also for the small class sizes and the chance to learn more about life in the [United] States.

The presence of black mentors and role models plays an important part in some students' decision to enroll in HBCUs.

Being here has been a great experience [said Culmer, 21, whose parents attended Fisk]. Where I'm from, I'm part of the majority, and other races fit in with us. So, for me, coming here was not so much about black and white.

In part, the plight of private HBCUs mirrors that of many other private colleges—particularly those in rural areas—which are facing keen competition from large state schools with huge endowments, government support, popular sports teams and expansive campuses.

Students want to go where all the action is [said James Rogers, executive director of the Southern Association of Colleges and Schools]. With the private schools, the customers—the parents and the students—are starting to ask: What are we getting for the additional money we are paying?

Rogers noted that private schools once served a niche—minorities, women and religious faiths, among others. But now social integration has made them less essential.

All of the private HBCUs on probation with the Southern Association made the list primarily due to financial problems. Morris Brown's problems, said the association, were "financial" and "academic preparation of faculty."

An important experience

Despite the problems, the black-college experience remains important for many. And private colleges still offer that experience.

Over time, the privates will be our last great hope for black colleges in this country because the public HBCUs are shifting their enrollment and becoming more racially diverse [said Brown, of Penn State]. I think we need to come together and talk about what is needed so we can begin to build constructive strategies.

Some private HBCUs are still doing well. Michael Lomax, president of Dillard University in New Orleans and former chairman of the Fulton County Commission, said:

We have no trouble being selective [Lomax said]. For the fall of 2002 [he said], 3,000 students applied for the 600 slots in Dillard's freshman class. There are hundreds of thousands of African American high school graduates who need a college education and who will be best served by a historically black college because we know best how to produce high-performing black graduates.

Senior Unique Robinson said she believes she has done better at Fisk than she did at her Ohio high school, which was about 8 percent black. "I felt ignorant about black history and that sort of thing before I came to Fisk," said Robinson, 21, a third-generation Fisk student. "There's just something about being at a black institution. I think I've grown a lot here." Still, the question remains: In an era that's a generation removed from Jim Crow, how many private historically black colleges and universities does the country need? The student market seems to say the nation will support some private black schools, but not all 39.

> *Do HBCUs or other minority organizations run a risk of discouraging social integration? Or might they actually help encourage it?*

> *Dillard University was founded in 1935 and was named after the white philanthropist and educator James Hardy Dillard.*

> *The term "Jim Crow" refers to the discrimination against and segregation of blacks from the 1870s to the 1950s. The term originated in a song performed by a white minstrel show entertainer called Daddy Rice in the 1830s. Rice blacked his face and performed a song and dance routine that caricatured black people.*

THE CASE FOR ALL-BLACK COLLEGES
William H. Gray, III

NO

HBCUs train more than 35 percent of black lawyers, 50 percent of black engineers, and 65 percent of black physicians.

For the past 150 years, historically black colleges and universities have prepared African Americans for the economic, social, and political challenges of America. The majority of African Americans who hold Ph.D. degrees, medical degrees, law degrees, federal judgeships, and officer rank in the U.S. military did their undergraduate work at these institutions. Every year about one-third of all African Americans who get a college degree graduate from these schools, even though they enroll only 16 percent of all African American college students.

Distinguished graduates

Long lists are a good way to support a case, but should be used in moderation.

Graduates of these colleges and universities are among the most distinguished Americans and include such familiar names as the Rev. Martin Luther King, Jr., Supreme Court Justice Thurgood Marshall, former Virginia governor Douglas Wilder, opera diva Leontyne Price, former U.S. Ambassador to the United Nations Andrew Young, filmmaker Spike Lee, actor Samuel L. Jackson, former Secretary of Health and Human Services Louis Sullivan, Director of the Centers for Disease Control David Satcher, U.S. Air Force General Chappie James, and astronaut Ronald McNair. But their graduates are not only the famous: They are business leaders, schoolteachers, doctors, lawyers, civil servants, elected officials, poets, and artists who enrich the lives of America's cities and towns by their contributions to all our prosperity and well-being.

Throughout their history, historically black colleges and universities (HBCUs) have prepared leaders for America through a quality education at an affordable cost in a nurturing environment. The 103 HBCUs vary in geography, type, size, and curricula just as white universities and colleges do. There are 53 private and 50 public HBCUs, 14 2-year colleges, and 3 professional schools. Included in this array of institutions are single-sex, coeducational, church-related, research, liberal arts, small, large, undergraduate only, undergraduate and graduate, predominantly African American, and predominantly white.... West Virginia State, Bluefield State, and Kentucky State, all established as colleges

Bluefield State has the largest white enrollment. Whites make up 91 percent of the students and 96 percent of the faculty.

to educate blacks only, are now predominantly white in student enrollment and faculty.

In fact, HBCUs as a whole are more integrated and diverse racially than the rest of America's colleges and universities. Eleven percent of their students are white, compared with the 6 percent of students at other colleges who are black. About 20 percent of faculty at these schools are white, while only 2 percent of faculty at other colleges are black. And more than 10 percent of the administrators are white, compared with the paltry 1.5 percent of administrators at other colleges who are African American. HBCUs are more integrated racially and have always been.

There are currently 1.6 million blacks enrolled in U.S. colleges, accounting for 11 percent of all college students in the United States.

Origins in the 19th century

These amazingly productive educational institutions trace their origins to the 19th century. Prior to the end of legal slavery, approximately 4.4 million African Americans lived in the United States; 90 percent were slaves. They were barred from the basic rights of education and citizenship, and in many places educating slaves was illegal because whites feared it would foster slave revolt.

Three HBCUs were founded in Ohio and Pennsylvania prior to the Civil War: Wilberforce, Cheyney, and Lincoln. However, the majority of HBCUs were established after the Civil War in the South where America's black population was concentrated. In the states that made up the old Confederacy, private black colleges were founded by ex-slaves, free blacks, religious and missionary organizations, and philanthropic organizations with abolitionist roots. Their initial mission was to improve the condition of the newly freed slaves through education.

Wilberforce University was founded in 1856, Cheyney in 1837, and Lincoln in 1854. The Civil War ended in 1865.

Following the Supreme Court ruling in *Plessy v. Ferguson* in 1896, the doctrine of "separate but equal" became the basis for the establishment of a new group—the public HBCUs. By 1927 the U.S. Bureau of Education reported that 77 African American institutions in the United States offered college-level degree programs. Although a small number of African Americans attended other colleges in the North, Midwest, and West, the HBCUs were the educational institutions that provided the vast majority of America's college-trained African Americans. In fact, 8,000 HBCU graduates served as commissioned officers, pilots, and nurses in World War II.

This remained the case until the Supreme Court reversed *Plessy v. Ferguson* in 1954 with its *Brown v. Board of Education* decision. However, even after court rulings and congressional legislation, by the mid-1970s, three-quarters of African American college students were still attending

The Supreme Court ruled in Brown v. Board of Education *that legally segregated schools were inherently unequal. But it was not until the Civil Rights Act was passed in 1964 that any real attempt was made to dismantle the dual system.*

HBCUs. The next 20 years saw a major shift as traditionally white colleges began to recruit, accept, and support students from the black community. Thus, by the 1990s, HBCUs, which represented only 3 percent of the nation's colleges and universities, enrolled only 16 percent of all African American college students.

A rise in enrollments in HBCUs

Recently, the enrollments of HBCUs have grown significantly above the national average. This can be attributed to several factors. First, African American student enrollment is up at all colleges and universities due to higher high school completion rates and African Americans' increasing recognition of the importance of a college education. Recent data show that African American youths believe that a college education is important for economic mobility, and new census figures state that a college education does help to overcome the "race gap" in income—the median income of African Americans with a college degree is 92 percent of that of white college graduates. Newly released figures also show that African American high school completion rates hit an all-time high of 73 percent, compared with 81 percent for white Americans. Thus, it is not surprising that approximately 300,000 students are now attending HBCUs (this includes non-black students). In addition, African American students at other colleges and universities are at an all-time high of nearly 1.4 million.

Secondly, the growth rate of HBCUs has outdistanced the national rate because they are educational bargains for a community that is overwhelmingly low income. With the average African American family income at $32,826, access to higher education is usually determined by cost. Although many colleges and universities have attempted to address this issue through special scholarships and government student loans, the fact is that there are not enough resources to meet the demand. With the ever-rising cost of higher education, African Americans will increasingly be attracted to the affordable, high-quality education offered by HBCUs. A recent analysis by Harold Wenglinsky of the Educational Testing Service shows that the average 4-year HBCU student pays 58 percent less tuition than the average 4-year student at another institution. The cost factor is also one of the leading reasons why increasing numbers of white, Hispanic, and Asian students are attending HBCUs.

Thirdly, HBCUs are centers of excellence with unique capabilities to address African American needs. Of the 20

Black enrollment at HBCUs rose 21 percent between 1976 and 1994. It rose 40 percent at other colleges.

From 1990 to 1998 white enrollment at HBCUs increased by 16 percent.

colleges that graduate the most African American students who go on to earn Ph.D.s, 9 of the top 10 are HBCUs. While only 16 percent of African Americans attend HBCUs, 45 percent of recent African American Ph.D.s received their undergraduate degrees at HBCUs. The leading four colleges in America placing African Americans into medical schools are HBCUs—Xavier, Howard, Spelman, and Morehouse. When this is combined with the fact that over one-half of all African American professionals are graduates of HBCUs, then, increasingly, young African Americans will be drawn to these centers of affordable higher educational excellence where they can find role models, a nonhostile and nurturing environment, professors who expect them to succeed and achieve academic excellence, and where the president and professors know them by name—and sometimes have even memorized their parents' telephone numbers.

> The author uses statistics in many places in the article to add weight to his argument. Statistics can often make a case more convincing, but equally, too many examples can lessen the impact of the argument.

Indeed, it is in such environments that HBCUs do their transformational work. These institutions have proved themselves capable of taking students who have received modest or inadequate secondary education—or those whose aptitude was not discovered using traditional assessment methods like the SAT or ACT tests—and producing talented, contributing citizens. They know how to take diamonds in the rough and make them more brilliant, as Harvard and Stanford do. But they also know how to do something other colleges cannot do. They know how to take a lump of coal and turn it into a diamond by mentoring, expecting excellence, and hands-on teaching by faculty who have been there and care.

> In 1999 Harvard University had an endowment of $7.02 billion. Of the HBCUs Howard University had the top endowment of $152 million.

> Given the subject of the article, do you find Gray's metaphor appropriate?

HBCUs are important to all Americans

That is why these valuable educational institutions are still important, not just to African Americans, but to all Americans. Demographers predict that in the twenty-first century, 85 percent of all new workers will be women, minorities, and new immigrants. By the year 2020, one-third of this nation will be made up of African Americans and Hispanic Americans. By 2050, more than one-half of all Americans will be the people we call minorities today.

If America is to prosper in the global marketplace and maintain our economic strength, we will have to rely on the skills and productivity of that twenty-first century workforce. Thus we need to support the educational institutions that know how to take not just the best and brightest, but also the talented and intelligent, and give them the skills America will need....

Summary

In a society fast moving toward racial integration, especially in the field of education, the relevance of historically black colleges and universities (HBCUs) is being questioned. The first article, by Janita Poe, claims that HBCUs should be phased out since they no longer serve a purpose. Focusing on Fisk University, a private HBCU, Poe argues that until the 1970s, Fisk was an excellent black-only college, but it has lost the "funding, faculty and esteem associated with being an academic leader." The school has financial problems, and enrollments have fallen. In a bid to stay afloat, the school has been forced to attract nonblack students. Poe's article emphasizes that with integration, single-purpose colleges have become redundant.

William H. Gray, however, does not agree that there is no room in today's society for black-only colleges. The list of distinguished and successful black Americans who have graduated from HBCUs is just one reason why the colleges should continue, he says. He challenges the view that enrollments have dropped in HBCUs, asserting that they have in fact grown faster than the national average. With a higher rate of school completion and changing attitudes to higher education among the African American community, there is a greater demand for tertiary institutions. HBCUs, with their lower fee structures, attract large numbers of black students, primarily from low-income households. With growing cultural diversification in society it is more important to have institutions that reflect the values of minority groups. These values, argues Gray, can best be given by HBCUs.

FURTHER INFORMATION:

Books:

Grimes-Robinson, Kyra M., *No Ways Tired: The Public Historically Black College Dilemma*. Bloomington, IN: 1stBooks Library, 1998.

Ross, Marilyn J., *Success Factors of African American Women at a Historically Black College*. Westport, CT: Praeger Publishers, 2003.

Willie, Sarah Susannah, *Acting Black: College, Identity, and the Performance of Race*. New York: Routledge, 2003.

Useful websites:

www.hbcu-central.com/siteLogin.cgi
HBCU Central features news, information, and links.
www.hbcunetwork.com
HBCU Network has news and opinions and links to articles.
www.cnn.com/2003/EDUCATION/03/17/morris.brown.reut/index.html
"Black Colleges Suffer Financial Strain," March 17, 2003.

www.nydailynews.com/news/ideas_opinions/story/66917p-6231c.html
"Wrong Time to Shut Down Black College" by Karen Hunter, March 3, 2002.

The following debates in the Pro/Con series may also be of interest:

In *Individual and Society*:
Topic 6 Should affirmative action continue?

Civil rights timeline, 1942–1992, pages 34–35

Affirmative action policies, pages 84–85

SHOULD BLACK UNIVERSITIES BE PHASED OUT?

YES: Black universities arose out of the need to provide higher education for black students; and since segregation does not exist, the universities are outdated now

YES: It is important to teach people to live and work with each other regardless of their race or color; black universities work against that idea

SEGREGATION
Are black universities an anachronism since segregation no longer exists?

RACISM
Do HBCUs perpetuate racism?

NO: Most black colleges and universities provide a good education for black students who might not be able to receive education in nonblack colleges

NO: HBCUs are important because they instill in black students a sense of identity and culture and also give them much needed confidence

SHOULD BLACK UNIVERSITIES BE PHASED OUT?
KEY POINTS

YES: Many black students are given preferential treatment in colleges and schools, and the need for separate places to educate them has long gone

YES: HBCUs were historically inferior universities; and since affirmative action has allowed blacks into mainstream universities, HBCUs should be disbanded

AFFIRMATIVE ACTION
Have affirmative action policies made HBCUs irrelevant?

NO: Affirmative action policies do not work, and statistics show that HBCUs are still much needed

NO: Most HBCUs provide a very good education and should not be dismissed so easily

Topic 16

ARE UNIVERSITIES DOING ENOUGH TO PREVENT PLAGIARISM?

YES

"LESSONS IN INTERNET PLAGIARISM"
HTTP://TMS.PHYSICS.LSA.UMICH.EDU/214/OTHER/PAPER/
062801INTERNETPLAGIARISM.HTML
JUNE 28, 2001
KATIE HAFNER

NO

FROM "DOWNLOAD. STEAL. COPY. CHEATING AT THE UNIVERSITY"
THE DAILY PENNSYLVANIAN, NOVEMBER 27, 2001
MARY CLARKE-PEARSON

INTRODUCTION

According to Merriam-Webster's Collegiate Dictionary, "plagiarism" means either "to steal and pass off (the ideas or words of another) as one's own," "commit literary theft," or "to use … without crediting the source."

Throughout history people have accused others of copying their work. Despite the strengthening of copyright law in the 20th century, the advent of the Internet has greatly increased the ease with which information can be directly copied.

While the most high-profile cases often involve large-scale copyright infringement, in the music industry, for example, for some people a key part of the debate concerns the increased incidence of plagiarism in U.S. schools and colleges since the 1980s. Universities, in particular, are suffering from mounting allegations of plagiarism—so much so that they have

also been accused of not taking the issue seriously enough. But is that really the case?

Many critics argue that plagiarism is inevitable. Siri Carpenter, in "Plagiarism or Memory Glitch?" reports on the difficulties faced by teachers who try to outwit plagiarists. Carpenter concludes that inadvertent plagiarism or "cryptomnesia" is such a common occurrence that many people do not think it is wrong. Dr. Jamie McKenzie also argues that many plagiarists do not think they are cheating. He claims that a lot of students are not trained in academic discourse, and ignorance and lack of proper instruction, rather than a deliberate attempt to steal intellectual property, have led people to plagiarize.

Even if that is the case, critics argue, perpetrators have to be punished; otherwise, how will they learn that plagiarism is a serious crime? It is not enough, they assert, to mark term papers down or temporarily suspend students from classes: Plagiarists must be made aware that they are cheating and should be taken to court.

Plagiarism cases are reportedly on the rise, and critics claim that proves the problem is not being addressed. The Internet and access to a greater range of information from a multitude of sources have further fueled the issue.

"By necessity, by proclivity, and by delight, we all quote."

—RALPH WALDO EMERSON

(1803–1882), ESSAYIST

In the 1990s Professor Stephen Davis conducted a study of academic dishonesty. He discovered that as many as 60 percent of the student population have committed plagiarism at larger universities. Moreover, a study performed by Duke University's Center for Academic Integrity reported in the article "Universities, Schools Fight Plagiarism" that the number of college students who admitted cutting and pasting text from the Internet without citing sources jumped from 10 percent in 1999–2000 to 41 percent in 2001–2002.

A recent study by professors at the Rochester Institute of Technology disagrees with those conclusions. Around 700 undergraduates were surveyed at nine colleges and universities. The evidence showed that 16.5 percent of students "sometimes" plagiarized from the Internet, but that only a further 8 percent did so "often" or "very frequently." Some 50.4 percent of students reported that their peers "often" or "very frequently" did the same. It concluded that online plagiarism was comparable to conventional plagiarism. While the total proportion of students who admitted that they plagiarized from the Internet at least "sometimes" was 24.5 percent, 27.6 percent did so from conventional texts—and around 90 percent of students believed that their peers at least "sometimes" plagiarized from conventional sources.

So, what can universities do to stop this problem? Dr. John Barrie, founder of Turnitin.com, a plagiarism-detection service, believes that the growing number of services such as his own provide the answer. Critics of services such as Turnitin.com, however, argue that it promotes distrust between teachers and students, and assumes that people are inherently dishonest. They claim that the problem lies less in detecting plagiarism than in the failure to impose sufficiently harsh penalties on anyone caught cheating.

In the following two articles Katie Hafner, in the first, argues that universities are doing their utmost to stamp out plagiarism. She focuses on the different measures that institutions are taking to prevent the spread of the problem.

Mary Clarke-Pearson, on the other hand, firmly disagrees. She argues that statistics show an increase in the number of students who opt out of conventional research in favor of online paper banks. Her belief is that universities are not doing enough: An honor code is not sufficient. "Having an honor code is one thing—upholding it is a completely different story."

LESSONS IN INTERNET PLAGIARISM
Katie Hafner

To a student at Spring Lake Park High School, outside Minneapolis, it seemed like a formatting problem: the margins on the research paper he was trying to print out for an English class this spring were not aligning correctly. But when he complained to Jane Prestebak, a librarian whose duties include running the school's computer labs, she immediately suspected the actual cause.

Ms. Prestebak took the first five words of text and put them in a search engine. Up came the Web site from which the student had taken the paper, in its entirety, margin formatting and all.

> Do you think increased computer training could better enable teachers and other school staff to detect plagiarism?

When she confronted the student, he was taken aback to be caught so swiftly, by a 43-year-old school librarian of all people. "Maybe a teacher who wasn't as computer literate as I am wouldn't have known to be suspicious," Ms. Prestebak said. She alerted the student's teacher, who decided to turn the incident into a lesson in scholarly ethics.

"The student needed a wake-up call," Ms. Prestebak recalled. "His teacher allowed him to rewrite it and hand it in again a week later. It gave us a chance to reteach him."

At a time when Internet literacy seems in inverse proportion to age, a new generation of students is faced with an old temptation made easier than ever: taking the work of others and passing it off as one's own. In this era of cut and paste, hundreds of sites offer essays and research papers on topics as abstruse and challenging as Shakespeare's "Troilus and Cressida" and Sartre's "Being and Nothingness," some at no charge. And e-mail has made it simpler for students to borrow from one another's work.

> This article was published in June 2001. See www.cbsnews.com/stories/2001/05/10/tech/main290674.shtml for further background on the University of Virginia story.

Research shows scale of problem

Indeed, a scandal last month at the University of Virginia, where 122 students are being investigated for possible plagiarism of term papers for an introductory physics course, not only revealed how precarious the notion of an honor system can be, but also painted in sharpest relief how easy cheating has become.

Donald McCabe, a management professor at Rutgers University in Newark who conducts periodic surveys on cheating at college campuses, recently surveyed 4,500 high school students at 25 schools around the country. When it comes to plagiarizing from the Web, he found, high schools seem to present a far larger problem.

More than half of the high school students surveyed admitted either downloading a paper from a Web site or copying a few sentences from a Web site without citation. On the college level, Dr. McCabe said, just 10 to 20 percent of those surveyed acknowledged such practices.

See www.aaup.org/ publications/Academe/ 02JF/02jfmcc.htm for an article by Donald McCabe and Linda Klebe Treviño discussing this research and giving further background on previous studies into plagiarism.

The telltale signs

Often, teachers are suspicious from the start. "If a student hasn't done a lick of work or produced anything during the stages of a research paper, then suddenly this beautifully typed-up paper materializes, that's a sign," said Cathy Aubrecht, an English teacher at Hononegah High School in Rockton, Ill[inois].

Students have different ways of working. Do you think Aubrecht's assessment is a fair one?

At other times, the problem presents itself in a more subtle fashion. "I have kids every year who have a hard time understanding that ideas can be plagiarized as well," she said. "If you get a good idea from someplace, or a concept is related to you via a book or Internet site, it needs to be recognized. But they assume that everything is public domain."

Dr. McCabe said he was deeply concerned about the cavalier attitude toward plagiarism among students coming up through high school and beginning to enter college. "Many students say, 'We're way ahead of our teachers when it comes to the Internet,'" Dr. McCabe said. "And they say, 'Everybody's doing it.'"

Serious repercussions

In high school, moreover, the consequences are not so grave as they are in college. High school students caught cheating are usually given a stern lecture or, at worst, a failing grade. On rare occasions, seniors will not be allowed to graduate. College students caught plagiarizing, especially at institutions with strict honor codes, are often suspended and may even be expelled, Dr. McCabe said.

Information on the purpose and operation of honor codes at universities can be found at www-cse.stanford. edu/classes/cs201/ projects-00-01/ honor-code/honor codes.html. A page from Duke University (www.duke.edu/web/ Archives/history/ honor_system.html) gives an interesting history of the ideas behind the system.

Dr. McCabe said he believed there was less cheating in college than in high school not only because of the consequences but also because students take college more seriously.

At the same time, Dr. McCabe said there was a "steady erosion" of students' sense of right and wrong when it came to plagiarism. When he reads the comments accompanying his surveys, he said, he is struck by how readily students place the blame for their cheating on societal problems and pressures.

"The college students say, 'When Clinton can do this,' or 'When Milken can do that,' who can blame them for what they do? It's very, very pervasive."

This is a line of justification Dr. McCabe said he increasingly saw among high school students as well. "High school students tend to blame the competitiveness of the college admissions process," he said.

Fighting back

At the same time, the Web has made it much easier to catch plagiarists. A growing number of educators routinely use Web-based services for detecting unoriginal work.

See www.salon. com/tech/feature/ 1999/06/14/ plagiarism/print. html for an article comparing Turnitin.com with other sites offering a similar service.

Turnitin.com, a popular service, offers a simple method that allows both teachers and students to submit papers to electronic scrutiny. The service compares the paper against millions of Web sites, a database of previous submissions and papers offered by the so-called term-paper mills. Turnitin.com then sends a report with the results to the teacher. High schools using this service pay around $1,000 a year for an unlimited number of submissions. colleges pay roughly $2,000.

Dr. John M. Barrie, a founder of Turnitin.com, estimated that of all the work submitted to the site, nearly one-third is copied in whole or in part from another source.

"When it comes to cheating, at the top of the list is plagiarism, and at the top of that list are students cutting and pasting, mostly from the Internet," Dr. Barrie said. He said about 1,000 institutions subscribe to the service. Roughly 60 percent are high schools and the rest are colleges. A handful of middle schools subscribe to the service, and Dr. Barrie said he has also had inquiries from some elementary schools. Such services are surprisingly effective, especially as a deterrent.

Dr. Steven Hardinger, a chemistry lecturer at the University of California at Los Angeles, said he had students submit their own papers to Turnitin.com, with the results sent to him.

"The use of Turnitin.com as a deterrent is perhaps much more valuable than as a way to ferret out plagiarism," Dr. Hardinger said. "We really hate to see plagiarists and hate to punish them, but we want them to know we're watching."

Dr. Jamie McKenzie, editor of *From Now On: The Educational Technology Journal*, an online publication … said he saw a more disquieting problem associated with youthful plagiarists—what he calls "mental softness."

"Students are caught up in a cut-and-paste mentality that relates to an old belief that longer is better," Dr. McKenzie said. "They're confusing the size of their pile, of what they've accumulated, with wisdom. Instead of finding the right stuff, they're just finding lots of stuff.... They don't think of it as cheating. They are simply collecting information and don't understand the whole concept of intellectual property."

Challenging attitudes

Even when caught, many high school students are relatively blasé about their transgression. Dr. Peter G. Mehas, superintendent of schools in Fresno County, Calif., blames parents, at least partly. He said he was chagrined to see a shift in parents' attitudes over his 30 years as an educator.

"Some of the teachers who have stood up and said, 'This is cheating,' are accused of being too harsh and too strict," Dr. Mehas said. "I have some parents complain, saying, 'Why give the kid an F just because he plagiarized four or five points?'"

Each spring, he receives about 200 calls from parents, "asking why someone's little darling isn't graduating," Dr. Mehas said.

"In the cases where the child has been caught plagiarizing," he added, "what I hear is, 'Well, it's really not cheating, he just didn't cite all the sources.'"

But Dr. Mehas stands firm on his decision to deny graduation to plagiarists.

He said that many school districts remain silent about the problem because it reflects poorly on them. "It's our responsibility to say there are consequences when you sign your name to something you have not produced," he said.

When confronted with the notion of serious consequences, high school students do appear to pay attention. Nancy Breedlove, the writing center coordinator at Hononegah High School, told a group of students about a sports writer for the local newspaper, *The Rockford Register Star*, who was recently fired after he admitted using quotations from an article in *The Star Tribune of Minneapolis* without attributing them.

"We wanted to let them know that not just in the academic world, but in the professional world, it could hurt them," Ms. Breedlove said. The story had an impact. "You could have heard a pin drop in the room."

Ms. Breedlove said she was willing to do whatever it took to reinforce her point. "I just hope that somehow the kids do get the message," she said, "because this new temptation has been put out there, and it begins with www."

"Intellectual property" refers to anything a person creates originally. It is divided into two categories— "industrial property," such as inventions (patents), trademarks, and industrial designs, and "copyright," including literary and artistic works, such as novels, films, musical works, drawings, and paintings.

Is it fair for an assignment to be given a failing grade because of plagiarism? Should students be made to redo the assignment instead?

Can you think of other examples in which plagiarism in the professional and commercial world can have serious consequences?

DOWNLOAD. STEAL. COPY. CHEATING AT THE UNIVERSITY
Mary Clarke-Pearson

NO

Pearson begins her piece with a strong image that will immediately capture the attention of her audience.

Writing a term paper usually involves jamming a semester's worth of research into one week, writing 15 pages in a night and emerging from a computer lab with bloodshot eyes and a stack of empty coffee cups.

But for a few students, the task is hardly this draining. All it takes is a click of the mouse.

Downloading papers from the Internet, combined with the upsurge of other incidents of cheating, has been a growing concern for the future of academic integrity in higher education....

These students aren't the only ones who have opted out of conventional research and turned to online paper banks, amid the "cut and paste plagiarism" trend at universities nationwide.

The Center for Academic Integrity (www.academicintegrity.org) aims to "identify, affirm, and promote the values of academic integrity."

According to a 1999 survey conducted by Donald McCabe, a Rutgers University professor and the founder of the Center for Academic Integrity at Duke University, more than 75 percent of college students admit to some form of cheating. About one third of the 2,100 participating students admitted to serious test cheating, and half admitted to one or more instances of serious cheating on written assignments.

Problems start early

The pattern for high school students, the next generation of college-goers, is disturbingly similar.

The Josephson Institute of Ethics, based in California (www.josephsoninstitute.org) aims to promote "principled reasoning and ethical decision making."

Eighty-four percent of the students surveyed last year [2000] by *Who's Who Among American High School Students* said that cheating was common among their high-achieving peers. Moreover, studies conducted by the Josephson Institute of Ethics show that the percentage of students who admitted to cheating on a test has risen from 61 percent in 1992 to 71 percent in 2000. Research conducted by the Educational Testing Services suggests that this jump is partially due to the pressure cooker environment of high schools....

In the spring of 1999, a University Honor Council survey found that only 54 percent of Penn students considered copying homework to be cheating. Moreover, 61 percent of the students indicated that they would not report a case of cheating to the Office of Student Conduct.

National ... implications [of the findings] at Penn are pretty clear: acts of academic dishonesty are on the rise at universities and Internet plagiarism is "in." Judging from the incoming wave of technology-savvy high school students, breaches of academic integrity aren't abating....

The technology is indeed simple—just typing a topic name into a search engine can result in vast amounts of information. And the hundreds of term paper banks online— from superior-termpapers.com to geniuspapers.com— make it even easier....

These days, universities across the nation are struggling to confront and combat this new form of plagiarism. While part of the solution lies in redefining the concept of academic integrity, a lot of it involves preventing "cut and paste plagiarism" before it occurs.

See www.coastal. edu/library/ papermill.htm, a page from Coastal Carolina University, for an analysis of what "paper mills" provide and how their business operates.

The importance of honor

Developing an honor code that clearly lays out a university's standards for honesty and the consequences for violating these rules has been a good starting point, according to McCabe.

His research shows that academic honor codes effectively reduce cheating. In several university surveys over the past decade, McCabe concluded that serious test cheating on campuses with honor codes is typically one-third to one-half lower than on campuses that do not have honor codes.

"I really think it matters what sort of community you create on your campus and how students perceive the issue," McCabe said. "What an honor code does is to transfer the issue to the responsibility [of] the students. Honor codes have students thinking about the issue and struggling with the issue. They get some moral education."

Having an honor code is one thing—upholding it is a completely different story.

At Penn, for example, the Code of Academic Integrity defines seven acts—ranging from plagiarism to multiple submissions of a single paper—that interfere with the pursuit of knowledge. Yet a 2000 University Honor Council survey showed that only 6 percent of students were aware of the official rules. Forty-five percent of the students said that they never even read the code.

As a result, the 24-member organization has been making more concentrated efforts over the past year and a half to

Do you think it is as simple as that? What other methods could a school or university employ to reduce plagiarism?

Go to www.upenn.edu/ osl/acadint.html to see the University of Pennsylvania's Code of Academic Integrity. Do you think that the code is enough to prevent Internet plagiarism? Should it be more specific?

educate the student body. The council declares an "Academic Integrity Week" every fall and lets incoming students see the Code of Academic Integrity when they sign a "pledge card" promising not to cheat....

While some have celebrated the council's efforts, others feel as though Penn's administration could be doing a better job addressing this issue.

What might the reasons be for lax enforcement of the honor code? Why might universities have an interest in playing down the problem?

"The problem lies on the enforcement side," said Rebecca Kowal, a political science teaching assistant. "The cases are detected, and Penn does not seem to punish offenders of plagiarism very strongly, so you have cases where the offender has plagiarized multiple times and is still not expelled."...

Communication counts

Diane Waryold, executive director of the Center for Academic Integrity, suggests that university professors need to openly address the issue of plagiarism with their students.

"They're the folks who can create climates in their classrooms that can get it on the radar screen," Waryold said. "If they talk about it and build relationships with their students, then people won't cheat."

Do you think this is a good way to approach the problem? Is explanation key to dealing with plagiarism?

Sociology Professor Nathan Sivin, for instance, passes out a style guide to students, detailing how to acknowledge sources. As a result, according to Sivin, students have no excuse for not citing their research properly.

"In large lecture courses, I have to remind students that they can do themselves irreparable harm by giving in to temptation, and that it is very likely that they will be caught," he said. "In seminars, when we discuss research use of the Web, I take care to mention that if a student can find something to copy, an instructor can find it even quicker."

Choosing not to rely solely on their professors, many universities have invested in high-tech tools that detect plagiarism. Over the past year, a growing number of institutions have signed up for a service called turnitin.com, which scans student papers to see if material has been copied from the Internet or from other papers in its database.

While this software has proved very effective at some universities, there is some concern at Penn.

Should all papers be screened so all students' work is treated the same, or should instructors be selective to avoid becoming bogged down in checking rather than teaching?

"There's a possibility that it would send a message to our students that we're not trusting," Goldfarb said. "Plus, there's a potential for inconsistency. Unless you make it mandatory, which is unlikely at a school like ours, what you've got is an opportunity for real disparities in treatment."

The increases in reported plagiarism at Penn might demonstrate a need for such technology.... "I have run fairly regularly into plagiarism, and even more often into cases where I could tell it had taken place but couldn't make an airtight case," Sivin said.

A professor who asked to remain anonymous has observed a lapse of academic integrity among students, as well. "How much cheating and plagiarism occurs today I don't know, but I do know the opportunities to cheat and plagiarize have been on the rise over the past 20 years," the professor said.

A student, who also wished to withhold his name, said that it was easy to get away with cheating at Penn, especially in large classes. "When you have an exam in a big lecture hall, it's not too hard to position yourself with a good view of another person's test," he said. "I've done it before. I think a lot of people have."

What practical steps could be taken to make it harder to cheat in the exam room?

The struggle to maintain integrity

Apathy toward cheating—and the notion of integrity in general—has left many wondering whether it is the values of college students that should be challenged.

"Many people treat academic integrity as being very trivial," said Education Professor Joan Goodman, who co-teaches a freshman seminar on integrity. "If you're willing to cheat, then you're going to find a lot of other offenses that you're comfortable doing...."

The professor argues that if someone is willing to cheat, they will be likely to commit other offenses. Do you think that this is necessarily true? Is it not just an opinion rather than a fact?

Philosophy Professor Rahul Kumar expressed his frustration with this casual attitude. "I have had to deal with cases of cheating and am always disturbed by how unrepentant students have been," Kumar said. "Aside from the usual pro forma apologies, students exposed of cheating usually behave like children who have been caught with a hand in the cookie jar."

A teaching assistant who asked to remain anonymous said she attributes students' lapses in academic integrity to their outlook on learning. "I have noticed that students at Penn are more interested in doing well than learning a subject," she said. "Given their goals, I think students weigh their ability to 'get away with it' over any moral objections they might have to being dishonest."

Why do you think students go to college? Because it is important for their future success? Or because they want to learn more about a subject?

At any rate, sooner or later students will have to move on into a world where they won't be coddled. "The University is a very protected environment in which to learn how to live in the world," Sivin said. "Of those who don't get caught cheating here, many will get caught later, and that will be the end of promising or successful careers."

Summary

Are universities doing enough to prevent plagiarism? The article "Lessons in Internet Plagiarism" suggests that universities are attempting to minimize the flow of plagiarized material by a two-track approach: by teaching students to take responsibility through an honor system, and by using electronic aids to detect plagiarism. The article also claims that students do not consider plagiarism to be cheating—"they are simply collecting information and do not understand the whole concept of intellectual property." Therefore, the article concludes that when students are made aware of the issue and are held accountable for their own actions, teachers are able to bypass the issue of trust by encouraging students themselves to take full advantage of services such as Turnitin.com, which are becoming a very valuable deterrent against plagiarism.

In the second article Mary Clarke-Pearson argues that students are becoming increasingly adept at using the Internet to download term papers. The increasing pressure on students to succeed, caused by the cost of education and the importance of qualifications to their careers, also makes it more likely that they will try to cheat in this way. The article goes on to criticize educational establishments for their soft touch with students who are caught cheating. If, the article argues, students are given a clearer definition of what is expected of them, then this needs to be reinforced by all concerned, especially schools, colleges, and universities.

FURTHER INFORMATION:

Books:

Decoo, Wilfried, *Crisis on Campus: Confronting Academic Misconduct*, Cambridge, MA: MIT Press, 2002.
Johnson, Doug, *Learning Right from Wrong in the Digital Age: An Ethics Guide for Parents, Teachers, Librarians, and Others Who Care about Computer-Using Young People*, Worthington, OH: Linworth, 2003.
Lathrop, Anne, and Kathleen Foss, *Student Cheating and Plagiarism in the Internet Era: A Wake-Up Call*, Englewood, CO: Libraries Unlimited, 2000.

Useful websites:

 www.caslon.com.au/ipguide15.htm
Caslon Analytic's *Intellectual Property Guide* gives an overview on plagiarism issues and resources.
http://bms.westport.k12.ct.us/lmc/plag.htm
Bedford Middle School's article on "Tips on Finding Plagiarized Material on the Web." Specifically aimed at schools.

www.virtualsalt.com/antiplag.htm
Robert Harris's "Anti-Plagiarism Strategies for Research Papers," with links to detection sites.
www.citejournal.org/vol1/iss4/currentpractice/article2.htm
Jill Suarez and Allison Martin's article "Internet Plagiarism: A Teacher's Combat Guide."

The following debates in the Pro/Con series may also be of interest:

In this volume:
 Issues in U.S. education,
pages 8–9

In *U.S. History:*
Plagiarism,
pages 86–87

ARE UNIVERSITIES DOING ENOUGH TO PREVENT PLAGIARISM?

YES: Plagiarism is theft, and as such, offenders should be prosecuted and fined

YES: It is not a serious crime, and schools and universities go overboard when they discover an offender

PUNISHMENT
Should people who plagiarize be punished?

CHEATING
Are people taking plagiarism too seriously?

NO: People who plagiarize often do so unwittingly. They should be chastised, but they should be taught how to use research materials properly. It is teaching that is at fault.

NO: Recent studies have shown that plagiarism is a growing problem and must be taken seriously. Students do not see it as a crime when in fact it can be an intellectual property offense with serious consequences

ARE UNIVERSITIES DOING ENOUGH TO PREVENT PLAGIARISM?
KEY POINTS

YES: People have unlimited access to a large range of sometimes uncredited material, and it is inevitable that plagiarism occurs

YES: By installing this software, the school, college, or university is implying that they expect students to cheat

INTERNET
Has the Internet made plagiarism inevitable?

NEW TECHNOLOGY
Is using new plagiarism-detecting technology an abuse of trust between student and teacher?

NO: The Internet is blamed for everything. Plagiarism has always existed.

NO: Unfortunately it is a necessary reality and has helped stop many people from committing this crime

GLOSSARY

accountability in the context of education, the responsibility that schools and teachers have to ensure that educational standards are met.

affirmative action policies and initiatives designed to end discrimination based on race, color, gender, or religion. Also known as "positive action."

assimilation a term describing the process by which the traditions and culture of a minority ethnic group are absorbed by a dominant culture.

bilingualism the ability to speak two languages; the term also refers to a system of education in which non-English speakers are taught in their native language.

binge drinking drinking a large quantity of alcohol in a short period of time, usually for the purpose of getting drunk.

charter school a type of public school that is granted a certain amount of freedom (determined by state law and local charter) in decision-making regarding its structure, curriculum, and educational emphasis.

common school movement a social and political movement that emerged in the early 1800s and advocated that a good education was essential to the nation's democracy. Today's public schools evolved from the movement.

constitution a written codification of the basic principles and laws under which a government or other body operates.

creationism the theory that the Earth and all living things were created in the process detailed in Genesis in the Bible.

cryptomnesia inadvertent plagiarism that results from lack of awareness of academic discourse and lack of proper instruction rather than a deliberate attempt to steal intellectual property.

curriculum a framework of learning directives and teaching strategies that make up an educational course.

Darwinism a theory of organic evolution claiming that new species arise and are perpetuated by natural selection.

discrimination the act of treating others unfairly on the basis of their color, race, gender, sexuality, nationality, religion, education, or economic status.

Equal Protection Clause part of the Fourteenth Amendment to the U.S. Constitution that prevents states from denying any person within their jurisdiction equal protection.

Establishment Clause part of the First Amendment to the U.S. Constitution, which makes it illegal for the government to establish an official religion or to prefer one religion over another.

evolutionism a set of theories or a theoretical school in sociology based on the assumption that human societies tend to develop into higher and higher forms.

First Amendment article of the Constitution that protects from government interference the right to freedom of religion and freedom of expression.

fraternities or "brotherhoods," social organizations with male members at colleges; because most have names made up of letters from the Greek alphabet, they are also known as "Greek letter societies."

freedom of speech the right to the free expression of views and opinions.

hate speech verbal abuse of a person or group on the basis of their race, religion, national origin, or sexual orientation. *See also* freedom of speech.

hazing term for the harassment, abuse, or humiliation involved in some initiation rites, for example, to join a fraternity.

home education education of school-aged children at home rather than at school.

illiteracy an individual's inability to read, write, speak in English, compute, and solve problems at levels of proficiency necessary to function in school or at work, in the family, and in society.

literacy an individual's ability to read, write, speak in English, compute, and solve problems at levels of proficiency necessary to function in school or at work, in the family, and in society.

marginalized a term that describes a person or a group of people that is ignored, relegated, or excluded to the outer edge of a group, community, or society.

No Child Left Behind Act an act passed in 2001 that develops the assessment and accountability system put in place under the 1994 reauthorization of the Elementary and Secondary Education Act. It reformed the federal role in education to give states and local school districts greater flexibility in the use of federal education funds in return for increased accountability.

parental responsibility the notion that parents should provide for the welfare of their offspring and teach them the concepts of right and wrong behavior. In legal terms, the liability of a parent if their child's behavior causes damage to another person or property.

phonics a method of teaching reading and spelling that stresses symbol–sound relationships, used especially in early instruction. It is based on recognition of the different sounds that make up words and the realization that words are made up of sequences of these sounds. See also whole-word or whole-language.

plagiarism stealing or passing off as one's own the words, ideas, or images created by someone else.

Pledge of Allegiance promise of fidelity and loyalty to the United States and the principles on which it is based. "I pledge allegiance to the flag of the United States of America and to the Republic for which it stands, one nation under God, indivisible, with liberty and justice for all."

private schools privately controlled and financed schools, as opposed to public schools.

privatization the transfer of services performed by public employees to private businesses, a process also sometimes known as "contracting out."

public schools schools supported with public funds or operated by an education agency or state education agency.

racism the belief that some races are inherently and naturally superior to others, which gives rise to discrimination against or harassment of certain races.

religious freedom the freedom to practice one's own religion without the interference of the state.

school vouchers credit notes issued by the government to parents enabling them to pay for their children to be educated at the school of their choice, including private schools.

segregation the practice of separating out a person or group of people from the rest of a community or society.

sororities or "sisterhoods," the female version of fraternities. The first sorority was Adelphean, later Alpha Delta Pi, founded at the Wesleyan Female College, Macon, Georgia, in 1851.

syllabus outlines the goals and objectives of an educational course.

tenure the name given to a term in office, for example, of a college professor; it comes from the Latin tenere, meaning "to have or hold in possession."

union an organization of workers joined to protect their common interests and improve their working conditions.

whole-word or whole-language a method of teaching children to read which stresses overall understanding of a piece of writing rather than word-for-word learning and accuracy. Some critics consider it less effective than phonics, but many schools use a combination of both methods.

Acknowledgments

Topic 1 Can the No Child Left Behind Act Work?

Yes: "News from the Committee on Education and the Workforce" by George W. Bush, Radio Address, March 2, 2002. Public domain.

No: From "All Children Tested, But Many Left Behind" by Nick Weller, Cascade Policy Institute, Policy Perspective No. 1021, March 2002. Copyright © 2002 by Nick Weller. Used by permission.

Topic 2 Has the Federal Class Reduction Program Improved Student Performance?

Yes: "Yes, Smaller Class Sizes Are a Key to Educational Success" by Kerry Mazzoni in *Spectrum*, the Journal of the Council of State Governments, Summer 1998 (www.cpec.org/forum/yesforum.html). Used by permission.

No: From "The Debate over Class Size, Part 2: The Critics Have Their Say" by Gary Hopkins, education-world.com, February 23, 1998 (www.education-world.com/a_admin/admin051.shtml). Used by permission.

Topic 3 Is Swearing Allegiance to the Flag in Schools Unconstitutional?

Yes: From "What Is Wrong with the Pledge of Allegiance?" by Blair Scott, Atheism Awareness (www.home.att.net/questions/pledge_allegiance.htm). Used by permission.

No: "Under God" by Dr. George M. Docherty, Sermon, New York Avenue Presbyterian Church, Washington D.C., February 7, 1954. Used by permission.

Topic 4 Do School Vouchers Work?

Yes: From "Do School Vouchers Violate the Establishment Clause? Are They Good Public Policy?" by Elizabeth J. Coleman, Rutgers Journal of Law and Religion website (www-camlaw.rutgers.edu/publications/law-religion/debate_3.htm). Used by permission.

No: "Do School Vouchers Violate the Establishment Clause? Are They Good Public Policy?" by Stephen D. Sugarman, Rutgers Journal of Law and Religion website (www-camlaw.rutgers.edu/publications/law-religion/debate_3.htm). Used by permission.

Topic 5 Should Private Businesses Run Public Schools?

Yes: From "Classrooms, Inc.: Will Privatization Save Public Schools?" by Rebecca Pollard, *Ed.* magazine, Fall 2002, Vol. XLVI, No. 2. pp.12-17. Reprinted by permission of The Harvard Graduate School of Education.

No: "Private Operator of U.S. Public Schools Facing Financial Crisis" by Peter Daniels, World Socialist Website, May 29, 2002 (www.wsws.org/articles/2002/may2002/edis-m29.shtml). Used by permission.

Topic 6 Do Charter Schools Provide a Better Education than Traditional Public Schools?

Yes: From "Charter Schools Pledge Success" by Tamara Henry, *USA TODAY*, November 14, 2001. Copyright © 2001 by *USA TODAY*. Used by permission.

No: From "Charter Schools Take Us Backward, Not Forward" by Heather-Jane Robertson, CCPA Education Monitor, Summer 1997 (www.policyalternatives.ca). Used by permission.

Topic 7 Is Home Education an Acceptable Alternative to Public Education?

Yes: From "Teach Your Own Children ... at Home" by John Holt (www.bloomington.in.us/~learn/Holt.htm). Originally published as "Plowboy Interview" in the July/August 1980 edition of *The Mother Earth News*. Used by permission.

No: "School's Out: Does Homeschooling Make the Grade?" by Katherine Pfleger, *The New Republic*, April 6, 1998. Reprinted by permission of *The New Republic*, copyright © 1998 by The New Republic, LLC.

Topic 8 Should Illegal Immigrant Children Get Public Education?

Yes: From "Responding to Undocumented Children in the Schools" by Susan C. Morse and Frank S. Ludovina, Eric Clearinghouse on Rural Education and Small Schools, EDO-RC-99-1, September 1999. Public domain.

No: From "We Are Overwhelmed" by Jerry Seper, Part 2 of *Border Wars*, *The Washington Times*, September 24, 2002. Copyright © 2002 by News World Communications, Inc. Reprinted with permission of *The Washington Times*.

Topic 9 Do Teachers' Unions Hinder Educational Performance?

Yes: From "Teachers' Unions: Are the Schools Run for Them?" by James Bovard (www.libertyhaven.com). Used with permission.

No: "How Unions Benefit Kids: New Research Dispels Myths about Unions" in *New York Teacher*, the official publication of New York State United Teachers, March 28, 2001. Used by permission.

Topic 10 Is Phonics Instruction the Best Way of Teaching Students to Read?

Yes: "Phonics Teaching Gets Top Grade" by Mike Bowler, *The Baltimore Sun*, April 14, 2000. Used by permission.

No: From "The Reading Debate: Has Phonics Won?" by Stephen Krashen, originally published in *Substance* 27 (2): 24, 21, 2001. Copyright © 2001 by Stephen Krashen. Used by permission.

Topic 11 Should Public Schools Teach Creationist Theory?

Yes: From "Creationism v. Evolutionism in America's Schools" by Alex Rainert, *Trincoll Journal*, 1997.

No: From "The Creationism Controversy" by the Anti-Defamation League (www.adl.org). Reprinted with permission of the Anti-Defamation League.

Topic 12 Should Religion Be Taught in Schools?

Yes: From "The Bible & Public Schools: A First Amendment Guide" by the National Bible Association and First Amendment Center, www.teachaboutthebible.org, November 1999. Used by permission.

No: "Eleven-Year-Old Muslim Girl Harassed after Declining Bible from School Principal, ACLU of LA Charges" by American Civil Liberties Union, www.aclu.org, April 10, 2001. Used by permission.

Topic 13 Does Tenure Protect Incompetent Teachers?

Yes: "Profs Do Better on Shorter Leash, Study Concludes," NewsMax.com, March 12, 2002. Used by permission of NewsMax.com. All rights reserved.

No: From "Tenure and Academic Excellence" by Linda L. Carroll. This article is reprinted with permission from the May–June 2000 issue of *Academe*, the magazine of the American Association of University Professors.

Topic 14 Should Fraternities and Sororities Be Banned?

Yes: "Without Reform" by Emmanuel Ortiz, *The Minnesota Daily*, October 14, 1996. Used by permission.

No: "What Is 'Tens of Millions' Good For?" by Alexander Wilson, *The Dartmouth Review*, February 17, 1999.

Topic 15 Should Black Universities Be Phased Out?

Yes: "Black Colleges Under Pressure to Change or Close" by Janita Poe, *The Atlanta Journal-Constitution*, November 14, 2002. Used by permission.

No: From "The Case for All-Black Colleges" by William H. Gray, III, *The Eric Review*, Vol. 5, Issue 3. Used by permission.

Topic 16 Are Universities Doing Enough to Prevent Plagiarism?

Yes: "Lessons in Internet Plagiarism" by Katie Hafner, June 28, 2001. Copyright © 2001 by The New York Times Company. Used by permission.

No: From "Download. Steal. Copy. Cheating at the University" by Mary Clarke-Pearson, *The Daily Pennsylvanian*, November 27, 2001. Used by permission.

The Brown Reference Group plc has made every effort to contact and acknowledge the creators and copyright holders of all extracts reproduced in this volume. We apologize for any omissions. Any person who wishes to be credited in further volumes should contact The Brown Reference Group plc in writing: The Brown Reference Group plc, 8 Chapel Place, Rivington Street, London EC2A 3DQ, U.K.

Picture credits

Cover: Corbis: John Henley; **Corbis: Bettmann**, 148; **Getty Images:** 6/7, 105, 144; **Popperfoto:** Rebecca Cook, 167; **Richard Jenkins:** 46/47; **Topham Picturepoint:** Michael Greenlar, 179, 188/189, Jack Kurtz, 158, Tannen Maury, 13

SET INDEX

E